A SLICE
THROUGH TIME

A SLICE THROUGH TIME

Dendrochronology and precision dating

M. G. L. Baillie

B.T. Batsford Ltd, London

© M. G. L. Baillie 1995

First published 1995

All rights reserved. No part of this publication may
be reproduced in any form or by any means, without
permission from the Publisher

Printed and bound in Great Britain by The Bath
Press, Bath

Published by B.T. Batsford Ltd
4 Fitzhardinge Street, London W1H 0AH

A CIP catalogue record for this book is available from
the British Library

ISBN 0 7134 7654 0(limp)

Contents

Illustrations

Preface

During the 1970s and 1980s I had the great good fortune to be heavily involved in the construction of some of the Old World's first long tree-ring chronologies. These year-by-year records of mean oak growth, stretching back some seven millennia, offer not just the opportunity to date some ancient sites and artefacts very precisely, but additional opportunities to investigate the stored information within a parallel biological system, parallel, that is, to the human populations who inhabited the earth over the same period. The environmental potential of these tree-ring chronologies is immense and I have been lucky enough to be one of the first workers to have an opportunity to look into some of these past records. Having witnessed the large and expanding literature on dendrochronology, and its related disciplines, dendroecology and dendroclimatology, I feel that there is room for someone to draw together some of the disparate sources and produce a text which is narrative in character and which will serve to draw the student, or the interested lay reader, into the subject.

Inevitably, I have drawn heavily on work with which I have been personally involved. Much of the information has been published in separate articles over the years, and this book is an opportunity to draw elements from several of these together into a single text. However, as will become clear to the reader, there is nothing insular about Irish dendrochronology. Information from tree-ring work is inherently international in character. This is because, being underpinned by precise calendrical dating, tree-ring studies allow real-time comparisons from one region to many others; lessons learned in one area are often universally applicable. Indeed, the range of information covered in the following text would not have been possible without the efforts of many other individuals around the world. I would like to acknowledge the debt I owe to the many scholars who have helped make this text possible. Inevitably some will be left out and to them I apologize in advance.

The Tree-Ring Laboratory at Queen's University, Belfast, has always been closely associated with Queen's Radiocarbon Laboratory and much of the driving force behind the construction of the oak chronologies came from involvement with Dr G.W. Pearson and the radiocarbon calibration work in Belfast. The tree-ring work was greatly facilitated by generous grants from the Science-Based Archaeology Committee of the Science and Engineering Research Council in Britain and latterly by support from The Wolfson Foundation. It would not have been possible without the involvement of a whole list of research assistants, though for brevity I shall mention only the last four: Ms Elizabeth Halliday, Dr Martin Munro, Mr Andrew McLawrence and most importantly Mr David Brown whose measurement and organizational abilities underpin the Belfast tree-ring operation. I have been greatly assisted by interchange of data and information, particularly from Ms Jennifer Hillam and Ms Cathy Groves, at the Sheffield Tree-Ring Laboratory; Mr Ian Tyers at London; Dr Ann Crone at Edinburgh; Dr Keith Briffa at Norwich; the late Dr Bernd Becker at Stuttgart; Dr Burghart Schmidt at Köln; Professor Dieter Eckstein at Hamburg and Dr Hubert Leuschner at Göttingen, though many others could be mentioned. Important wood samples have been supplied by many workers in different geographical areas and in numerous different disciplines, and I must acknowledge their generosity. Of particular importance are Mr Mike Harvey who introduced us to Croston Moss, Lancashire; Dr Malcolm Hughes and Dr Pat Leggett who donated their Lancashire sub-fossil collection; Mr Richard Parr and the staff at the Godwin Laboratory, Cambridge, for supplying their East Anglian sub-fossil collection and the Staff at the Nottingham Tree-Ring Laboratory for the original river gravel oaks from the River Trent.

Preface

As will be evident in the following text, my excursions into the possible environmental effects of some major, ancient, volcanic dust-veil events have led to interchange of information and ideas with a wide range of scholars in other disciplines. Among others I would like to thank Dr Sturt Manning, Dr Mike Rampino, Dr Steve Self, Dr Kevin Pang, Dr Greg Zielinski, Mr Richard Warner, Mr Leroy Ellenburger and Mr Don Carleton. I have enjoyed many hours of useful discussion with my colleagues Professor Jon Pilcher, Dr Jim Mallory, Dr Valerie Hall and Dr Gerry McCormac. Much of the content of Chapter 9 is taken from *Dendrochronology and Past Environmental Change*, read in February 1991 at a joint symposium of the Royal Society and the British Academy, published in *Proceedings of the British Academy*, vol. 77, *New Developments in Archaeological Science* and I am grateful for their permission to reproduce it here. Similarly, I would like to thank the Ulster Museum for their permission to re-publish Figure 1.

I cannot leave these acknowledgements without reference to the late Professor Valmore C. LaMarche Jnr of the Laboratory of Tree-Ring Research in the University of Arizona at Tucson. Val, together with Dr Kathy Hirschboeck, first drew attention to the date 1627 BC and suggested that the tree-ring effects in that year might be due to the Bronze Age eruption of Santorini in the Aegean. The fall-out from that story occupies almost half of this book. If we think of their date as a solitary signpost, pointing back into the mists of time, it was that signpost which set me off on the strange but fascinating journey into aspects of archaeology, volcanology and ancient history which I describe in Chapter 5 and thereafter.

Finally, this book is about hard information and soft information. Hard information is that which is precisely dated and where relationships can be worked out with some confidence. Soft information is more or less everything else which is not precisely dated – much ancient history, almost all prehistoric archaeology, quite a lot of volcanology. This realization, based on chasing the past effects of ancient eruptions, brings one to the conclusion that, in reality, we know almost nothing about the past – almost nothing, that is, at annual resolution. To take but one example:

> The Great Cycle of the Maya Calendar which began in darkness on 13 August 3114 BC will come to an end . . . on 23 December AD 2012 . . . on that day, the ancient Maya scribes would say, it will be 13 cycles, 0 katuns, 0 tuns, 0 uinals and 0 kins since the Beginning of the Great Cycle. (Coe 1992)

So what happened in 3114 BC to start off a Great Cycle for the Maya? Was it a date pulled out of the air purely by retro-calculation? Was there any kind of natural event which acted as a trigger? Ancient history, archaeology and even Greenland ice-core records can't help: in terms of conventional study there is absolutely no information available about that year. The only real information about 3114 BC is locked up in the cellulose of the tree-rings which grew in that year. That information is available in the form of bristlecone pine samples, from the western United States, and oak rings from Ireland, England, Germany and Switzerland. If we want to study the past in real detail, tree-rings are the essential starting point.

Introduction

During the 1980s the science of dendrochronology came of age in Europe. Long reference chronologies for oak were completed for most of the later Holocene and, as a result, for the first time precise calendrical dating became available across a swath of the Old World.

The implications of that success are only now beginning to dawn on the scientific community. The work has been well known to archaeologists and to people working in the field of radiocarbon; however, there are still surprisingly large numbers of people who have never heard the term 'dendrochronology' and their reaction on having it explained tends to be at the level 'wouldn't it be nice if such a method could be produced but have you thought of the following problems . . .'. Frequently it is an uphill battle to explain that, yes, of course there were problems and chronologies took many years to build but they are here, they are completed and replicated and producing precise dates for a range of both archaeological and naturally preserved timbers. On occasion this message is best driven home by pointing out that, if the reader cares to give any calendar date in the last seven millennia, dendrochronologists can now supply a sample of wood which grew in that year – a time capsule of biological material. Indeed, dendrochronologists can supply not one but many biological time capsules for any year in the last seven millennia. Moreover, for many periods these precisely dated time capsules exist over a wide geographical area and for a variety of substrates.

Take as an example the year 1492 BC. A worker interested in studying cell size or cell density or isotopic composition or trace element concentrations in that year could be supplied with samples of oak wood which grew in northern or southern Ireland, in western or eastern England, in northern or southern Germany and in Switzerland. If there was necessity, samples could be supplied from 10 different trees in each of these areas. If that worker was willing to contact dendrochro-nologists in the United States he could be supplied with samples of bristlecone pine or foxtail pine which grew in Nevada in that same year.

Such precisely dated samples have already been used to duplicate the calibration of the radiocarbon timescale by providing samples of cellulose, of precisely known age, for the analysis of its residual radiocarbon content; so the scientific community already has a continuous measure of variation in the amount of radiocarbon in the atmosphere in the past. Moreover, not only has this work been done, it has also been duplicated using wood samples supplied by different workers and the radiocarbon concentrations have been measured in different laboratories – so the calibration is already a replicated system. The radiocarbon calibration curve, produced primarily with the view of allowing archaeologists to refine their understanding of chronology, also forms one of the best proxy records of variation in solar activity with time; itself a fundamentally important parameter in any study of past variations in earth climate.

Now obviously, for someone who has only just been introduced to the concept of dendrochronology, the astonishing fact is the discovery that it is more than just a concept – it already exists. Intuitively a method which offers calendrically precise dating should always have been a 'holy grail' for both archaeological and environmental dating – something to be striven towards. Instead, in a single leap, in the mid-1980s, the grail was reached in Europe.

One irony is that dendrochronology, aimed at the calibration of the radiocarbon timescale, has tended to expose the limitations of radiocarbon dating. Tree-ring dates have started to accumulate for historic and prehistoric sites and structures and have shed a new hard light on chronological issues. Moreover, ancient history which had regarded itself as possessed of a superior chronological system, for the Mediterranean at least, suddenly has a competitor. The hard questions which dendrochronology poses have implications even for the Egyptian historical chronology: is that house truly in order?

So, as the existing chronologies feel the chill wind of a precise dating method, dendrochronologists are sprinkling a new crop of precise dates across northern Europe. The implications are only beginning to be assessed but the first signs are that the new story is not the same as the old. The old chronologies by their very nature tended to smear information through time; radiocarbon by virtue of its inherent errors; archaeology and indeed ancient history by their need to fill up time. Dendrochronology, in contrast, is an independent method capable of absolute precision, which allows us to see events in *real time*. When we see things in real time they are not always as expected; the past appears more punctuated than previous dating methods led us to believe; indeed, the past may never be the same again.

This book tells something of the story of the completion of the tree-ring quest. It is necessarily a story of pioneers because dendrochronologists are the first people to be able to view aspects of the ancient past at annual resolution. Its principal aims are to describe the processes by which dendrochronology has been brought to its present state and to expose the reader to the current limits of chronological resolution. By facing up to chronological issues at very high temporal resolution, and seeing the problems of chronological interpretation encountered *when dates are known*, the reader is exposed to dating in real time. I believe it is fair to say that, in terms of scientific chronology, all other methods and situations are inferior: they might offer wider applicability, but their results cannot rival the precision offered by dendrochronology. So, if there are chronological questions which cannot be answered when tree-ring dates are available, it is virtually certain that they cannot be answered at all.

As far as possible, the book is structured in the order in which things happened; I hope this will help to make it readable as a narrative. With this in mind, Chapter 1 reviews the situation up to 1980 in order to give some historical depth to the story. At that time the principal European oak chronologies were still under construction and a number of problems were dogging the various

workers in Ireland and Germany. This review is, in effect, a precis of *Tree-Ring Dating and Archaeology* (Baillie 1982) which looked in detail at the early stages of chronology building in Europe, particularly Ireland. This should prepare the reader for Chapter 2 where two issues are covered. First, the completion of the long European oak chronologies back to 5000 BC and beyond; itself a milestone in the history of chronological studies. Second, the outlining of a 'second-generation' long, prehistoric, chronology in England. Second-generation refers to the placing of chronology sections with reference to pre-existing, in this case Irish and German, absolute chronologies. Such chronologies can be constructed much more quickly than the original, first-generation – or pioneering – chronologies which, of necessity, had to be independent and self-replicating.

Chapter 3 covers the resolution of the long-standing art-historical problem, associated with art-historical tree-ring chronologies in England, which had refused to cross-date with any other chronologies from the British Isles, and the clear identification of their exotic origins.

All of the above is very positive. Being able to date things is fun and the story of the past is being significantly padded out by the results of tree-ring dating: we have, as noted above, acquired the chronological holy grail. However, there is another side to all this. Dendrochronology creates its own demand. If sites or events *not* dated by dendrochronology are 'second class', then workers increasingly want dendrochronology to be applied to their material. Unfortunately, in Europe, dendrochronology currently really only works on long-lived oak samples. The danger is that the demand for such dating will force workers to toy with attempting to date short-lived samples, those with, for sake of argument, significantly less than 100 rings. The problem is that the methodology which has led to successful chronology construction, and much successful dating, is based on long-lived oaks – oaks with often 150 or 250 or 350 growth rings, sometimes more. There is no established methodology for definitively dating short-lived oak samples. An analogy would be the difference between trying to identify an individual human from a complete thumb-print (which could be done with a high degree of certainty) as opposed to a partial print containing only two whorls. So, there are problems associated with the wholesale application of dendrochronology and, following the solution of the art-historical problem, Chapter 3 reviews some of the lessons, and dangers, associated with uncontrolled tree-ring dating. The reason for including this section is largely because of the important position which dendrochronology is destined to hold in many areas of chronological and environmental study in the future; there is no point in being unrealistic about the method. Dendrochronology may be potentially extremely powerful, it is also of extremely limited applicability.

With the tree-ring chronologies complete, for a period which includes all of human history since the development of agriculture, Chapter 4 looks at the way in which dendrochronological dates are impinging on the archaeological record. Much of the information is self-evident, and reflects the routine status which the method is rapidly developing; oak timbers are being dated, from all periods back to the Neolithic, over a large part of northern Europe. This is rapidly tightening up chronology and exposing the inadequacy – the second-class nature – of other 'datings' on other sites. So, dendrochronology is opening up a new window on the past and it is surprising that it has not yet been christened the 'tree-ring revolution'. Interestingly, some of the dates being produced by dendrochronology don't, at first sight, come out as expected. For example, in Ireland we seem to see unnatural clusters of dates and curious depletions and it quickly becomes apparent that the past is in no way uniform. This punctuated record is partly the result of seeing things in real time and moving away from the 'smeared' chronologies which were inevitable when the principal dating tool was radiocarbon. Apart from dating sites, dendrochronology also allows direct dating of timbers within structures, thus defining, usually for the first time, true chronological relationships; such dating sometimes demonstrates how previous attempts at archaeological interpretation might have been fundamentally flawed.

A chapter on precise dating also seems an obvious place to introduce high-precision radiocarbon dating, especially in the form of high-precision 'wiggle matching'. This is the state-of-the-art radiocarbon method which can allow dating to 'within a few decades' in real time. So in Chapter 4 we see how, as a by-product of the shape of the radiocarbon calibration curve, we can date some sites almost as well with radiocarbon as we could with dendrochronology itself.

Chapter 5 looks at perhaps the strangest tree-ring excursion of the 1980s: the volcanic dust-veil story. Who would ever have thought that Irish bog oaks would hold records of major volcanic dust-veils? Well, actually, I should! In *Tree-Ring Dating and Archaeology* it was pointed out that

> one of the clearest signatures in northern Irish oaks was a consistent narrow ring for the year 1816. . . . it later transpired that this cold, dark summer was a direct result of a massive volcanic eruption which occurred in Tambora [*sic*] in 1815 and gave rise to widespread cooling the following year.

So Irish trees did record the environmental effects associated with the largest volcanic eruption in recent times. In retrospect, why shouldn't earlier and more sensitive trees record earlier large eruptions? In fact, it turns out that they do. Moreover, when they do, they specify the dates of these major dust-veils for the *first time*. That turns out to be the important twist. Volcanologists have never previously known the exact date of any prehistoric volcano. Nor, for that matter, have they ever known the exact date of any volcano-related environmental effects in prehistoric times. However, if you can't date the eruptions and you can't date the effects, then you can't tell *which* eruptions cause *which* effects! So it turns out that volcanologists have been in a bind when it comes to assessing the effects of large ancient volcanoes. What turns out to be really interesting is this: when you do date some large ancient dust-veils exactly, you suddenly discover that the dates seem to mean something to archaeologists and ancient historians studying the human past. Almost immediately, previously unconnected observations start to make possible sense: volcanoes, famines, plagues, Dark Ages . . . who would have thought that some natural

13

phenomena could have effects right round the northern hemisphere? Yet the story makes sense because volcanic dust-veils do circle the globe. Date them in one place and they are dated wherever their effects are observed.

So involved does this volcano story become that it fills two further chapters – Chapters 6 and 7 – with case studies relating, first, to an apparently traumatic event around AD 536–45 and, second, to attempts to date the major Bronze Age eruption of the volcano Thera (Santorini) in the Aegean. Thera has everything. It occurred in a civilized area only three-and-a-half millennia ago and is of major interest to archaeologists; it may have had significant environmental consequences; it is a testbed for volcanological understanding of the environmental effects of large explosive eruptions and it has received a lot of dating attention. The problem is that the true date is proving to be very elusive indeed. The subject exposes virtually all of the current problems of chronology: the inadequacies of the ancient historical record; the inadequacies of the archaeological record; the inadequacies of the ice-core record and of attempts to date the eruption by conventional radiocarbon dating.

The ability of dendrochronology to produce much more than simple dates is expanded in Chapter 8. When precise dates begin to accumulate it frequently becomes possible to see suggestions of real processes – archaeological and environmental and socio-economic – within the body of information. Often this information is a bonus and casts light on periods of human activity or inactivity. To give but one example, it is now possible to 'see' the Black Death in Europe as a clear building hiatus which would have aroused suspicions of a pandemic even in the absence of written history.

The time-capsule idea, noted above, is taken up in Chapter 9, where some of the results of tapping into the stored environmental information in tree-rings is reviewed. Environmental reconstruction is a massive research area and this chapter does no more than scratch the surface. To gain some deeper perspective on this topic, there are two substantial volumes edited by Jacoby and Hornbeck (1987) and Cook and Kairiukstis (1990) which deal respectively with the current dendroecological and dendroclimatological

aspects of tree-rings. They are recommended to anyone interested in looking further into the complexities of environmental reconstruction from tree-rings.

My interest is in trying to extract proxy environmental information from the tree-ring story, rather than the more detailed 'instrumental style' records sought by climatologists and others. This probably reflects my archaeological interests which, currently, seem best served with qualitative rather than quantitative information. At present, archaeological chronology is still so ill-defined that we only want to know when things were 'good' or 'bad'. Most workers studying the past are a long way from being able to handle monthly temperature reconstructions; rather they would welcome some hints on bad decades or centuries! It is fair to say that the initial environmental results look quite promising and, of course, the environmental information gleaned from a precisely dated system is immediately compatible with the precisely dated archaeological, and indeed sub-fossil, stories coming directly from the act of dating sites and events by dendrochronology.

In Chapter 10 I take a somewhat light-hearted look at two key ancient chronologies – the Shang in China and the New Kingdom in Egypt – and consider their dating in the light of some of the tree-ring evidence in Chapters 5, 6 and 7. It may come as a surprise to many readers to realize that before c. 800 BC the only truly known dates in the world, with the exception of a handful of astronomical retrocalculations associated with ancient Chinese records, derive from dendrochronology. The historians of ancient Egypt so beloved of statements such as 'Nefer died in 2400 BC' or 'Waty, who was buried here in 2372 BC' are beginning to come clean on the errors associated with their chronology. If there is at least some flexibility in the Egyptian chronology then it seems appropriate to ask just how it is dated. In Chapter 10 this is one of a number of general chronological issues discussed in some detail. Having gone from hard chronology to speculation on related chronological issues, the final summing up relates to the quite apparent inadequacy of our knowledge of the past. Now that we can date some ancient environmental happenings very precisely, it is obvious how little we know about the causes – how do we separate the effects of several, large, coincident volcanic eruptions from the effects due to a cometary impact on an ocean?

Finally, I feel that there are some observations which have no other logical place in this book; I record them here for what they are worth. One lesson of the 1980s is that people shouldn't try to push trees around. You can't tell a tree what it should or should not have recorded in its rings. You can't tell a tree where it should have grown. In Chapter 3 we see the consequences of one worker's attempts to tell several hundred oak panels that they had grown in England. They hadn't – which was why their ring patterns refused to match with native patterns from the British Isles. In retrospect the trees were telling anyone who was willing to listen that they were exotic to England.

There are other examples in Chapter 2 where Hollstein tried to tell German oaks when they were felled: they 'knew' when they were felled and they 'told' Baatz, which led to the unravel-

ling of that problem. When Hollstein did the same thing again, those trees told their Irish cousins there was something wrong and again led to the solving of the puzzle. There's nothing supernatural about this; it's just that trees are rooted in the real world (*sic*). Each ancient tree only grew once and only grew in one place. When they tell us where and when those places and times were – when their ring patterns are cor-rectly cross-dated against appropriate chronologies – they tend not to lie. When the trees told Val LaMarche that there had been a major volcanically related environmental event in the 1620s BC, some people accused them of lying – but they didn't lie then either (see Chapter 5). I would like to formalize the statement: '*The trees don't lie.*'

A final note: one convention used in this book is that all tree-ring or historical dates are AD/BC. Uncalibrated radiocarbon dates are noted as BP. Any other usage will be made clear in the text.

1 The tree-ring dating method

Basic principles

In concept, tree-ring dating is still an extremely simple method. It relies, like most dating methods, on a natural clock; in this case the natural clock provided by the annual growth rings of trees. For the sake of discussion the following descriptions will concentrate on the characteristics of oak, because, in northern Europe, oak underpins the tree-ring method. Many of the comments could be applied in a general way to a number of other species. Most temperate trees put on a single ring of new wood each year. This ring is formed immediately under the bark and, in the case of trees such as oak, forms a visually apparent band on a cut or polished cross-section of the main stem. The annual bands of new wood accumulate over the lifetime of a tree into a year-by-year record of the tree's life – its ring pattern. To some extent this ring pattern must record the conditions under which the tree grew. We might expect, and herein lies the basis of the dating method, all trees of the same species in the same 'climatic area' to record at least some aspects of common growth conditions. If such common records do exist, and clearly they do because the method works repeatably, it becomes possible to compare the pattern of rings from one tree to its neighbour and, as importantly, to overlap patterns back in time. In practice, widespread studies of oak growth patterns have shown that there is a strong common element to the patterns over surprisingly large areas.

Fig. 1.1 illustrates the process of chronology building. The ring pattern of the modern tree is anchored at the present – the date of its last growth ring is known. The pattern of its inner rings are overlapped with the outer rings of an ancient specimen; in this case from an historic building. This process is carried on through the

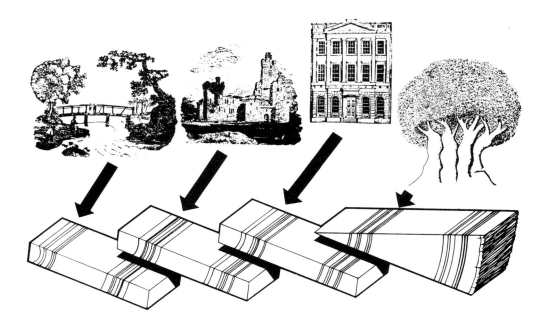

1.1 Schematic representation of the principle behind dendrochronology

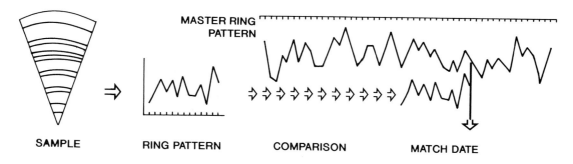

SAMPLE   RING PATTERN   COMPARISON   MATCH DATE

1.2 Schematic representation of the dating process

patterns of successively older timbers from buildings, from archaeological sites and, ultimately, from natural sources such as lake margins, submerged forests, peat bogs and river gravels. As a result, and we will look at this in some detail in Chapter 2, very long master chronologies can be constructed, with lengths of seven–nine millennia. The master chronologies do not of course depend on the patterns from single trees. If we consider oak, many individual ring patterns are cross-dated for every period and the master pattern is therefore a year-by-year record of average oak growth, for a particular region.

From a dating point of view, once a master chronology is available, the next stage is to analyse a timber of unknown age. This involves preparing the transverse surface of the specimen in such a way that the ring pattern is clearly visible. Once prepared, the width of each individual ring, from the centre to the outside of the specimen, is measured using one of a range of measuring devices. The resulting list of consecutive ring widths – the ring pattern of the specimen – can then be compared with the master chronology for the appropriate area and species (**Fig. 1.2**). In concept, there are strong similarities with the fingerprinting of humans. In tree-ring studies the comparisons are made both visually and statistically. Statistical computer packages represent an invaluable aid to the dendrochronologist and are mostly based on the same general principles. A correlation coefficient is calculated at every position of overlap between the specimen ring pattern and the master pattern. If the specimen is of the correct species, if it is from the same area as the master chronology, and, if it is suitably long, then often it will be possible to find a

unique matching position, i.e. only one position where the pattern fits the master visually and with a really high correlation value. The correct matching position will be where the year-by-year record of the specimen refers to the same span of years in the master. If the pattern matching is successful, the date of the last ring on the specimen can be read off with exact calendrical precision from the master. To compound the fingerprinting analogy, if enough points of similarity are established between a tree-ring sample and a master pattern, the sample's *time* is identified.

Such a dating method is breathtaking in its elegance and simplicity and, of course, the real joy is that it has been found to work, and work repeatably, in many areas and for a number of species. Different workers have built chronologies and arrived at the same answer when attempting to date test samples. The following chapters will be liberally sprinkled with examples which show the levels of replication which are possible between chronologies and the almost unbelievable accuracy of the results. Many sites yield specimens where the time of felling is restricted to about six months: 'the timbers used in the construction of the Corlea 1 trackway (in Co. Longford, Ireland) last grew in 148 BC and were felled either late in 148 BC or early in 147 BC' or 'the main activity at the Sweet Track was in the winter/spring of 3807/6 BC'. Occasionally it is possible to specify felling in the early part of the summer, i.e. to within about two months. Here then is a tool which can be used to resolve historical and archaeological questions, on the one hand, and which can give information on such diverse topics as river gravel formation, bog growth and past environmental conditions, on the other.

17

Historical elements

Dendrochronology has come a long way in the last 90 years. The first half of this century was largely monopolized by work in America by A.E. Douglass and his followers. Because of the nature of the method, Douglass' descriptions of his pioneer work are still fresh today (see, for example, Douglass 1919). While there may be differences in detail the basic elements of chronology building never change. Douglass was the first to face up to putting together the main elements of master chronologies, contending with gaps in the record due to sampling deficiencies, ironing out problems – worse for him because his stressed pines from the arid south-west of the United States frequently missed rings – and checking for replication to prove the chronologies. Douglass' completion of the first, great, classic, chronology-building exercise, involving many overlaps through successively older yellow pines, ensures his position as the 'father' of dendrochronology (Robinson 1976; Baillie 1982).

The work initiated by Douglass continued and expanded, mostly at the dedicated Laboratory for Tree-Ring Research in the University of Arizona at Tucson, with eventual chronologies for bristle-cone pine running back to beyond 6000 BC (Ferguson and Graybill 1983). In comparison, European work developed slowly from the 1930s onwards with the main European flowering coming only in the last twenty years. From the late 1960s a whole generation of workers dedicated themselves to the construction of long master chronologies. It is undoubtedly the case that these long chronologies form the backbone of the subject. When Ferguson published his bristle-cone pine chronology in 1969 the longest published tree-ring chronologies in Europe extended only as far as AD 822 and AD 832 (Hollstein 1965; Huber and Giertz 1969). Now there are continuous records for Ireland back to 5479 BC (Brown and Baillie 1992), for England back to 4989 BC (Baillie and Brown 1988), for south Germany back to 7237 BC (Becker and Schmidt 1990) and for north Germany back to 6200 BC (Leuschner 1992). Leuschner also reports that Becker's south German chronology has now broken the 10,000-year barrier. Overall, dendrochronology is now based on a well-tried

and tested methodology. The remainder of this chapter examines the main elements in both the working of the method and chronology construction. This is a necessary section for those not previously familiar with tree-ring dating. Although only an outline, it should be sufficient to give the newcomer a feel for the methodology which underpins the results in the following chapters.

Sampling

As dendrochronology deals with ring patterns, clearly ring patterns have to be acquired for study. The requirements are extremely simple. Sampling is about extracting ring patterns – the widths of all the successive rings from the pith to the bark of a tree. The tree can be standing, felled, cut up and built into a building, buried in an archaeological site or natural deposit. It may be in a secondary position, for example, a jumble of timbers from a demolished building or a pile of tree-trunks recovered from some drainage operation. The optimum method of obtaining the ring pattern of a timber will always be the cutting of a complete cross-section (i.e. transverse to the original direction of growth) and this is straightforward when dealing with timbers out of context.

Sampling problems arise mostly where the dendrochronologist has to be as non-destructive as possible. This is certainly the case with living trees and with timbers in important or occupied buildings. Obviously it is also important when attempting to extract the ring patterns of valuable museum objects, such as panels in furniture or those supporting paintings. Methods include wet and dry coring, X-ray analysis, ultrasonic probes and body scanners on the one hand, through to simple photography and contact 'lifting' on the other. I was introduced to this latter procedure by Hubert Leuschner and it nicely demonstrates the empirical nature of tree-ring studies.

In a word dendrochronologists need ring patterns and it doesn't much matter what sort of Heath Robinson device is used to get them, as long as, at the end of the day, an accurate set of numbers is available from the timber. For example, the 'lifting' procedure involves making a thin strip of a child's moulding clay. The strip is then laid along the ring pattern (the edge of a panel, for instance) and pressed firmly on to the wood. Dust present (or applied in the form of chalk) in the spring vessels of each ring is transferred to the strip and remains as a well-defined image when peeled off. Moreover the material can be rendered permanent by heating in a domestic oven, thus providing a useful record for storage purposes. The procedure works particularly well on oak with its ring-porous structure and large spring vessels. So samples can end up in the laboratory as everything from complete cross-sections of trees, sections of beams, cores, charcoal, X-ray plates and photographs to strips of modelling clay. If the sample is wood, as most inevitably are, it can be wet, dry, solid or decayed. The job of the dendrochronologist is then to extract from the sample that all-important ring pattern.

Preparation and measurement

Since the principal aim is to extract an optimum ring pattern from the sample, it is important that the individual growth rings be rendered clearly visible. Different workers favour different methods when dealing with wood samples, depending on whether the sample is wet or dry. With wet samples paring or planing is the preferred technique and certainly paring renders the structure of the wood visible down to the level of individual cells. With dry samples, sanding often produces optimum results and the surface can be rendered highly visible by the application of successively finer grades of abrasive. Normally pared or sanded specimens are treated with chalk dust or some other agent, which highlights the spring vessels and ring boundaries.

Since the most useful dates produced by dendrochronologists will be those which specify the felling year of the timber, it is important, whenever possible, to take samples which run out to the bark surface (see also under 'sapwood', below). In oak the stem is made up of an inner cylinder of robust, consolidated, heartwood and an outer, unconsolidated, layer of sapwood. So, since the sapwood runs out to the underbark surface, complete sapwood is vital for really precise dating. Unfortunately the unconsolidated sap-

wood readily suffers damage due to insect attack (in buildings) or rot (in buried specimens). As a result, difficulties can be experienced with both dry samples from buildings and wet samples from archaeological contexts. When coring building timbers it is important to extract subsidiary samples of complete sapwood so that the ring patterns can be reconstructed out to the felling surface. With wet archaeological samples the sapwood is often so de-natured that it can be damaged simply by the weight of the sample itself. In this latter case it is wise to measure the ring pattern in the sapwood as soon as possible to guard against either physical damage or damage due to differential drying.

So procedures for dealing with particular sample conditions are largely a matter of common sense and experience. The same can be said for measurement. In essence the idea is to measure the width of each ring in the sample from as close to the centre (pith) as possible, to as close to the felling surface (bark) as possible. Although the individual rings should be measured radially, there is no rule which dictates measurement along a single radius. The governing factors are:

(i) that the measurement of the individual ring should clearly reflect the relative width of the ring being measured to the width of the previous ring;
(ii) that the overall pattern should reflect measurement where the rings are most 'regular'.

These factors arise out of experience and represent an optimizing of the ring pattern. An alternative procedure would be always to measure in an exact radial line and take the mean of three such radial measurements. In the course of measurement it is essential to mark the pattern at regular intervals – normally every tenth ring, with additional marks to highlight each fiftieth and hundredth ring – to facilitate subsequent checking of the sample and to guard against losing one's place during measurement.

Once an optimum ring pattern has been produced for a sample, the ring widths are plotted against a scale in years. Different procedures are used depending on preference, some workers using raw ring widths while others employ semilog plots. The end result is a graph for the

19

individual tree with a scale in years which can subsequently be converted to calendar dates once the sample is precisely dated. The graph will also carry annotations on such things as problem rings, anomalous rings, the position of the heartwood/sapwood boundary and the condition of the felling surface (if it exists). Having sampled and prepared the timber and having measured the ring pattern, the original wood sample is converted to a graph and a set of numbers. The sample itself can then be stored for future reference. This is where dry samples, photographs and even modelling clay do prove an advantage as they can be stored indefinitely. Wet samples tend to take on a life of their own! Even if frozen, they remain dependent on someone supplying money for electricity; wet they play host to a wealth of organisms bent on recycling the cellulose.

Cross-dating

Cross-dating is the art of dendrochronology. The sample has been fingerprinted: its ring pattern has been taken. Now the dendrochronologist must identify that ring pattern against other individual ring patterns or against a master chronology. The course of action will depend on particular circumstances. If one is dealing with a group of timbers from a single context, it will often be possible to cross-match the individual ring patterns visually by examining the graphs superimposed over a light box. Often an internally consistent site chronology can be constructed purely by visual matching. A site master chronology can then be constructed by meaning the individual ring patterns together at their correct relative positions. A site master has the advantage of ironing out a lot of the 'noise' associated with individual samples and concentrating the matching 'signal'. Indeed, experience shows that site masters have a higher dating success rate than individual timbers. In practice extensive use is made of cross-correlation computer programs which calculate some sort of correlation coefficient on the high-frequency (year-to-year) component of the ring patterns. Statistics such as the German 'coefficient of parallel variation' (w) values (Eckstein and Bauch 1969) or t values obtained from programs such as CROS (Baillie and Pilcher 1973) or Cross-84 (Munro 1984) are still in widespread use. Attempts have even been made to combine these two measures of correlation to assist with the identification of a single position of strongest correlation (Schmidt 1987). It is almost certain that this latter approach has little validity to a statistician – combining two statistics which are not themselves independent. However, this in itself helps to highlight an aspect of dendrochronology which is widely misunderstood. When a dendrochronologist uses a computer-based

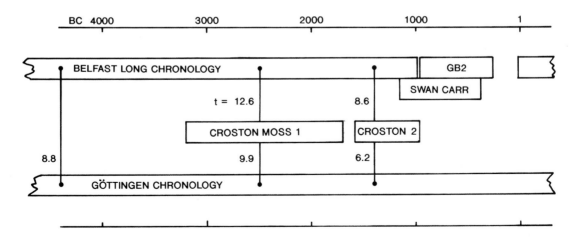

1.3 Completely integrated correlations between independent chronologies. The long sections of English chronology from Croston Moss, Lancashire, match at exactly the same date against both the Irish and German master chronologies, with highly significant correlations

correlation program 'to pick out possible matches' he or she is using the correlation coefficients as a *guide*. Matches between ring patterns, whether between individual trees or between master chronologies, are not perfect 100% matches. The practised dendrochronologist is looking for matches which he/she is willing to accept, based on experience, as correct matches between long ring patterns (see also below).

Misunderstandings between statisticians and dendrochronologists have always centred on this cardinal point: the statisticians are talking about 'statistical tolerances and significance levels', while the dendrochronologists are talking about 'guides' as to where to look for significant matches (Orton 1983). Of course it is nice, when a computer match between a 200-year ring pattern and a master chronology is $t = 8.5$ with a statistical tolerance of $p = 0.0000000002$; however, it is not necessary for the dendrochronologist to have this level of correlation in order to establish an absolutely correct match. The secret is that the dendrochronologist has relevant experience and a repertoire of multi-match back-up, in the form of *replication*. The dendrochronologist is seldom looking at a single match and a single correlation value. Most of the time there are multiple correlations, all of which have to be self-consistent to make the match acceptable. So, for example, when the English Croston Moss chronology matches with both the independent German and Irish master chronologies at self-consistent positions with significant t values (**Fig. 1.3**), it is no longer a case of statistical tolerances, it is a case of absolute certainty. Purists would argue that, since the probabilities are multiplicative, the probability of such a self-consistent set of correlations being wrong becomes vanishingly small.

So, correlation programs are extremely useful and this is particularly the case with some of the reference chronologies which are thousands of years in length. In such cases it would not be practical to search for matching positions by eye. High-correlation positions are checked visually and, where appropriate, backed up by replicative matches. It should be pointed out that other approaches to the problem of cross-dating have been suggested (see, for example, Wigley *et al.* 1987 and Yamaguchi and Allen 1992, among

others). Unfortunately, in none of these cases have working programs gone into general usage. This is a direct reflection of the fact that the method works repeatably, and to the satisfaction of the peer group, using variants of the existing w and t programs, in combination with visual matching and replication. (Anyone wanting to perfect a computer program which will give absolutely certain matches is presumably working towards a black box system which will automatically measure and cross-date samples and eliminate the subjective human element in dendrochronology. I wish them luck!)

Sapwood and interpretation

Let us imagine that the dendrochronologist has successfully sampled, measured and cross-dated either one timber or a group of timbers. In an ideal world each timber would be complete to its felling year and interpretation would be straightforward. In **Fig. 1.4a** we see examples of this ideal situation. Each sample last grew in the same year and any interpretation devolves to discussions of possible storage or seasoning – or the relationship of the timbers to the building in which they occurred. All such arguments are secondary to the dating: we know the exact felling dates. In **Fig. 1.4b** there are two clear felling phases and any interpretation falls to the archaeologist or building historian. The tree-ring evidence is unequivocal. In these complete sapwood cases interpretation is essentially trivial. Indeed, it is in these cases that one is drawn into the minutiae of the *season* of felling. In oaks, the large spring vessels at the beginning of a ring are normally the product of growth in April–May. So a timber felled in the early summer will show a ring pattern truncated immediately after the spring vessels of its last ring. On the other hand, if its summer wood appears complete, then it could have been felled at any time between roughly September of its final growth year and March of the following year. Hence there is a fine distinction between the 'last year of growth' and the 'felling year' of a tree. As such examples accumulate, dendrochronologists become more punctilious in their language. Note how the Sweet Track timbers 'last grew' in 3807 BC and

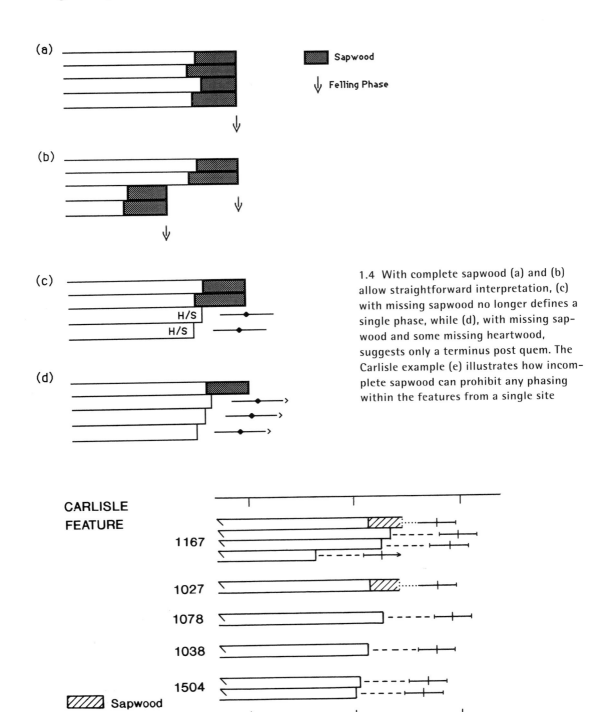

1.4 With complete sapwood (a) and (b) allow straightforward interpretation, (c) with missing sapwood no longer defines a single phase, while (d), with missing sapwood and some missing heartwood, suggests only a terminus post quem. The Carlisle example (e) illustrates how incomplete sapwood can prohibit any phasing within the features from a single site were felled late in 3807 BC or early in 3806 BC (Hillam *et al.* 1990). It often seems laughable that dendrochronologists are worried about a semantic nicety which, at most, might make a difference of about four months. However, tree-rings are about absolute precision. In a case like the Sweet Track it is wrong to say that the timbers were felled in 3807 BC because they might, in fact, have been felled in 3806 BC! Perhaps this tendency to exactitude is brought about by the summer-felled trees where one is no longer talking about years but about 'felling in May or June' of a particular year (Baillie 1982: 162).

Unfortunately, given the friable nature of sapwood, the felling date of many archaeological samples cannot be specified to the year; there are a whole series of retreats from the precise dating scenario. Sapwood can be partially present or totally absent. These are several possibilities:

i) where a small amount of the sapwood is damaged or missing;
ii) where most of the sapwood is missing but one or two definite sapwood rings remain;
iii) where all the sapwood is missing but other evidence suggests that *only* the sapwood is missing and the heartwood is complete;
iv) where all the sapwood plus an unknown quantity of heartwood is missing.

In each of these cases attempts to rescue dating accuracy involve the use of some estimate of the expected number of sapwood rings. However, with sapwood there is good news and bad news. An estimate of the number of sapwood rings on an oak can be made by measuring a lot of examples with complete sapwood. Unfortunately it transpires that the sapwood estimates are very variable both within an area and between areas. In Ireland the 68% confidence limits on oak sapwood are 23–41 years (95% confidence 14–50 years) (Baillie 1973, 1982) while in England Hillam *et al.* (1984, 1987) propose a 95% range of 15–50 years. While these estimates are consistent they have to be viewed against average sapwood numbers around 20 years in Germany (Hollstein 1980) and as low as 14±3 in Finland (Baillie *et al.* 1985).

So, with the loss of sapwood there is an immediate and serious step-down in dendrochronological accuracy from those marvellously precise examples where the sapwood was complete. Fig. 1.4 illustrates the problem. In **Fig. 1.4c** we see two timbers with complete sapwood and two with definite heartwood/sapwood boundaries. In this case the estimated felling dates are 'not inconsistent with' all the timbers having been felled in the same year. However, that is quite different from being able to say that they *were* all felled in the same year, the case with Fig. 1.4a. In **Fig. 1.4d** we have several timbers without any trace of sapwood and in each case felling could be within the range of the sapwood estimate *or later*, i.e. the estimated felling range is only a *terminus post quem*. In this case sensible interpretation rapidly breaks down: the timbers without sapwood could easily have been felled later than the sample with complete sapwood. Such problems can be accommodated where the timbers are all from a single structure and/or where archaeological information would infer simultaneous use. However, when timbers from different structures all have missing sapwood it can become impossible to assign any kind of relative dating.

An example of this is shown in **Fig. 1.4e** where the felling dates of timbers, from an early analysis of different Roman structures at Carlisle, could not be separated by tree-ring analysis (Eckstein *et al.* 1984). Interestingly, a later detailed analysis of a large sample of timbers from Carlisle, by Cathy Groves at Sheffield, did allow the isolation of detailed Roman building phases at Carlisle, starting in AD 72/73 and earlier than the traditional historical date of AD 79 based on Tacitus (Hillam 1992). From the point of view of this discussion, the building phases in AD 72/3–85 and AD 93–7 could only be separated with timbers with complete sapwood.

Such are the problems with incomplete samples, and other examples will be encountered below. The important point is that these interpretive difficulties are not in any way semantic. There are many quite genuine examples where potentially serious dating errors could occur if the concept of missing heartwood rings is ignored. In an early example from Hillsborough Fort in Co. Down, two timbers cut from the same parent tree, felled around AD 1660, had final heartwood rings at 1585 and 1488. Failure to recognize that truncation was a significant factor

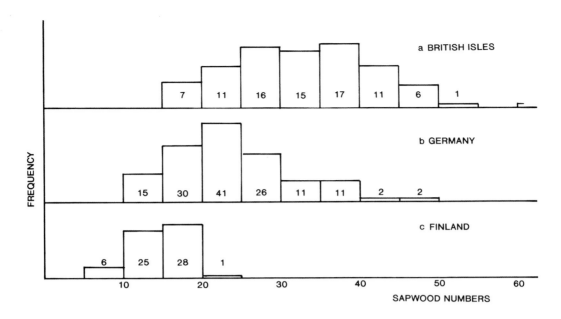

1.5 Sapwood numbers for oaks from different areas within Europe showing an apparently systematic decrease with distance from the Atlantic (Baillie et al.1985)

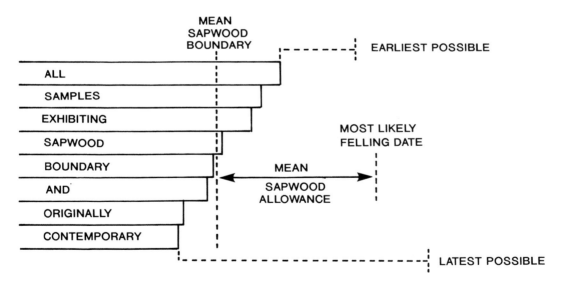

1.6 Hollstein's proposed method for assessing the closest felling date from a group of timbers with missing sapwood (Hollstein 1980)

in this case could have led to estimated felling ranges of 1617±9 and 1520±9 respectively; dates too early by two and seven human generations. In such cases, where no evidence for sapwood exists, it is essential to state the uncertainty by adding 'or later' to any felling estimate, i.e. provide a *terminus post quem*.

Additional information on the effects of woodworking practice on sample completeness is given below (see Island MacHugh in Chapter 4). The subject of sapwood can become even more difficult when account is taken of factors such as importation. When making sapwood allowances it is obviously quite important to know the area of origin of the timbers involved (**Fig. 1.5** and Chapter 3).

Finally, on the subject of sapwood allowances, it is sometimes possible to rescue dating accuracy where a number of samples from a single phase all have clear heartwood/sapwood boundaries (**Fig. 1.6**). With the provision that only the sapwood is missing, and assuming that the timbers were originally felled at the same time, then the outermost heartwood years should be at distances from the felling date governed by the sapwood estimate and standard deviation (range). This approach essentially involves finding the *mean* sapwood boundary and adding on the *mean* sapwood allowance. Although this approach seems eminently sensible, the fact that sapwood estimates are mostly skewed distributions complicates the issue somewhat (Fig. 1.5).

Building a chronology

Having outlined the ways in which the dendrochronological method works, we can, by way of an example, trace the development of chronology construction in the British Isles during the 1970s. What follows is essentially a précis of *Tree-Ring Dating and Archaeology* (Baillie 1982, from here on referred to as '*TRDA*'). This serves two functions. It acts as an extended introduction for those not familiar with dendrochronology and it sets the scene for several aspects of the remainder of the volume.

The first stage in building an indigenous tree-ring chronology is to choose a suitable species. The requirements are stringent:

1) The species has to be long lived – or it will never be possible to significantly extend the chronology, all the overlaps being taken up in the matching process.
2) The species has to be available from all periods – otherwise a continuous chronology will be impossible.
3) The species has to be a good subject for

dendrochronology – it has to exhibit cross-dating.

These three criteria have so far restricted most north European dendrochronology, and the really long chronologies, to oak. However, other species have received attention in Germany, Scandinavia and Switzerland where extensive use has been made of conifers (Schweingruber 1983). One recent climate reconstruction has been based on a Fennoscandinavian pine chronology which extends back to AD 500 (Briffa *et al.* 1990) and it is reported that a 7000-year chronology has been outlined in the area with only one or two gaps (Keith Briffa and Pentti Zetterberg pers. comm.).

Modern trees

Having selected a species for chronology building, modern samples are acquired to form the anchor in time. These modern samples of known felling or sampling dates also allow the cross-matching properties of the species to be investigated (a variety of corers exist which allow non-destructive sampling of living trees). Clearly, if the method is not capable of cross-dating known-age test samples there would be little hope of building a long chronology. In most European studies the modern samples have also supplied some information on tree-age, measurement difficulties, missing or absent rings and, in the case of oak, sapwood properties.

The choice of study area is potentially critical. For example, having chosen to build a long chronology in Ireland, in part because of the large numbers of prehistoric bog oaks, it turned out that Ireland, for complex reasons, has no really long-lived modern oak trees. The oldest Irish oak, so far discovered, ran back only to 1649. In Scotland, living trees were found with ring patterns which stretched back to 1444 (from Cadzow near Hamilton), while in England Sherwood Forest specimens ran back to 1425. However, while it might have proved easier to build a medieval chronology in Scotland, it would have been next to impossible to extend that chronology into the prehistoric period. So, while the medieval section may have been more

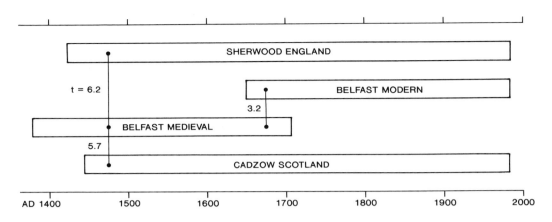

1.7 Placement of the original Belfast medieval chronology was based on a 68-year overlap with a t value of only 3.2. This was later confirmed to be correct by consistent links to two living-tree chronologies from Britain

difficult in Ireland, it was a necessary precursor to the long bog-oak chronology. In retrospect, the difficulties experienced with medieval overlaps in Ireland forced us to face all the questions associated with cross-matching at an early stage (Baillie 1973). Constructing a chronology back to 1380 required the linking of ring patterns from living trees to historic timbers, a link which could subsequently be tested by direct cross-dating to the English and Scottish living-tree chronologies (**Fig. 1.7**). This is a classic example of how

extensive replication can confer *absolute certainty* on the dating of a section of ring pattern.

The Middle Ages

By the mid-1970s, with an Irish chronology successfully extended back to the fourteenth century, another problem was encountered. Chronologies existed for both the north of

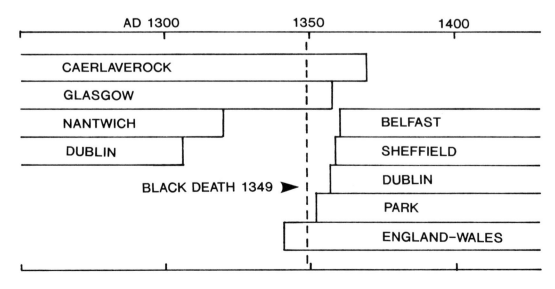

1.8 Oak chronologies from the British Isles show clear evidence for a major regeneration phase, just at the time of the Black Death, in the mid-fourteenth century

Ireland and the Dublin area covering the tenth–fourteenth centuries. It proved extremely difficult to bridge back across the fourteenth century to link with these earlier chronologies. It became apparent that there was a 'depletion/regeneration' phase *c.* 1350 (**Fig. 1.8**). The same problem had shown up elsewhere, in both England and northern Germany, and it was possible to suggest that this tree-ring hiatus was due to the effects of the Black Death which swept through Europe just at that time. The difficulties associated with attempting to build chronologies across both the seventeenth and the fourteenth centuries in Ireland were the first clues that tree-ring studies could give information of a 'socio-economic' character (see Chapter 8).

Although it took a considerable time, timbers were eventually found in Ireland which allowed the chronology to be extended across the fourteenth century. By 1977 the Belfast chronology ran back to AD 1001 (Baillie 1977a), while the Dublin medieval chronology ran back to AD 855 (Baillie 1977b). This Dublin section was dated not only against the Belfast chronology but also against a parallel chronology from Scotland, which spanned AD 946 to the present (Baillie 1977c). (This Scottish chronology was the source of some considerable irony. While work had gone on from 1968 to 1977 to construct a Belfast chronology back to AD 1001, all the tim-

bers required to construct a similar chronology in Scotland were acquired in a matter of a few months!) So, by 1977 chronologies had been produced in Ireland of an equivalent length to the pre-existing German chronologies of Hollstein and Huber-Giertz.

Replication

One highly significant finding, involving the Dublin chronology, related to the ultimate proof of the whole chronology system. It was discovered that there was a strong cross-correlation between the Dublin chronology and an English medieval chronology, Ref. 6 (Fletcher 1977), which had previously been dated against the German oak chronologies. This observation showed that a section of English chronology could be dated to the same end-year, 1193, against both Irish and German chronologies. QED: both chronologies must be in precise synchronization (**Fig. 1.9** shows the correlation values involved).

So it was possible to check the correctness of a chronology by replication against an independent chronology. This is termed *tertiary* replication. It was to become increasingly obvious that replication was the secret to successful chronology building. It occurs at three levels:

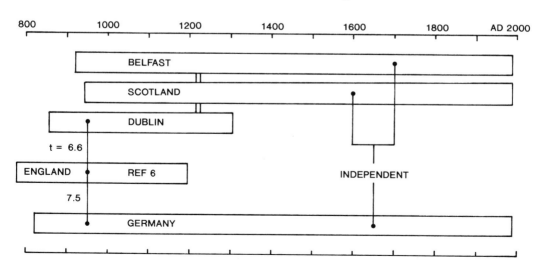

1.9 An early example of tertiary replication between independent chronologies. The English Ref 6 chronology dates to AD 1193 against both Irish and German chronologies

1) Primary replication is provided by the matches between the individual ring patterns which go to make up a site chronology.
2) Secondary replication is provided by comparisons between independent site chronologies which tend to be both longer and, because of their internal replication, more robust than individual ring patterns.
3) Tertiary replication, which provides the ultimate test, involves correlations between the chronologies of independent workers; see Chapter 2.

Replication is the factor which allows dendrochronologists to have confidence in their procedures. A dendrochronologist can not only claim that a chronology is precisely correct on the basis of in-house primary and secondary replication, but can demonstrate independent verification using tertiary replication.

The first millennium AD

With the Irish chronology pushed back to the ninth century AD, another gap problem was encountered. A long archaeological chronology was known, on both general archaeological grounds and on radiocarbon evidence, to span approximately the first eight centuries AD. Continuous sample collection throughout the 1970s failed to provide any link between the Dublin chronology (which ran back to AD 855) and this Dark Age chronology (Baillie 1979). It was clear that the problem was centred on the ninth century AD. At this stage in chronology construction no continuous oak chronologies were published for this period from any part of Europe. Becker and Delorme (1978) had formalized the case for central Europe, showing chronological breaks in the third century and around AD 800. So pushing back into the Dark Ages was literally stepping into the dark!

However, it was noted by Jennifer Hillam that the Dublin chronology cross-dated extraordinarily well with a chronology from Exeter, in the south-west of England, which in turn matched with a chronology from Tudor Street, London, which spanned AD 682–918 (Hillam 1981). Combined with the successful stepwise correlations from Dublin to Ref. 6 to Germany, it seemed possible that the solution to the ninth-century Irish gap lay in links to English chronologies. The crucial breakthrough came in early 1980 when a new chronology, from Ballydowane West, Co. Waterford, cross-dated against both the existing Irish Dark Age chronology and against Tudor Street. This link, from the south-east of Ireland, confirmed that the Dark

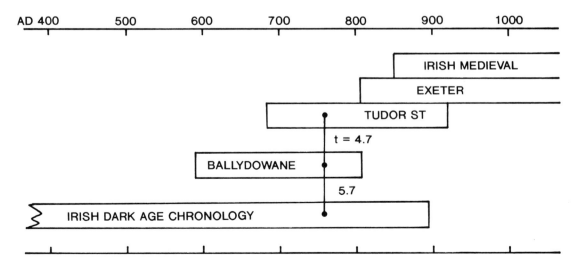

1.10 English chronologies, from Tudor Street, London, and Exeter, provided a key link across the ninth-century Irish 'gap'

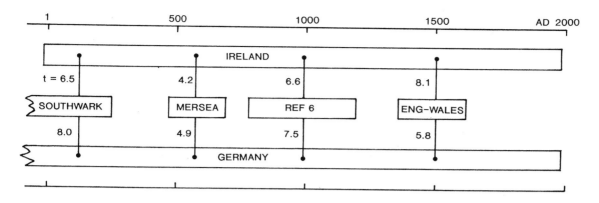

1.11 Full tertiary replication of the European oak chronologies for the last two millennia showing consistent stepwise correlations from Ireland to England to Germany

Age chronology spanned AD 894–13 BC (**Fig. 1.10**). So the chronology had overlapped, by 40 years, with the older end of the Dublin chronology; an overlap much too short to serve as a basis for a substantive dendrochronological link.

As with so much research, any glory associated with the completion of a two-millennia chronology was short-lived: in 1980 Hollstein published his German oak chronologies back to 724 BC. However, this independent German chronology, and others dated against it, did allow confirmation of the dating of the Irish chronology by further stepwise correlations (**Fig. 1.11**) (Baillie 1982). So 1980 saw a major consolidation phase in the dendrochronology of the first millennium AD in northern Europe. Precise dating was available, against replicated chronologies, for the whole of the last 2000 years.

Prehistoric chronologies

During the 1970s, while a lot of effort was going into the completion of the AD chronologies, workers in Ireland and Germany were pushing ahead with the construction of long prehistoric oak chronologies. There were different reasons for the work in different areas. In Ireland the principal aim was high-precision radiocarbon calibration, with archaeological dating viewed as a natural spin-off. In Germany there was a wide range of motivation, which included radiocarbon calibration and studies of river valley development as well as quests for palaeoecological and archaeological information.

The approach to building prehistoric chronologies was necessarily different from that applied to the last two millennia. In the AD era most of the timbers were archaeological and at least some general time-control was available from archaeological evidence and building history. In the prehistoric period most of the timbers were sub-fossil. These are naturally preserved oak trunks which occur in two principal contexts, namely peat bogs and river gravels. In the former case the oaks originally grew on the surface of peat bogs; though just to complicate matters some grew on mineral soils and were subsequently buried in peat. After death and burial, bog oaks were preserved as stumps or trunks at the spot where they grew. With river-gravel oaks the trees were presumably washed out from eroding river banks by fluvial action so that they are no longer *in situ*. Such different sources suggest that different types of environmental information may be recorded by these trees, in terms both of climate response and the information contained in their accumulated growth initiation and death phases.

The approach to building sub-fossil chronologies was conditioned by the fact that most of the trees came without stratigraphic or other dating information. As a result they had to be treated as random samples. However, it was quickly apparent that 'random' did not imply 'completely different dates'. It was observed that trees from one location tended to cluster in time, i.e. many of their ring patterns cross-dated. In retrospect this is sensible because, at any given location, the

29

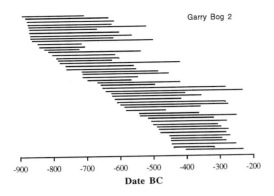

1.12 The individual tree-ring patterns making up the Garry Bog 2 chronology, plotted by start-year, showing regeneration over five centuries

trees were originally part of a regenerating system. This is demonstrably the case because at most sites the trees not only cluster but tend to be staggered through time (**Fig. 1.12**).

Inevitably all workers aimed towards the construction of robust site chronologies, exploiting the regenerating character of the assemblages. Sub-fossil site chronologies could be much longer than the lifespan of individual trees and were, of course, more robust units because of their internal replication. So workers built site chronologies and used these long series as the building blocks of the overall chronology. Computer comparisons allowed the testing of every possible position of chronology overlap. Matches between site chronologies extended site chronologies into major units of chronology, while further site chronologies provided secondary replication confirming established links,

and so on.

By 1980 it was clear that the Irish and German prehistoric chronologies were at a very similar stage of near completion (**Fig. 1.13**). The problem was, of course, that they were *not* complete. By that stage the whole nature of chronology construction had changed. While all the early work had relied on random sampling to 'fill up time', by 1980, with only a few specified gaps remaining, it became necessary to find timbers of specific ages to bridge those gaps. That posed a whole new set of problems; for example, where do you go to find timbers which grew across the tenth century BC? Were the gaps purely a sampling problem, whereby more and more samples would eventually bridge the remaining gaps, or was there something more to the gaps? Was it possible that environmental events had interrupted the survival of oaks so severely at some points that it would prove impossible to complete the chronologies? These were some of the questions which were current when *TRDA* (Baillie 1982) was being written.

1980 conclusions

It is interesting from the perspective of the 1990s to look back at the conclusions which were written in 1980. Firstly, there were questions hanging over the completion of the long chronologies. If the gaps in the Irish chronology, in the first centuries BC and in the tenth century BC, were due to some sort of widespread depletions, then it might never be possible to bridge those gaps within Ireland. There is no doubt that at that time there

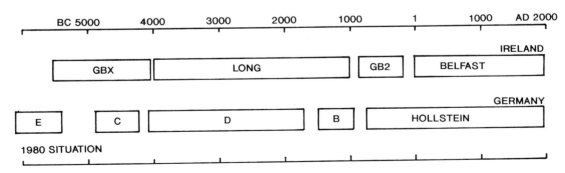

1.13 The 1980 status of the European long chronologies showing almost equal progress, and very similar distributions of remaining gaps. Chronology sections E, C, D and B from Becker and Delorme (1978)

were grounds for pessimism.

The failure to complete the prehistoric chronologies left another piece of unfinished business. Until the European oak chronologies were complete and replicated, it was not going to be possible to complete the high-precision radio-carbon calibration curves. As an independent European calibration was necessary to check the original Suess calibration (Suess 1970), the completion of the tree-ring chronologies was fundamentally important.

The one other outstanding problem, in 1980, was that relating to the so-called art-historical chronologies in England (Fletcher 1977, 1978a). These chronologies, constructed from art-historical boards, failed to show any cross-dating with the other, apparently indigenous, oak chronologies from the British Isles. One obvious solution was that the art-historical chronologies represented imported timbers from an 'exotic' source. Unfortunately, because such a suggestion had implications for the dating of the same

chronologies, this suggestion was bitterly contested. This was obviously a question which was going to have to be resolved (see Chapter 3).

The two other future projections, back in 1980, related to the possibilities of climatic reconstruction and chronological coverage. It is interesting to see statements such as 'It seems likely that between the three methods, widths, densities and isotopic ratios, notwithstanding other approaches which may become available [*sic*], it should be possible to make adequate reconstructions for the last thousand years with thinner but none-the-less useful extrapolations well back into the post-glacial' (Baillie 1982: 250). In some ways we are only marginally further forward today although one of those 'other approaches' does appear to have paid off handsomely (see Chapters 5, 6 and 7). In the following chapters I will deal with the unfinished business from the early 1980s and show how dendrochronology has moved forward on many fronts.

2 Oak dendrochronology comes of age

This chapter will review some of the basic work in dendrochronology which took place during the 1980s. There is no doubt that long, replicated chronologies form the backbone of the tree-ring method. It was important to have this backbone in the form of precisely correct, year-by-year records before the full power of the method could be employed. We have to remember that only when we have completed chronologies, far back into prehistory, can we begin to exploit their dating potential in at least three ways: we can date archaeological remains and begin to see exactly when people were doing things; we can begin to look for evidence for environmental change both from the point of view of attempting to assess the limits of natural variability and also to see if any environmental changes affected human populations; and we can supply those precisely dated time capsules of wood for isotopic, elemental and other analyses.

The chapter treats the final stages in the completion of the first long oak chronologies in Europe. This took place between 1981 and 1984 with the resolution of some of the problems which had seemed insuperable in 1980. The power of dendrochronology to date things precisely opens up a whole new window into the past and so significant are the results destined to be that it is important to see how the chronologies were constructed in the first place. The final section reviews progress with the construction of a second-generation oak chronology, i.e. one which is not independent in the sense of the original Irish and German chronologies but derivative in that the chronology sections are placed in time by cross-dating with the established chronologies. This is the way most European chronologies will be constructed in the future and it is interesting to see just how rapidly a long, *c.* 5000-year chronology can be put together when there are neighbouring chronologies against which to cross-date.

The completion of the Irish and German oak chronologies

Work on the construction of a long Irish oak chronology had started seriously in 1970. At that time the only significant chronologies in Europe were those of Huber (Huber and Giertz 1969) and Hollstein (1965), both of which ran back to the ninth century AD and made extensive use of timbers from structures of approximately known age. There were no publications which dealt with the concepts involved in producing long prehistoric chronologies, but clearly the problems were going to be different; it would not be possible to go out and acquire successively older timbers, as was the case in medieval times. Instead the approach had to be based on random sampling and the construction of 'site' chronologies. It was always intuitively obvious that, if a large number of sub-fossil trees were recovered from one small area, some of those trees were likely to be contemporary. There are two reasons for this logic. First, trees do not spring from nowhere; they naturally tend to be part of a regenerating system. Second, if you have 50 trees and each, on average, has a ring pattern of 200 years, then if *none* is contemporary those 50 trees would represent some 10,000 years of chronology! Both pieces of logic, particularly the latter, suggested that overlaps were to be expected between ring patterns from a localized site. In fact it was quickly discovered that groups of even 10–20 trees from a single location tended to provide multiple overlaps and yield site chronologies of 400–800 years in length. This was the finding at Belfast (Pilcher *et al.* 1977; Baillie 1982) and independently in various German laboratories (Becker and Schirmer 1977; Schmidt 1981; Becker and Delorme 1978). So the 1970s saw a rapid 'filling up' of time as site chronologies were constructed and shuffled into chronological order. By 1980 there were four main centres concentrating on the completion of long chronologies: Stuttgart, Köln, Göttingen and Belfast.

The Irish Long Chronology

In Ireland, some major sites provided chronologies up to 1500 years in length. This was helped, for example at Garry Bog, Co. Antrim, by the occurrence of many trees which had individual lifespans of 300–350 years – a major boost to chronology construction. For humans, especially archaeologists, it is sobering to consider that these individual trees were growing on the surface of Irish peat bogs for one-third of a millennium – some 15–20 human generations!

Just as the individual ring patterns formed the building blocks of the site chronologies, so the site chronologies formed the new robust building blocks for the overall chronology. As they were being constructed, cross-dating was found between site chronologies from different bogs, thus consolidating major pieces of chronology. By 1980 there were only three gaps remaining in the last 6000 years. These were estimated to fall in the first/second and tenth centuries BC and around 4000 BC (Fig 1.13) (Baillie 1982). The first two gaps were worrying for various reasons. They had stubbornly refused to yield to the large-scale random sampling exercises which had provided, and indeed replicated, the bulk of the chronology. The gap around the tenth century BC was particularly worrying because it showed up in material from a number of different sites and suggested some sort of environmental hiatus. The obvious danger was that the hiatus might be so general as to imply that the chronology could never be completed within Ireland alone. It was possible to envisage a situation where, around the tenth century BC, a large number of trees had been blown down, or killed by dramatic inundation. If this caused a depletion in the number of trees, and if there was immediate regeneration following the event, it could result in an 'end-to-end' chronological situation for the dendrochronologist. The concept of a prehistoric hurricane may have seemed fanciful; however, the October 1987 experience in southern England demonstrated all too graphically how

even the tail-end of a hurricane could deplete a tree population. Dealing as we are with the ancient past we don't need to envisage all trees being killed to create a tree-ring gap. Since only a statistical sample of the original tree population comes down to us – due to the vagaries of preservation and recovery – any depletion in the original tree population could result in a chronological gap.

The most recent gap, that in the first centuries BC, was equally serious. No bog oaks appeared to belong to this period and no archaeological sites of the first or second centuries AD were known in Ireland which might provide timbers to bridge back to the prehistoric chronology (which was estimated to end around 200 BC). This was the situation which existed in 1980 when *TRDA* was being written. The exact situation at that time in Ireland was that we had a complete chronology from the present back to 13 BC and a long 2990-year sub-fossil chronology – called the Long Chronology – which was believed to span approximately 4000–1000 BC on radiocarbon evidence. Between these lay the 719-year Garry Bog 2 (GB2) chronology which had to be younger than the Long Chronology. It was clear that, because it failed to cross-date with either the absolute chronology or the long chronology, it had to fall somewhere between 1000 BC and 13 BC. Indeed, radiocarbon evidence suggested that GB2 might span the approximate period 900–200 BC.

A lot of effort had been expended in attempting to link the GB2 chronology to the younger end of the Long Chronology. This had proved a total failure. There was no significant matching between either the chronologies or their constituents. This was taken as significant because trees from Garry Bog (indeed trees found together) were significant elements of both the younger end of the Long Chronology and GB2. The failure to find any cross-dating reduced the possibilities to two – either the two chronologies overlapped slightly (perhaps up to 60–80 years) and this overlap was too short for us to identify, or the chronologies occupied an end-to-end situation with some unspecified gap between them.

By 1980–1 the Belfast work had reached this impasse. Additional samples from the north of

33

Ireland served only to duplicate the existing chronology sections, with no progress in bridging the two gaps. Clearly some new initiative was necessary, and two strategies were devised. By this stage it was known that the prehistoric chronologies in Germany were in an essentially similar state of completeness: again something like two gaps in the last 6000 years (Becker and Delorme 1978). Would it be possible to bridge the gaps by some sort of stepwise matching from Ireland to England to Germany? After all, such stepwise correlations had been found for the various sections of the AD chronologies (see Fig. 1.11). In order to set about testing this, a random batch of bog oaks was acquired from East Anglia in December 1980. From this collection – from Lakenheath and several sites adjacent to West Row – one well-replicated chronology of 509 years was constructed. A significant tree-ring match was found against the Belfast Long Chronology suggesting that this English chronology section lay in the third millennium BC, and indeed, this was supported by a radiocarbon determination. Unfortunately at that stage there was no access to suitable German chronologies for comparison, with the result that the East Anglian chronology was premature. It would, however, prove useful later.

In addition to the East Anglian bog oaks, approaches were made to the excavators at Roman Carlisle where it was already known that timbers of the first and second centuries AD were being uncovered. It was suggested that if they supplied samples of Roman oak to allow the construction of a site chronology, this might assist in bridging the first centuries BC. Equally such a chronology could be used for archaeological dating. So pressure was being applied to the two gaps in the hope of some eventual breakthrough. Meanwhile, sampling within Ireland had not been abandoned completely. Around this same time extensive processing of new material and re-processing of the earlier – fifth and sixth millennia BC – chronologies yielded a continuous 1550-year chronology designated Garry Bog X which was eventually joined to the older end of the Long Chronology. This meant that the Long Chronology now extended for 4341 years. New radiocarbon dates, being produced for calibration purposes, suggested strongly that the younger end of this chronology was likely to lie within about 10 years of 940 BC (Baillie et al. 1983).

So the original suggestion of the Long Chronology ending c. 1000 BC, which had been made on the basis of a scatter of routine dates, remained essentially unaltered from the dendrochronological point of view. We would not know the true dates of the Long Chronology until both the remaining gaps were closed with

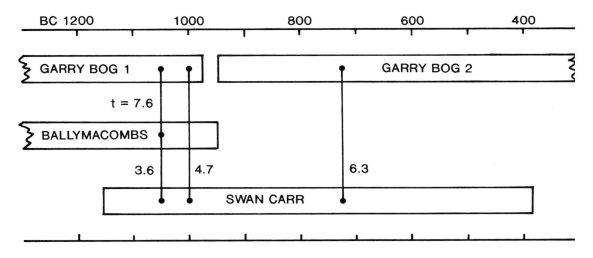

2.1 The Swan Carr sub-fossil chronology from north-east England formed a critical link across the tenth-century BC gap in the Irish chronology, with consistent correlations to two Irish site chronologies (Baillie et al. 1983)

significant *tree-ring links*. Only then would we know if the radiocarbon suggestions were even remotely correct. After all, if we found that the true placement of the Long Chronology was wildly at odds with the placement suggested by calibrated radiocarbon dates, then we would know that Suess' calibration was not applicable worldwide. Were that to have been the case, the Belfast calibration would become the accepted radiocarbon correction curve for the Old World! If, on the other hand, tree-ring connections were found which were in line with the suggested radiocarbon placement, then this would confirm that the Suess curve was effectively universally applicable.

The first major break came with a remarkable stroke of luck in March 1981. An international conference on 'Climatic Change in Later Prehistory' was held in Durham. Travelling to Durham by train from London, I happened to see a large heap of bog oaks on low-lying ground just south of the junction between the A689 and the A1(M). Given such an excellent grid reference it was easy to locate the trees at Swan Carr about 10 miles south of Durham. That summer a fieldtrip was organized and 20 trees were sampled from the heap. These samples yielded a robust 775-year chronology which immediately cross-dated with the Garry Bog 2 chronology and extended it back in time by 208 years. It was quickly apparent that this extension gave a direct correlation (t = 4.7) to the Long Chronology (**Fig. 2.1**). Here, more or less by accident, we had found an English site which bridged one of the gaps in the Irish chronology (Baillie *et al.* 1983). The situation is all the more remarkable because of course the Swan Carr oaks could have been of any age and were merely collected in the hope of linking the Long Chronology directly to the German chronologies at some stage. To find material which bridged a difficult gap in the Irish chronology was remarkable, to say the least. The Irish prehistoric chronology now spanned 5061 years with only the 'Roman' gap remaining. A final bizarre note on this particular gap-bridging exercise was the fact that the gap between the Long and GB2 chronologies was a single year! We now know that the Long Chronology ended in 949 BC and GB2 started in 947 BC.

The completion of the Irish chronology

There were two strands to the completion of this story. One related to in-house attempts to bridge across the final gap in the Irish chronology, in the first centuries BC. The other involved direct cooperation with those dendrochronologists in Germany who were involved in remarkably similar attempts to complete their long chronologies.

From 1980 the Carlisle excavators had been supplying Roman oak timbers for study. This material, much of which came from late first- or early second-century AD levels, proved extremely intractable. The kindest thing which could be said of it was that it gave the impression that it had come from a variety of different sources. However, that disguises the difficulties. Although we had worked extensively with timbers from quite wide geographical areas, we had never experienced anything like the Carlisle timbers. We began to wonder if the Romans created stores of wood from all over the Empire and then sent wagon loads, suitably mixed, to outposts like Carlisle! From a chronology building point of view, we ended up with a chronology of 18 trees which appeared to span AD 90–247 BC. At least the chronology did fall in the pre-existing gap in the Irish material. The preliminary dating relied upon a link to a Roman London chronology (New Fresh Wharf) which had been constructed by Ruth Morgan (1977a).

As a basis for dating a section of the Irish Long Chronology this was very unsatisfactory, for the following reasons. The 5061-year prehistoric Belfast chronology had been built completely independently – thanks to Swan Carr – and at no point did the Irish chronology depend on any of the German chronologies. Given this situation it was to be hoped that the Irish chronology could be completed independently. This was potentially very important because comparisons between the Irish and German chronologies could then form the third-level replication which would ultimately prove European dendrochronology. Because of this need for independence, we retained misgivings about attempting the Ireland to England to Germany bridging exercises mentioned above. In an ideal world such comparisons should only take place *after* both chronologies had been completed independently. So the prob-

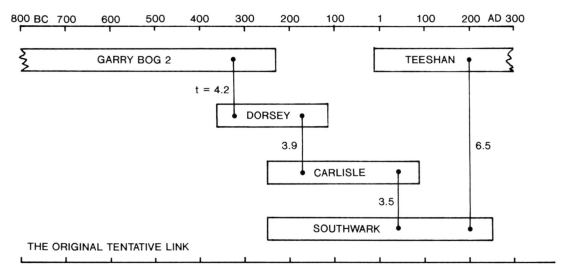

2.2 The logic-chain which marked the tentative completion of the Belfast chronology in 1982. At that time, the English Roman chronologies bridged a 116–13 BC gap in the Irish series

lem with New Fresh Wharf was that it had been dated against German chronologies. Fortunately this situation was later rectified when Ian Tyers constructed a complete Southwark chronology which spanned AD 255–252 BC (Sheldon and Tyers 1983). This chronology cross-dated directly with the older part of the Irish AD chronology and with Carlisle (**Fig. 2.2**).

So, the situation by 1982 was that in Belfast we had an absolute chronology back to 13 BC. We had access to two Roman chronologies running back to 252 BC (Southwark) and 247 BC (Carlisle). We had a 5061-year prehistoric chronology running, on radiocarbon evidence, from c. 200–5200 BC. Fortunately we had one other chronology up our sleeve. I have already mentioned that in Ireland there are essentially no known archaeological sites of the first few centuries AD, certainly no timber-bearing sites. However, two early Iron Age sites had turned up timbers during the 1970s. These were the ritual 'temple' at Navan Fort, the ancient capital of Ulster, and the earthwork enclosure called The Dorsey to the south of Navan, both in Co. Armagh. By chance (see Chapter 4) the timbers from these two sites were indistinguishable in date and they formed the Dorsey/Navan chronology, initially of 246 years. Again on both archaeological and radiocarbon evidence it was likely that this chronology fell in the first few centuries BC. Interestingly, there were reasonable visual matches and significant *t* values which suggested that the Dorsey/Navan chronology ended in 116 BC and ran back to 361 BC and that Garry Bog 2 ended in 229 BC and ran back to 5289 BC (Fig. 2.2). Technically, the Irish chronology was complete. However, the strung-out logic of this series of links made us uneasy about announcing the result without supporting evidence. This was where the German chronologies enter the story.

The German oak chronologies

In 1980 Hollstein had published a German oak chronology back to 724 BC. In 1981 and 1982 a series of publications (Schmidt 1981; Schmidt and Schwabedissen 1982; Becker and Schmidt 1982) indicated that the overall German chronology complex had been extended first to 1462 BC and then to 2061 BC. This had come about very rapidly by the amalgamation of Becker's mostly south German chronologies with those from northern Germany constructed by Schmidt at Köln. So, ostensibly, the German workers had beaten us to the punch and had completed their chronology first. In the spring of 1982 it was agreed with both Bernd Becker and Burghart Schmidt that the time was right for a mutual exchange of data in an attempt to confirm the

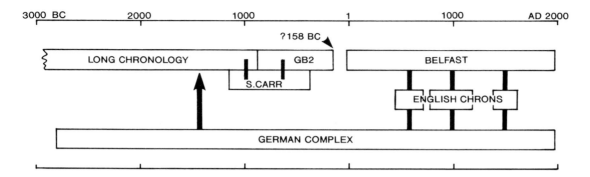

2.3 The Irish–German link which raised questions about the integrity of the German prehistoric chronology. While Fig. 2.2 suggests an end-date for the Irish GB2 chronology at 229 BC, the link to Germany suggested 158 BC

Irish and German chronologies. As a first step chronologies for the second millennium BC were exchanged. What follows is a necessary simplification of a complex series of matching and cross-correlation exercises. In reality each laboratory had many chronologies and sub-chronologies and a great deal of time was involved in making comparisons and looking for consistent replication. However, the essence of the exercise was that almost immediately Schmidt was able to demonstrate a long section of consistent cross-dating between one of his north German chronologies and the Irish chronology. This agreement was sufficiently good to imply that our whole 5061-year chronology ended in 158 BC (**Fig. 2.3**). If correct, this direct link to the absolutely dated German chronology should have bypassed the problems in the first centuries BC, and in theory the arrival of Schmidt's telex with the news of the match should have marked the 'eureka' finish to the whole long chronology programme. Unfortunately, as outlined above, the Southwark to Carlisle to Navan/Dorsey to Garry Bog 2 logic-chain suggested that GB2 ended in 229 BC! We had no evidence to support a 158 BC end-date for Garry Bog 2.

This presented a serious dilemma in the Belfast laboratory. All our chronology building had been based on the assumption that, when we had long overlaps between chronologies from our area, then we could find visually and statistically significant cross-dating at the correct relative positions. Now, if this German dating were correct, we had overlaps between Garry Bog 2,

Navan/Dorsey and Carlisle, but no significant visual or statistical *cross-dating* at the 'correct' positions! Worse still, the suggested shortening of our overall chronology implied that we were failing to find even *longer* overlaps than we had actually used. This raised the question: if our procedure had broken down here how were we to know that it had not broken down elsewhere? So the ramifications of this disagreement were potentially profound for Irish dendrochronology.

This was the situation in which we found ourselves in late 1982 and into 1983. There was, however, some hope. For one thing we knew that our procedures were robust enough to build a chronology back to 13 BC which was totally independent of the German chronologies and which dated with them exactly – to the year – via English chronologies (Fig. 1.11). It could be argued therefore that there was nothing wrong with our procedures, which tentatively indicated an end-date for the 5061-year chronology at 229 BC. But we also agreed that our prehistoric chronology matched the German chronology directly in the second millennium BC. Was it possible therefore that there was something amiss with the German chronology? It was known that the German workers had a replicated system back to around 400 BC (Hollstein 1980; Becker 1981), so any problem really had to be between 400 BC and 1000 BC. Examination of the relevant data showed that the weakest point in the German complex had to be around 550 BC where *neither* Schmidt nor Becker had continuous chronologies. At that point the German complex relied on

37

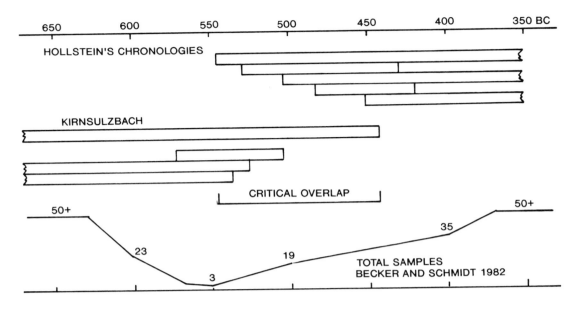

2.4 The weak link in the 1982 German prehistoric complex. Since Becker and Schmidt had no link across 550 BC, everything depended on Hollstein's doubtful Kirnsulzbach chronology (Hollstein 1973)

Hollstein's chronology which ran back to 724 BC (**Fig. 2.4**). Further scrutiny showed that at the critical point the whole chronology relied on the placement of Hollstein's Kirnsulzbach (KSB) chronology (Hollstein 1980). So, if there was going to be a weakness in the German chronology complex it had to centre around KSB.

In a controversial position such as this there is a natural tendency to cast around for additional evidence. For example, by this time we knew that the high-precision calibration work was demonstrating a broad agreement between Pearson's work on Irish oak and Suess' original bristlecone calibration. Indeed the calibration performed on the old Long Chronology showed sufficient agreement with the Suess curve, by way of a 'wiggle match' (see Chapter 4), to make it likely that the 4341-year chronology ended 'within 10 years of 940 BC' (Pearson 1980; Baillie 1983a). Such a placement, if correct, implied that the end of the 5061-year chronology might be within 10 years of 220 BC. So radiocarbon evidence tended to support the Belfast '229 BC' placement rather than the '158 BC' German placement. Of course we could not rely totally on this radiocarbon evidence, for reasons given above (our aim had to be to test the bristlecone pine calibration). If we based the Irish, or indeed the European, chronol-

ogy on the bristlecone calibration we would inevitably be indulging in circular argument. No, all we could do was take comfort from the fact that the radiocarbon evidence tended to support our tree-ring logic.

There was another piece of evidence which also served to colour our judgement. This was the fact that Hollstein was known to have made a previous error in his 2700-year chronology (Schmidt and Schwabedissen 1978; Baillie 1982). That was the case where Hollstein had based the dating of his AD 369–486 BC chronology on historical 'evidence' for a Roman bridge at Köln. In dendrochronology this is a fundamental mistake. Tree-ring master chronologies should depend only on definitive tree-ring matches. However, Hollstein had made the mistake, and in due course Roman specialists showed that the earlier section of his chronology was producing impossible dates for early Roman sites (Baatz 1977). Subsequently, with help from Becker's work, Hollstein had to move the end-date of his chronology forward from AD 369 to AD 395 (Hollstein 1980). From a dendrochronologist's viewpoint this was an interesting logic error and it suggested that Hollstein had fallen into a very specialized tree-ring 'trap'. The trap relates specifically to the addition of ring patterns on to the end of pre-existing chronologies and it can be formalized as 'the dendrochronologist's dilemma' (see below and Baillie *et al.* 1983).

With the dendrochronologist's dilemma in mind we had a close look at Hollstein's KSB link. Reference to the original publication (Hollstein 1973) uncovered two very interesting points. The first was the very fragmentary nature of the KSB samples. Although there were seven timbers with a combined total of 634 rings, a total of 13,000 measurements were made – equivalent to measuring each sample 20 times! This unusual treatment in itself suggested some misgivings about the integrity of the ring patterns. However, the second point was potentially more fundamental. At the time KSB was being processed, the furthest extension of the middle-European master chronology was around 530 BC (remember all Hollstein's prehistoric dates were moved forward 26 years in the late 1970s to correct for the error in the Roman period) and Hollstein found himself in a classic 'dilemma' situation. He knew from archaeological information that the KSB timbers were somewhere in the mid-first millennium BC so they could either overlap with the existing chronology or they could come somewhere 'off the end'. Hollstein settled for an overlap of around 100 years and this apparently specified the date of KSB and extended the master chronology.

Looking at this situation with hindsight it is possible to see just how weak a link KSB represented in the overall German chronology. Here was a somewhat dubious chronology – because of the multiple measurements – which had originally been hung on to the end of the longest chronology in Europe (in a sense as the tail-end it may not have seemed all that important). However, by 1982, virtually the whole of German prehistoric dendrochronology depended on this critical link. So the answer to the Belfast problem presented itself as follows. Since Hollstein could only search for matches between KSB and the existing master, then, if the *true* position was 'off the end' of the master any match found would have to be spurious (this is the dendrochronologists' dilemma). The question reduced therefore to the reliability of the match between KSB and the components of the original master chronology. Analysis of the relevant overlaps using Hollstein's published data and the Belfast CROS program suggested that Hollstein's matching position was not supported by consistent *t* values and might well be spurious.

With this information, coupled with the Southwark to Carlisle to Navan/Dorsey to Garry Bog 2 logic-chain, and the radiocarbon back-up, the case was both published (Baillie 1983a) and presented to Schmidt and Becker. At around the same time Becker published an article indicating that the only point in the south-central German chronology *not independently replicated* was between 600 BC and 400 BC. He also noted that, when two of the German prehistoric oak chronologies were radiocarbon wiggle matched against the bristlecone calibration, their calibrated dates differed from their tree-ring dates by 73 and 67 years respectively (Becker 1983). Within months all concerned had accepted that the German complex had to be broken at 500 BC and the older section moved back by 71 years (Pilcher *et al.* 1984; Schmidt and Freundlich 1984).

Tertiary replication of the European oak chronologies

With the announcement of a consensus 7272-year European oak chronology in 1984 the first major phase of European dendrochronology was complete. Oak chronologies of comparable length to Ferguson's bristlecone pine chronology were available and represented an equivalent standard for the purpose of radiocarbon calibration. However, a lingering problem was that a section of the overall chronology was now *without* tertiary replication. At 500 BC the whole Stuttgart/Köln/Belfast chronology complex depended only on the Irish chronology. Had that situation remained static it would have been a continuing source of concern. For something of such fundamental chronological importance, full tertiary replication was essential.

We need not have worried. Tree-ring studies, like other branches of science, are ongoing and in 1984 we witnessed one of those examples of parallel work which are so frequent in the history of science. Just when it was needed, and unknown to any of the Belfast, Köln or Stuttgart workers, Leuschner and Delorme, at Göttingen, published

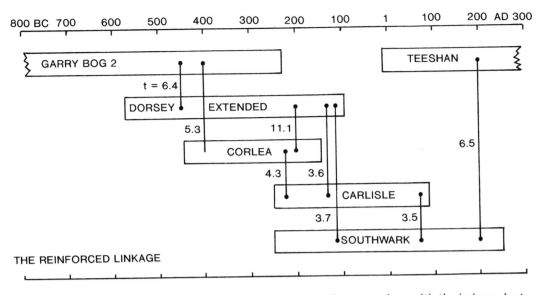

2.5 Although the logic-chain in Fig. 2.2 was proven correct by comparison with the independent Göttingen chronology (Leuschner and Delorme 1984), new and extended chronology linkages served to reinforce and confirm those originally available

a note on their completion of a separate German chronology from AD 785 to 4008 BC (Leuschner and Delorme 1984). Here then was the opportunity for an independent test of the Belfast chronology. In the spring of 1985 Hubert Leuschner kindly made available to us a continuous German chronology running, by that time, from AD 928 to 4163 BC. The results of running the various sections of the Belfast prehistoric chronology against the independent Göttingen chronology confirmed that both prehistoric chronologies were in precise synchronization. Despite the distances involved, the original Long Chronology gave $t = 8.8$ at 949 BC, Swan Carr gave $t = 8.45$ at 381 BC and even Garry Bog 2 gave $t = 3.6$ at 229 BC (Brown et al. 1986). Since that time numerous additional sections of English prehistoric chronology have shown consistent matching against both the Belfast and Göttingen chronologies (see Fig. 1.3 for examples). So the Göttingen chronology provided the ultimate tertiary replication necessary to prove the European oak complex. In the overall scheme of things it is remarkable that the independent announcements of the completion of long oak chronologies should have appeared in the same year.

However, as noted above, dendrochronology is not static. Already by 1985 fresh Irish material, from a major bog roadway at Corlea, Co. Longford (see Chapter 4), provided a chronology spanning 446–148 BC. This chronology confirmed all the main links in the original Belfast logic-chain. The Dorsey/Navan chronology has been extended and now spans 95–575 BC, confirming the original link to Garry Bog 2. And so it goes on (**Fig. 2.5**).

The development of an English prehistoric chronology

With the Irish and German chronologies acting as reference standards, it proved possible to outline a long English prehistoric chronology in a relatively short period of time. This type of secondary chronology construction will presumably become quite common as the grid of long chronologies gradually spreads. It is therefore interesting to trace the outline of the development of the English chronology and to compare the problem areas with those encountered in the construction of the original reference chronologies.

As was noted above, by the mid-1980s two sections of English bog-oak chronology had been successfully cross-dated with the Irish and German chronologies. These were the chronology from Swan Carr, Co. Durham, which spanned 1155–381 BC and a 509-year chronology based on bog oaks from two locations in East Anglia which spanned 3169–2661 BC (Brown *et al.* 1986). They had been constructed with the hope of establishing cross-dating links from Ireland to Germany at a time when it looked unlikely that the Irish chronology could be completed independently. So with the satisfactory completion of the Irish chronology there was no further need for English chronologies.

However, with the completion of the Irish and German chronologies, it quickly became apparent that we were in danger of creating a chronological hiatus. The hiatus would come about if prehistoric archaeological sites could be precisely dated by tree-rings in Ireland and Germany, while England continued to rely on chronology based solely on radiocarbon. Of course, even without a specific English chronology there was the possibility that some English site chronologies could be dated directly against Ireland or Germany (or both). Unfortunately, against that idea, was the evidence of a series of other chronologies, constructed by English workers, which had uniformly failed to date against Ireland or Germany. These included chronologies from the River Trent (Salisbury *et al.* 1984), from the Sweet Trackway in Somerset (Morgan 1988) and from Stolford (Heyworth 1978), all of which cross-dated into an English 'Neolithic' chronology (Morgan *et al.* 1987). The Neolithic chronology still showed no clear dating evidence against the Irish or German chronologies. This suggested that dating possibilities might be improved by the existence of at least an outline English chronology.

Several factors made the attempt on an English chronology feasible in the mid-1980s. At Belfast the laboratory was tooled up for chronology building, had recent experience in the field and possessed a radiocarbon facility. In England, workers at the Godwin laboratory in Cambridge had accumulated large numbers of sub-fossil oaks from the East Anglian fenlands while workers from the, then, Liverpool Polytechnic were in possession of substantial numbers of bog oaks from Lancashire. Both sets of workers were willing to make samples available for chronology building. The final ingredient was a substantial grant from the Science-based Archaeology Committee of the Science and Engineering Research Council to fund the research and sample collection. Serious work began in late 1985. As the sample collections were essentially random, the aim again was to construct robust site chronologies, using high-quality cross-matching between ring patterns as the sole means of establishing chronological relationships. The robust site chronologies would then become the building blocks for the overall area chronology. Such was the plan.

The first large batch of English sub-fossil oaks to be processed were the 300 plus samples from East Anglia. Here the pre-existence of the 3169–2661 BC Fenland chronology proved a considerable help. By the summer of 1986 it was clear that the Fenland material broke down into three main chronological units; one unit, based on the original East Anglian chronology was extended to 2618 BC. This included timbers from no less than *10* different locations. It was obviously of interest that randomly collected material, from this number of sites, fell into a 600-year period. This alone suggested elements of common history over a considerable area of the Fenlands. A second group of material consisted of 10 long-lived trees from Adventurer's Fen which yielded a 471-year chronology. This chronology could be dated directly against both the German and Irish chronologies and spanned 2151–1681 BC. The third unit was composed of timbers from seven sites and spanned 809 years. This chronology fell between the original East Anglian and the Adventurer's Fen chronologies.

By the time all the East Anglian material was processed, some 80% of all the usable trees matched into these three chronology sections. Thus, it was fairly clear that the vast majority of the Cambridge samples fell between 3200 BC and 1680 BC and we were not going to get any significant extension of the East Anglian chronology. This proved to be the case. What interested us was the fact that the samples might be random but they were not randomly distributed in time. The evidence pointed to East Anglia representing

41

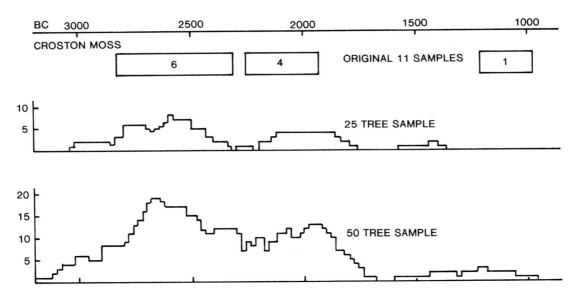

2.6 Repeated sampling of oaks from Croston Moss, Lancashire, illustrates the power of random sampling. The original eleven trees are a good indication of the distribution of the total population

a situation of diminishing returns from a chronology building viewpoint.

So in a relatively short time our attention turned to the Lancashire oaks. Here, yet again, we meet one of those unaccountable strokes of good fortune which can make, or whose absence can break, any research project. In November 1985 a letter was received from Mr Mike Harvey, a Lancashire science teacher, telling us about several good examples of bog oaks from the area between Leyland and Ormskirk and requesting relevant information. It transpired that he had contacted both Manchester and Liverpool universities before being directed to Belfast. As we would be passing the vicinity on the way back to Belfast from Cambridge, with one of the batches of Fenland oaks, we took the opportunity to call.

The results were fascinating. We took 17 samples from Mike Harvey's woodpile which turned out to be from 11 trees. When they were processed we found ourselves in possession of two chronologies of 527 and 334 years respectively. Moreover, both chronologies cross-dated with the Irish chronology, spanning 2832–2306 BC and 2257–1924 BC, with one single timber also dating to 1165–970 BC. This raised some interesting questions about the chronological potential of this site – called Croston Moss. It

was known that the oaks came from a very small area – a single low-lying field. It seemed unlikely that trees would have repeatedly colonized the spot; intuitively one would imagine a regenerating 'forest'. We knew from Mike Harvey that a large number of trees were still on the site. Did this imply that a larger sample would give a continuous chronology of around two millennia? In order to find out, the site was visited and 50 oaks sampled. This produced material which linked and extended the two original chronologies and some trees which matched the later second-millennium sample. The end result was a Croston Moss I chronology spanning 3198–1682 BC with Croston Moss II spanning 1584–970 BC. Oaks had been continuously present at Croston for over 22 centuries; the break in the seventeenth century BC being either a sampling deficiency or a reflection of some real drop in the number of trees growing at that time.

Because of our interest in an environmental event in the decade of the 1620s BC (see Chapter 5), we were particularly keen to find some trees at Croston which grew across this century. We sampled a further 25 trees which duplicated most of the chronology but still showed the gap (**Fig. 2.6**). The diagram is interesting and shows the power of random sampling. The first 11 trees gave a very good picture of the main distribution on the site. The 25-tree sample only marginally improved on the first 11 and still showed a gap in the main chronology unit. The 50-tree sample must be close to the total distribution. However, it does still leave the question as to just how many samples are optimum.

The gap in the seventeenth century was still a puzzle. Since a narrow-ring event showed up in Irish bog oaks in the 1620s BC, was it possible that some sort of depletion really had taken place at Croston at the same time? Would any amount of sampling yield even one tree across this episode? This caused us to try another approach. Most of the trees sampled were trunks which must have blown over and become buried over time (the trees are reputed to be found in the same orientation, so, because they fell over time, this must be a reflection of the prevailing wind direction). Was it possible that the trees we wanted were killed by rising water levels in the seventeenth century BC? If this was the case might the *relevant* trees have died standing upright (instead of being blown down) and therefore rotted away? Should we be looking for stumps, not trunks? We also tried this approach but to no avail. So, in both East Anglia and at Croston Moss we have low-lying sites which supported oaks from *c.* 3200 BC to *c.* 1680 BC. This must reflect some strong causal mechanism for the occurrence, or the survival, of these trees. The coincidence between these two date limits and the dates of two narrowest-ring events in the Irish bog oaks – at 3195 BC and 1628 BC – may well be significant (see Chapter 5).

By 1988, with East Anglia completed and with the addition of two chronologies from Jennifer Hillam at Sheffield which spanned 323–699 BC and 1362–1687 BC (Hillam 1987), we could list continuous English chronologies from 323 BC to 3601 BC with additional, patchy, coverage back to 4989 BC (**Table 2.1**). One of the things we realized as this work progressed was that trees from further north in Lancashire tended to be older than those from Croston. The acquisition and processing of large numbers of north Lancashire oaks resulted in two successes. First, the consolidation of a Lancashire chronology which extended Croston Moss back to 3807 BC (later 3916 BC); second,

the pulling together of a continuous chronology spanning 4165–4989 BC.

Table 2.1

323–699 BC Fiskerton Track/Hasholme Boat (Hillam 1987)
381–1155 BC Swan Carr
970–1584 BC Croston Moss II
1362–1687 BC Hasholme bog oaks (Hillam pers. comm.)
1681–3196 BC East Anglia
1682–3198 BC Croston Moss I
3109–3601 BC Eskham House Farm

Units of English prehistoric oak chronology in existence by 1988

At this point it became clear that there was something odd about the period very broadly 'around 4000 BC'. From 1980 to 1988 hundreds of random bog oaks had been acquired in England which had allowed the construction of chronologies for essentially the whole of the first five millennia BC. Why had none proved to be from this period around 4000 BC? What exacerbated the situation was the fact that the original Irish chronology had for many years stuck 'around 4000 BC' (Pilcher *et al.* 1977; Baillie 1982). We knew that Becker's A400 chronology for central Germany had for some time ended 'around 4000 BC' (Becker 1985) and indeed the Göttingen chronology had originally been published as ending in 4008 BC (Leuschner and Delorme 1984). Not only that, but the English Neolithic chronologies from the River Trent, from the Sweet Track and from the submerged coastal oaks at Stolford clearly represented 'different', non-bog, sources. Also – and this was hard to ignore – although these three English Neolithic chronologies matched each other, none of them was precisely dated. So while numerous bog-oak chronologies were datable against Ireland and Germany none of these 'different' chronologies was datable. They represented, as Hillam (1987) had pointed out, 'one of the major puzzles in British dendrochronology'.

In order to attempt a resolution of this problem, and in the hope of finally dating the 43

Neolithic complex, the Nottingham group kindly supplied the original River Trent timbers. In addition the Stolford timbers were resampled and Hillam began to rework the Sweet Track material. The detailed story has been published elsewhere (Hillam *et al.* 1990), suffice to say that a revised set of tree-ring measurements produced a new Sweet Track chronology of 396 years which gave $t = 4.9$ against the Belfast chronology at an end-year of 3807 BC. This was very much in line with some extremely good, high-precision radiocarbon evidence which was independent of the tree-ring match (Baillie and Pilcher 1988). However, it was felt that some additional tree-ring evidence was necessary for a final resolution. This resolution came simultaneously in late 1989 at both Belfast and Sheffield. At Belfast a new sample from Broad Lane, Lancashire, extended the 4165 BC chronology down to 4023 BC and matched with one of the Neolithic chronologies – again specifying the last year of the Sweet Track as 3807 BC. At Sheffield fresh river-gravel timbers from Beverley Long Lane, in Humberside, matched both the Belfast chronology and the Sweet Track chronology –

also specifying the last year of the Sweet Track as 3807 BC (Hillam *et al.* 1990).

So in a matter of four years, from late 1985 to late 1989, a complete year-by-year record of English oak growth had been pieced together for every year from 323 BC to 4989 BC. The chronology is not independent but represents a good working outline. It can already be demonstrated, in the case of several other River Trent chronologies, that dating against this English chronology can be successful when attempts against Ireland and Germany fail. It is now only a matter of time before even the least well-replicated joins in the outline chronology are reinforced and the areal coverage improved. It is inevitable that the main German chronologies will allow extended chronology construction across most of central Europe, as has already happened for Switzerland. In this respect only Peter Kuniholm, working in the eastern Mediterranean, is destined to have to complete his chronology in isolation. Though even there, the availability of radiocarbon wiggle matching does undoubtedly help general chronology placement (see Chapter 4).

3 Art-historical dendrochronology and the limitations of oak dendrochronology

If the completion of the long oak chronologies was a major issue in the early 1980s, one other significant dendrochronological issue related to the possible exotic origin of the art-historical oak chronologies constructed by the late Dr John Fletcher at Oxford. Late medieval paintings had frequently been performed on thin oak panels and Fletcher had been working on the ring patterns derived from such oak boards since the early 1970s. His interest in art-historical dendrochronology had almost certainly been inspired by a paper, by Bauch and Eckstein, at the British Columbia conference in 1970. Up to that time Fletcher had been interested in dating vernacular buildings and his approach had been to use his scientific training to find a 'better' dating method than that employed, for example, in the Tucson Laboratory. However, in the 1970s, having abandoned his previous line of research, Fletcher was building art-historical tree-ring chronologies in England (Fletcher et al. 1974).

To understand the art-historical story we have to go back to the beginnings of dendrochronology in the British Isles. In the beginning it was not known if dendrochronology would work successfully; it was not known if the British Isles represented a single tree-ring 'area' or two or ten. In Belfast, with the aim of a long chronology for calibration purposes, it was decided to build a chronology which was, as far as possible, based on oak timbers from the north of Ireland. Fletcher, working with panel paintings, chose to build a floating chronology which might be datable by 'tele-connection' to the existing German oak chronologies of Huber and Hollstein.

As it turned out, by the mid-1970s a number of medieval chronologies had been constructed in the British Isles. These included the local chronologies, constructed back from the present, in the north of Ireland and Scotland, and floating chronology sections from Yorkshire (Morgan 1977b) and the England/Wales Borders (Siebenlist-Kerner 1978), both dated against German chronologies. The other chronology was the art-historical MC18 (Fletcher et al. 1974), apparently dated against the German chronologies, but actually dated against another art-historical chronology, Netherlands II, built by Eckstein and Bauch at Hamburg (Eckstein et al. 1975). By about 1976 it was apparent that all the British Isles chronologies cross-dated with each other – with the exception of MC18. This art-historical chronology had been specified as spanning AD 1230–1546, but showed no meaningful correlation with *any* of the others at that date. This immediately made the art-historical chronology a bit of a puzzle. Moreover, because of a low correlation ($t = 3.0$) against the Belfast chronology – which suggested an end-date of 1550 for MC18 – Fletcher used this dating for a short time in 1975 (Fletcher 1975). Unfortunately there was no back-up for this '1550' dating against other chronologies and subsequently the chronology was moved back to the '1546' position (Fletcher 1977). So the puzzle was compounded in that not only was MC18 inconsistent, but its dating was apparently *flexible*.

In 1977 the discrepant nature of the MC18 chronology was pointed out (Baillie 1978a) and the suggestion made that MC18 might involve the use of exotic timbers. This suggestion had potentially serious consequences for the art-historical dendrochronologists. If correct, it called the dating of MC18 into question: if you don't know where your timbers are from, how can you know they are correctly dated? As a response to this challenge it was suggested, more and more strongly, that the art-historical timbers *were* English but, and here was the twist, they were 'different', i.e. they were from a 'different dendroecological zone'. This was an interesting idea with its implicit suggestion of mutually exclusive chronologies (Fletcher 1978a). In essence, this was the state of the ongoing debate when *TRDA* was published in 1982.

Now clearly this was an unsatisfactory situation because, if mutually exclusive chronologies did exist, it had serious consequences for dendrochronology within the British Isles and elsewhere. If mutually exclusive chronologies existed in such a small area how many chronologies were going to be needed to give good dating coverage? In addition, the concept of mutually exclusive chronologies present some philosophical difficulties for dendrochronologists (Baillie 1983b). So, the situation had to be resolved at some stage, and from 1982 some efforts were made in that direction. When the art-historical story was reviewed in detail, it was noticed that there was surprising flexibility in the dating of MC18 (by this stage MC18 had developed into Reference Chronologies 1, 2, 3 and 4 (Fletcher 1977)). Apart from the temporary 1975 use of the '1550' dating, later art-historical articles used dates of '1546' or sometimes '1545' (Fletcher 1980). Now on several grounds this was not acceptable. At its most fundamental it could be argued that trees only live once and their growth patterns must relate to a specific set of years; it is not possible to have flexible tree-ring dates. The varied datings raised the interesting possibility that the art-historical chronologies were not truly dated at all.

In 1984, after a detailed analysis of both the English and German art-historical chronologies, it was realized that there was a logical flaw in the art-historical dating (Baillie 1984). The secret of this first step in the unravelling of the art-historical problem lay in understanding how the dating had been arrived at in the first instance. Bauch and Eckstein had built the first art-historical chronologies in the Netherlands. They expected the chronologies to cross-date with the existing German chronologies, and indeed one – Netherlands I – did. However the other – Netherlands II – did not (Eckstein *et al.* 1975). So how was Netherlands II dated? Bauch and Eckstein knew approximately where the chronology must lie on the basis of known painting dates for many of the prestigious paintings which they had examined. They also knew that sapwood in Germany was normally around 20 rings. Since, in most cases, the sapwood had been removed by the original panel makers, they sought a matching position for their Netherlands II chronology 'approximately a sapwood distance back from the known painting dates'. The date they decided upon was slightly variable. 'Because at present the master chart [for Netherlands II] can only be proved with a precision of ±1 year, the curves for this chronology have not been published' (Bauch 1978). It was now clear that Fletcher's dating problem was at least partly derived from his dating of MC18 against Netherlands II. However, there were other factors. For example, although the English and Netherlands II art-historical chronologies matched each other, the same *dates* were not used: 'the Oxford laboratory has favoured and used dates two years earlier than those favoured by the Hamburg laboratory' (Fletcher 1978a).

Once all this was recognized, it was clear that the art-historical chronologies were not absolutely dated in a tree-ring sense. The problem then was, why did art-historical dendrochronology give such good results? Paintings dated against the art-historical chronologies clearly produced very acceptable dates. How could this be? How was it possible to use a system which could be 'wrong' and obtain dates which were 'right'? Some examples of the excellent dating results from art-historical dendrochronology are given in **Table 3.1**. The key to the solution of this whole problem was the realization that built into this art-historical complex was a logical flaw – a circular argument. By placing their art-historical chronology 'a sapwood distance back from known painting dates' and then adding the same sapwood allowance on to the date of the last existing ring of any new panel dated against the chronology, of course a good estimate of the true date would be achieved. The method would work *no matter what sapwood estimate was used!* For example, you could assume that sapwood represented about *1000* years; place the chronology 1000 years back from the known painting dates; add 1000 years to any date achieved against the chronology and a good dating estimate would be obtained for any new painting! So the method worked no matter what chronology placement was used. (For purists, the only exception is that if a 'too short' sapwood estimate is used, compared with the true amount of sapwood for the region from which the timbers were drawn, then some genuine paintings will give dates so late that they appear to be copies. However, and here is the joy of this erroneous procedure, some paintings could be *expected* to be copies. Thus, even when copies were uncovered, they would not cast doubt on the dating of the chronologies!)

Table 3.1

Painting	Dendro date	Signed
BR486	1622±5	1626
Tobias and Anna		
BR2	1630±5	1629
Rembrandt self portrait		
BR161/H	1631±5	1632
BR157/P	1632±9	1632
BR71/W	1636±5	1639

The estimated felling dates for a series of Netherlandish paintings produced by dendrochronological dating against the Netherlands II chronology compared with the dates of signatures (Bauch and Eckstein 1981)

In addition to the logical flaw, it was increasingly obvious that the origin of all the 'problem' art-historical chronologies was the eastern Baltic. Abram (1909) noted that there was a great increase in English commerce with the countries around the Baltic in the fifteenth century and mentions that Prussian timber was much needed in England. Salzman (1931) talks of common Hanseatic (Baltic) imports of wainscot boards into England. Symonds (1946) noted that wainscot 'meant boards of quartered, sawn or riven oak of the type grown in Russia, Germany and Holland . . . [and] . . . imported to England . . .

because it was recognised, by reason of its straight grain and even texture, to be infinitely superior to the majority of English grown oak'. This latter comment was particularly ironic because Fletcher had actually described his 'different' art-historical oaks as being 'elite' trees, specially sought out for panels. So, historical information suggested that Hansa traders had been shipping oak timbers from the Baltic into both the Netherlands and eastern England. Art-historical chronologies in the Netherlands and eastern England matched each other and nothing else: therefore the art-historical chronologies were Baltic chronologies. When this unravelling was suggested in print (Baillie 1984) a curious impasse was reached. Eckstein, who had originally noted that Netherlands II was 'different' from the other Dutch and German chronologies but had dismissed 'continuous importation of wood of the same provenance for over 200 years' (Eckstein *et al.* 1975), now came round to the Baltic hypothesis and instigated the construction of a north Polish chronology to resolve the issue. Fletcher, on the other hand, refused to accept the logic which he described as 'absolute nonsense' (Bunney 1985: 37).

As luck would have it, in late 1984, and before a Polish chronology could be completed, the final pieces of the jigsaw fell into place. Jennifer Hillam at Sheffield turned up some fresh timbers which again suggested the '1550' dating for the English art-historical chronologies. This dating was still hard to accept because it left such a short interval for sapwood. This is best seen in the effects a forward placement of the chronologies would have on the results in Table 3.1. Then some painting panels were processed at Belfast which suggested the same '1550' date. This amount of evidence was becoming overwhelming in favour of the 1550 placement. To try a resolution at that stage, all the art-historical chronologies were compared with all the available European chronologies at the 1550 position. It was immediately observed that the correlation values increased as one moved east across Europe (**Fig. 3.1**). The clinching factor was the analysis of sapwood on a group of southern Finnish oak samples collected by Keith Briffa in 1984. These samples had been brought to Belfast for quite different reasons but provided the first clear

47

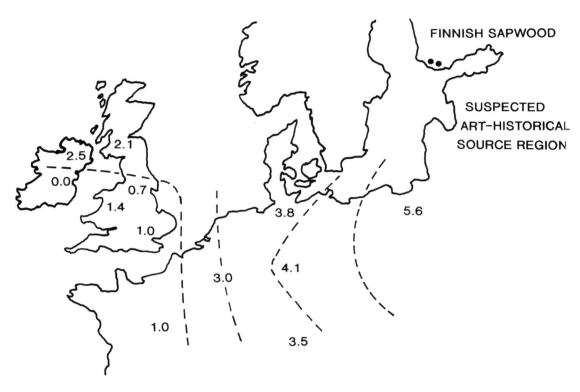

FINNISH SAPWOOD

SUSPECTED
ART–HISTORICAL
SOURCE REGION

3.1 The 'English' art–historical oak chronologies, when correctly dated, show increasing t values eastward across Europe indicating importation from a source in the eastern Baltic (Baillie et al. 1985)

evidence of short sapwood on Baltic oaks. The mean number of sapwood rings was 13.9 ± 3.2, much shorter than the Irish or German figures (see Fig. 1.5). The assembled evidence was published in 1985 (Baillie *et al.* 1985) and immediately accepted by all concerned (Eckstein *et al*; 1986, Fletcher 1986). The last serious anomaly in western European oak dendrochronology had been resolved.

In retrospect, Fletcher had been using dates for his chronology which were four to five years too old. Bauch and Eckstein had been using dates which were six years too old. Now there is a final twist to this tale. Bauch and Eckstein had used a *standard* sapwood allowance of 20±5 years. A more relevant sapwood value would be something like the Finnish 14±3. But, as they had used a dating position for their chronology six years too far back in time, these two factors self-cancel with the result that the Hamburg art-historical dates effectively do not have to change! This

demonstrates beautifully the way in which placing the chronologies 'a sapwood width back in time from known painting dates' worked in practice. Even with a wrongly dated chronology, excellent dating results could be obtained. Unfortunately, Fletcher had used a much more idiosyncratic approach to sapwood. Because the existing Irish and British sapwood estimates tended to be too long for sensible interpretation of his art-historical dates, he chose to estimate the amount of sapwood separately in each case (Fletcher 1978b). As a result, his dates are much more difficult to correct. So far, no complete revision list has been published; there may be some pictures where re-interpretation could radically affect the attribution and hence the valuation!

Finally, there are some cautionary comments which need to be made about the use of dendrochronology in art history. In a tightly controlled set of exercises, using well-authenticated paintings, Bauch and Eckstein, and more recently Klein, have achieved excellent results and even helped to refine the chronology of particular artists (Klein 1989). However, the question has to be asked, can dendrochronology be used to authenticate paintings? I would suggest extreme caution. Dating a panel – estimating the felling date of the tree from which the panel was cut – does not date the painting on that panel, nor does it specify who painted the painting. A modern painting on an old panel will after all give an old date. Fletcher allowed himself to become involved in just such authentication exercises. One in particular, the attribution of the painting *E Cosi Desio me Mena* to Holbein, stretches credibility to breaking point (Fletcher 1982). On the basis of the dating of the last ring of the panel to 1491, the date of painting is suggested to be in the 1520s. Then by assigning (on the most dubious logic) the panel to an origin in the same tree as panels used in two other Holbein paintings, inscribed 1527 and 1528 respectively, it is deduced that the painting was by Holbein and painted in Antwerp in 1526. Given that the only firm evidence is a date of 1495 or 1496 for the last existing growth ring (after correcting for the wrong placement of the art-historical chronology), the attribution of this painting has to be extremely suspect. Fletcher, in this, as in other cases, was practising a subtle blend of art history and tree-ring studies. No dendrochronologist could possibly justify the attribution of *E Cosi Desio me Mena* to Holbein and to 1526.

Tree-ring limitations

We have seen how certain assumptions about the origin of the art-historical timbers in England and the Netherlands led to a real problem in dendrochronology in northern Europe. Obviously importation raises the issue of the compatibility of any sample with 'local' chronologies. This would seem to be an appropriate point to address several other basic chronological issues which stem directly from the limitations of dendrochronology as a dating tool. To some extent these limitations are an in-house philosophical

issue for dendrochronologists: there are certain samples which the dendrochronologist either shouldn't handle at all or should treat equivocally. On the other hand, since the consumer – the person requiring dates – may, from time to time, have to face results associated with such doubtful samples, it is probably useful to understand some of the potential traps. What follows is mostly based on experience within the Belfast laboratory and relates to problems with short samples and sample isolates.

In each case recent empirical examples are used as vehicles for discussion of particular problems. Since some of the limitations, for example those associated with short samples, relate to experience with Irish oak, comments on them may not be immediately applicable to short samples from areas where the climate signal is 'stronger'. Nevertheless, it is to be hoped that the discussions will serve to warn archaeologists and others of the need to remember Crow's Law: 'Do not believe what you want to believe until you know what you ought to know.'

Short sample problems

There is no doubt that archaeologists, building historians or indeed others who get a taste for absolute chronology, become addicted to independent, absolute dating methods. In an ideal world samples could be plugged into a black box system which would supply totally independent and perfectly precise results. Curiously, radiocarbon in some ways comes closest to this ideal in the sense that any carbon sample submitted to a laboratory guarantees a 'date' even though the relationship of that 'date' to the true age of the sample is often tenuous (see, for example, Baillie 1990a). So with radiocarbon the results may be independent but they are usually limited by the accuracy of the method.

In the case of dendrochronology, which holds out the 'carrot' of extreme accuracy on the one hand, there is the 'stick' of its highly limited applicability on the other. The customer is quickly brought face to face with the limitations of the method: timbers must be of the correct species, must have long ring patterns, should be indigenous, etc. Even if all these conditions are satisfied there is still no guarantee that a date will be forthcoming for any particular piece of wood. This limited applicability is particularly distressing to customers who have developed a taste for the calendrical accuracy of dendrochronology. If half-a-dozen structures have been successfully dated, and thus related, it is hard to accept that the next cannot be dated at all. So customers tend to exert pressure for the dating of more marginal – particularly short-lived – samples. What follows developed, at least in part, from a discussion at an Athens workshop in 1984. The discussion centred around wood samples which are not immediately datable by dendrochronology. What, we discussed, are the possibilities of allowing archaeologists to use their available information to narrow the 'window' within which the dendrochronologist might search for a 'match' – a Bayesian approach? While this approach has certain attractions it also contains some hidden dangers, not the least being the loss of independence of the dendrochronological result. Some reasons for attempting to avoid such search procedure are set out below, together with some case studies. Some of these studies look at previous attempts to 'date' intrinsically undatable samples and go on to assess the consequences. I hope they illustrate why applying pressure to get a 'date' in such cases is probably not worthwhile and how, in at least some instances, it can be positively counter-productive.

The English art-historical chronologies in retrospect

We have looked at the resolution of the location and dating problems associated with the art-historical chronologies. We now know that the oak panels used in the construction of the 'English' art-historical chronologies had originated in the eastern Baltic. The result of this mistaken attribution was that for many years the art-historical chronologies were wrongly 'dated'. It is ironic that, even though the timbers were of Baltic origin, we now know that the dating attempts against western chronologies should have worked! For example, the first of the art-historical chronologies, MC18, actually gives t values of

3.3, 3.4 and 3.2 against chronologies from Göttingen, Hamburg and south Germany at the correct end-date AD 1550. By a quirk of fate, REF 4 (one of the later art-historical chronologies), although of Baltic origin, also gives a t value of 4.6 at the correct date against the most distant Belfast chronology! This consistency, were the exercise repeated today, would be taken as a strong case for consideration of the true dating position. However, it was ignored and the whole story took a lot of unravelling (see above). All of this happened during the development of European dendrochronology and forms a documented case which allows objective discussion of several important dendrochronological issues.

1. We know for certain that wood has been moved about in the past – where it is now may bear no relationship to where it grew.
2. Oak looks like oak no matter where it comes from (at least the sessile and pedunculate varieties) and so it is inherently impossible to source by appearance or physical characteristics. It is now accepted that the two sub-species cannot be separated on the grounds of wood anatomy (Dieter Eckstein, Bernd Becker and Fritz Schweingruber pers. comm.).
3. The cross-correlations between oak chronologies cannot easily be predicted in advance, thus the cross-correlation between the Belfast chronology and REF 4 at AD 1550 was correct but the match was not good enough (presumably because of the 1500km distance between the source areas) for anyone to accept it unequivocally. Now this specific example (readers can check it for themselves because the Belfast and REF 4 data are in print, as is the CROS program) leads us to the immediate realization that there are distinct types of information available to dendrochronologists:
(i) There are *cross-correlations* between ring patterns (either between the ring patterns of individual trees or between individual trees and master chronologies or between different master chronologies) where the computer checks every possible overlap position and calculates a

correlation coefficient at each. High values are suggestive of synchronization.

(ii) There is a *tree-ring match* where the dendrochronologist believes he or she can see meaningful synchronization between the ring patterns visually.

(iii) Finally we arrive at the situation where sufficient evidence – normally combining cross-correlations, visual matching and replication – is available to arrive at *cross-dating* between ring patterns. In this case the true relative position between the two ring patterns can be specified exactly.

If we take MC18 today and compare it with the most easterly European chronology, constructed in Poland by Thomas Wazny, we find that it gives a cross-correlation $t = 4.4$ with its end-year at AD 1550. It also matches the Polish chronology visually to the satisfaction of a practised dendrochronologist and indeed it dates to an end-year of AD 1550. We can be absolutely sure of this because later versions of the art-historical chronologies, e.g. Ref. 1234, give t values as high as 8.5 at the same '1550' position. We can compare this clear situation and those clear statements with the situation in 1974/5, before the Polish chronology was constructed and while British and Irish dendrochronology was in its infancy. At that time MC18 was mismatched against the published German chronologies. It gave a *cross-correlation* at the correct date against Belfast but did not constitute an acceptable *match*; and indeed it was not known to *date* to AD 1550 until 1985.

This tells us elegantly that any particular ring pattern must only be compared with relevant ('local') chronologies of the same species. It tells us that correlations in themselves do not date samples. It tells us that there can be spurious matches; hence a match in itself is not the same thing as a date. It reminds us that there is only one true date for any sample. One might at this point attempt a definition of sorts: 'anything other than the highest level of certainty associated with a date reduces it to a match or a cross-correlation, neither of which need be correct.'

Obviously the dendrochronologist has got to decide on a proper definition and a rigid termi-

nology when communicating with customers (it is actually very difficult to be consistent in the matter of terminology). For example: to say that 'MC18 dates to 1550' is correct because this result is now known with certainty. However, to say that 'MC18 correlates against Belfast at 1550' is also correct but does not mean the same thing – the latter correlation did not and could not define the true date. So correlation is a term which needs to be regarded with caution.

This preamble is to try to establish a realistic attitude to dendrochronology. Basically, when the method works – when a long ring pattern matches uniquely against an established and precisely dated master chronology for the same species – the result it produces is incomparable, because the last existing ring can be assigned to growth in a particular calendar year. It is unlikely that this level of accuracy will ever be surpassed. However, the problem for the customer is that, in what we might call classic dendrochronology, there is no fallback position. If there is no unique date for the long ring pattern, then the dendrochronologist says that the sample is undated.

This quantized character of the method – 'it either dates or it doesn't' – is hard to come to terms with. From the customer's viewpoint it is a lottery where there are no second prizes. However, the majority of dendrochronologists believe that this is the way things should be. Samples should be either dated or undated: there should be no half measures. Absolute cross-dating is the aspect which underpins all subsequent studies, i.e. if the dates are not absolute, all deductions based on them are suspect. This whole issue has to be seen against the calls from archaeologists and others to introduce secondary level 'dating' into dendrochronology – the demand for 'possible matches' and 'correlations' where unique dating proves impossible. At its most fundamental it is about the recognition that some samples are intrinsically undatable! And of course, any 'date' given for an intrinsically undatable sample will usually be wrong and probably can never be corrected. As will be demonstrated, particularly for short samples, you may get matches and/or correlations but these may not be dates.

The following series of cases will be used to develop this theme and to show some of the dangers in asking too much of the method. It is where samples fail to date unequivocally that the problems arise. It is then that pressure to assign some sort of ranking to a series of 'possible' matching positions becomes apparent. The pressure is like this: 'Can you not give some indication of the likely date?', 'Are there no correlations at all?', 'Could you let me have the correlations to see if I can decide which one might be correct?', 'If I tell you what date it's likely to be can you look around there?' etc., etc. All of these requests, in the final analysis, are asking for ranked dates.

Case 1 Ranked dating – the theoretical dangers

Let us imagine the sort of situation which might arise. A piece of oak is found in a context where dating appears relatively secure on the basis of coins/pottery or general association. The ring pattern of the piece of wood – for whatever reason (short ring pattern/poor response to signal/exotic origin) – fails to date uniquely. The dendrochronologist says, 'I cannot give a date for this piece of wood.' The response is some version of those above, e.g. 'If I can tell you the date of the context within a decade or so, can you see if there is a match there?'

No matter how it is put, the message is this: other evidence is being used to indicate, and narrow, the general date range of the context. The assumption is that, armed with this information, the dendrochronologist will be able to see where this piece of ring pattern fits against the master chronology. This assumes that the piece of wood contains enough clear, relevant tree-ring signal to be datable (it also assumes that the wood is in fact of broadly the supposed age). This is the fundamental mistake. It is possible to have a section of ring pattern which simply does not match with the master chronology over the period of years in which it grew. Leaving aside imported samples which are extreme cases, this failure of some samples to match is an empirically observed fact. By taking sections of ring pattern of precisely known age – either modern control samples or sub-sections from certainly dated long patterns – it is possible to demonstrate that dating can break down, especially for short samples. It is particu-

larly noticeable with samples containing less than 80 rings (Pilcher and Baillie 1987).

However, let us assume that the dendrochronologist is misguided enough (or is pressured enough) to acquiesce in this exercise. 'OK, I cannot uniquely date your sample but you tell me it is close to AD 1225. There are low correlation values with the last ring at 1137, 1201 and 1295 – I cannot say which, or indeed if any, of these positions is correct.' This would leave the customer in the following interesting position. The interpretation will (like it or not) go like this:

a) 1137 is clearly out of line with the other thirteenth-century evidence, so the customer can safely say, 'This is far too early, but even if it is correct it could be a re-used timber,' i.e. the early possibility is *explained away*!

b) 1295 is treated similarly: it is too late, therefore at best the timber is intrusive or a replacement. In neither (a) nor (b) will the customer allow the other dating evidence to be upset by what is, after all, a weak piece of dendrochronological evidence.

c) Having got rid of the other (awkward) possibilities the customer can now take comfort from the 1201 possibility which fits with his dating framework. It is the fact that, in these weak matching situations, it is possible to explain away all of the unpleasant possibilities which makes such exercises futile. Basically the customer is not willing to use the information in anything other than a reinforcing mode.

The dangers of this are obvious. Having gone through the above procedure the customer, having picked the date which fits his arguments, can now 'refine' the previous dating and, worse still, the dating appears more 'secure' because it *appears* to be based on dendrochronology. Moreover, because the piece of wood in question is more or less intrinsically undatable, no one is ever likely to be able to redate the sample with sufficient certainty to override the 1201 possibility. So by indulging in this type of exercise the customer builds a sort of cross between a 'circular argument' and an 'untestable hypothesis'.

Case 2 An actual example of ranked 'dates'

To see an actual example of the dangers of ranked 'dates' we can refer to Rigold (1975). Rigold asked John Fletcher to attempt to date an element from the Phase 1 structure at Eynsford Castle, Kent. Rigold says: 'Subject in each case to an addition of at least 20 years, in Fletcher's estimation, to cover a trimming deep enough to remove all traces of sapwood, four possible agreements were obtained, which gave, in order of preference a *date* [my italics] for the terminal ring at AD 1035, 1221, 1138 and 1046.' It is clear from this that Fletcher did not date the timber at all. What he did was list the four highest correlation values given by the computer when he ran the 132-year Eynsford ring pattern against a chronology from Westminster Abbey. So we immediately see the clear and definite distinction between a correlation and a date as discussed above. It is worth continuing with this particular example because it is an admirable demonstration of the role of the customer. Once Fletcher had listed the four highest correlations the ball was in Rigold's court.

Rigold goes on to state, 'Other archaeological considerations would seem to limit the possibility to 1138 . . .'. In other words, it does not matter whether the tree-ring correlation is intrinsically correct because archaeological considerations dictate that 1138 has to be correct. However, once the archaeologist (in this case) has exercised his archaeologial choice (because the choice is clearly archaeological not dendrochronological – the third preference correlation being selected), he immediately goes on to build upon this new evidence. This date

> . . . is important, taking the additional 20 years or more into consideration, in placing the reconstruction of the castle, with heightened curtain, gate-tower and enclosed, almost donjon-like, hall early in the reign of Henry II, in the full career of William de Eynsford III and presumably late in the archiepiscopate of his patron, Theobold, *rather than as historical but not archaeological factors might suggest* [my italics] in the time of Steven . . . (op. cit. 91)

Here we see the customer free to choose which tree-ring correlation is correct on archaeological grounds, using that 'date' to favour his or her own archaeological interpretation over a *pre-existing* historical interpretation. Rigold goes on to explain why the other correlation dates are unacceptable but that is not important. What is important is that an archaeologist, who has already made up his mind about the interpretation of his site, is indulging in pure circular argument. Dendrochronology should not be used in this way. To be objective, a tree-ring date must be independent of the archaeological/historical considerations. Only then can the method be used in its proper role of testing and adjudicating.

Case 3 Ships' timbers from Woodquay Dublin

This example is included to show the danger with really short samples. In 1977, on the Woodquay site in Dublin, a series of timbers were recovered from what had been a clinker-built boat of double-ended type. Originally the boat must have been up to 20m in length. Samples from a number of the radial oak planks were successfully dated against the Dublin oak chronology with t values from 9.6 to 13.7 (Baillie 1978b, Baillie 1982: 239). One of the planks, Q3137a, retained some traces of sapwood and the construction date could be estimated at AD 1195±9. All the evidence pointed to a late twelfth-century, locally constructed boat. The context of the remains suggested that they were deposited in the mid-thirteenth century, suggesting a life for the boat of about a half-century. Unfortunately, one of the timbers, Q3138, was attached to a small section of a further plank Q3138a. The two were held together by a large lozenge-headed clench nail and the hair calking was still in place between the two timbers (**Fig. 3.2a**).

Point 1: From an archaeological point of view it would seem reasonable to assume that 3138a was simply another 20cm riven plank which was broken off and weathered on its outer surface. It is possible therefore that the ring pattern of 3138a came from well in towards the centre of its parent tree (**Fig. 3.2b**), though there is the possibility

53

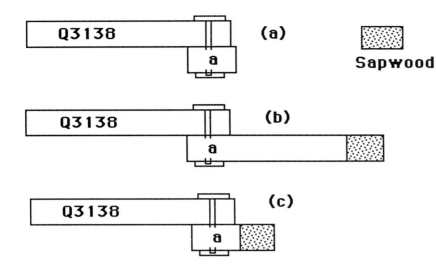

3.2 Two Dublin boat timbers (a) as found, (b) suggesting that Q3138a was the inner portion of a plank, (c) Q3138a as a bumper or rail

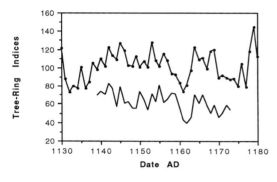

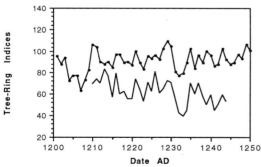

3.3 Possible 'matching' positions for short sample Q3138a. (a) at 1173 against the Dublin master chronology, (b) at 1244 against a general British Isles master

that the situation was as in **Fig. 3.2c** and that this small timber served some other purpose than simply another overlapping plank, e.g. a rail or bumper.

Point 2: Normal practice at Belfast (and in most other tree-ring laboratories) would have been to ignore this small piece, with its 35 rings, as intrinsically undatable – because of the dangers outlined above. However, for this exercise its ring pattern was measured. **Fig. 3.3** shows two positions where the 35-year ring pattern shows reasonable visual agreement with the published Dublin master chronology and a generalized British Isles chronology (Britim). It would be impossible for any dendrochronologist to say whether either of these positions is correct. For the purposes of discussion what would 1173 mean? Well, allowing for missing sapwood (32±9 years) we would be suggesting felling in the range 1205±9 or later; not so very different from the main phase of the boat. However, that would be on the assumption that 3138a is a small timber (e.g. a rail) with only its sapwood missing. We have no grounds for making that assumption. If 3138a were (as seems more likely) a plank, then there could be perhaps 80, or 100, or even more, heartwood rings missing. If we assume 3138a to be the inside of a plank, and we accepted the 1173 position, we might be considering felling around 1300, much later than the archaeological context. **Fig. 3.3b** shows 3138a at an end-year of 1244 compared with the generalized British Isles chronology. (The match is so good that it becomes hard, even for a dendrochronologist, to dismiss this position, i.e. it really looks as if 3138a matches at AD 1244.) The answer is 'Yes, it does match at 1244.' You don't have to be a dendrochronologist to see that (it also matched at 1173). However, and this is the nub of the dilemma, just because a 35-year section of ring pattern looks good against a master chronology does not mean that it actually *dates* to 1244. With short sections of ring pattern we can find matches in many positions. If we were to allow the particularly good match against Britim to swing us in favour of 1244 what would we be doing? We would be saying, 'Here is a small piece of wood, rigidly attached to a group of timbers, all of which match the Dublin chronology consistent with a late twelfth-century construction – which is a replacement timber and, because it matches better with Britim than it does with Dublin, may come from a *different area* from the rest of the timbers.' Now our 35-year ring pattern would be suggesting:

a) a later repair;
b) that repair in a different area;
c) a minimum lifetime for the boat of around 70 years (rail scenario) and quite possibly 170 years (plank scenario).

The situation is becoming truly horrible. Logic suggests that we have the inside of just another plank, but a 35-year tree-ring overlap is threatening to rewrite the whole story in glowing detail. The truth is that no one can put their hand on their heart and swear to a unique dating for such a short section of ring pattern. It *doesn't matter how good the match is*. The real danger lies in accepting such dubious matches when they *do* fit with other evidence. I would go so far as to

say that anyone trying to tell you that they have dated such a short sample is kidding both themselves and you. They may have matched it; they certainly cannot claim to have uniquely dated it!

There is nothing unique about this example. There are many cases where it has proved impossible to provide definitive dates for short samples. So extreme care has to be taken with such samples because there are grave philosophical problems associated with them: it's not that they don't match, it's just that they don't date. In almost every case the common factor is that a supposed tree-ring 'date' is being constrained by non tree-ring considerations – by making assumptions on the likely date from archaeological or other information. We have to be very careful how we treat such results. As discussed above there is no point in leaving the choice to the customer. A date given for a sample after the procedure has been heavily constrained by outside information is no longer an independent tree-ring date. It lacks the authority of an independent dendrochronological dating and should not be called the same thing.

Case 4 The isolated sample problem

From experience in Ireland, there is a potentially serious dendrochronological problem which is often encountered with individual tree-ring samples, or poorly replicated master chronologies, from isolated areas. The problem is a general one brought about by inadequate chronological coverage in time and space and applies particularly to the prehistoric period.

To illustrate the problem we can look at

3.4 While robust site chronologies can often be dated at a distance, there is a lower success rate with individual ring patterns

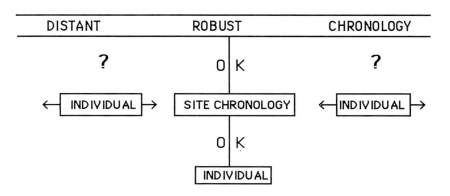

Fig. 3.4. In this figure we have to imagine that we have a well-replicated but distant master chronology and a robust and replicated site chronology. The site chronology has enough 'signal' to date directly against the distant chronology. However, individual samples from the site, without sufficient signal to date at a distance, can only be compared with the local site master. If, however, they fall outside the span of the local chronology, either earlier or later, then they cannot be dated. So dating at a distance carries with it the penalty of sometimes being unable to date individual timbers from later or substantially earlier phases of activity on the site. The individual samples appear to be simply undatable – yet may actually be the most important timbers on the site from an interpretive point of view. Both archaeologically and chronologically this is bad news. It would seem self-evident that, to understand the history of a site and the length of time it was in use, we need to be able to date earlier or later timbers from the site, not just a main phase. It would seem from Fig. 3.4 that this is just what, in many cases, the dendrochronologist can't do. This is a problem probably not appreciated by non-dendrochronologists; however, it is a relatively common problem and one which will only ease as the number of robust local chronologies grows and area coverage gradually improves.

In the same vein, it should be noted that, because of the need for significant overlaps between sample ring patterns and chronologies – at least 100 years or so – it can be very difficult to date samples around 'gaps' in chronologies. Take, for example, the fact that there is no Irish oak material between 95 BC and 13 BC (the gap being bridged with Roman chronologies from England). To extend a ring pattern into this gap, given the need for minimum overlaps of approximately 100 years, it must either extend back to *c*. 195 BC, or earlier, or forward to *c*. AD 87, or later. So the 95–13 BC gap in the Irish chronology is effectively a tree-ring gap from *c*. 195 BC to *c*. AD 87. Put more bluntly, the one-century gap in the Irish chronology is effectively a three-century tree-ring gap from a dating point of view!

Conclusion

The important thing about the art-historical question was that dendrochronology was capable of uncovering the problem with the chronology and eventually putting the whole issue to rights. It is interesting that little was heard from art historians during the debate. Presumably they were relying on the dendrochronologists to tell them which paintings were genuine and which were copies/fakes? Equally, it does have to be said that one author did pick up on the possible mis-datings after the initial problem was pointed out. David Starkey cited a painting, believed to be a Holbein by its elderly owner, which was 'proved' a copy by dendrochronology; the author's tone suggested that the elderly owner of the painting had died of a broken heart when he heard that 'the panel it was painted on dated from at least seven years after Holbein's death' (Starkey 1985). While it's impossible to be dogmatic with so little information, a possible solution in this case might be as follows. Fletcher seldom used an allowance of less than 20 years for sapwood, usually 20–30 years. Holbein died in 1543. So, if Fletcher said that the panel dated from 1550 (at the earliest), we could venture that the last heartwood ring might have been around 1520–30 (allowing for the missing sapwood). Redating the chronology forward by 4–5 years, puts the last ring of heartwood around 1525–35. Baltic sapwood range is 7–24 rings (Baillie *et al.* 1985). Therefore, it could be possible that a 'panel from at least seven years after Holbein's death' could have been painted on by Holbein.

This is also the place to say that the bottom line on dendrochronology – as late as May 1994 (at an international gathering in Tucson) – is that it is absolute dating which underpins everything else, i.e. there is no room in conventional dendrochronology for Bayesian or probabilistic dating. It is very important that customers, be they archaeologists, building historians, other dendrochronologists or dendroclimatologists, can rely on tree-ring dates being correct. Maybe just isn't good enough.

4 Archaeological dating and some ultimate chronological truths

Introduction

Chronology building tends to be a specialized activity and requires a single-minded approach, with the result that niceties of interpretation frequently have to be bypassed in the quest for links between chronologies and detailed replication. In addition, the vast bulk of the prehistoric material used in chronology construction is necessarily natural or 'sub-fossil' and, while this may ultimately yield environmental information, it has few direct archaeological applications. So, during the 1980s, while major effort was applied to the completion of the long prehistoric chronology in Ireland and England, relatively little effort was applied to addressing archaeological questions. Yet, even in chronology building mode, as the prehistoric chronologies were being pieced together, routine dating was adding to the list of precisely dated sites belonging to the last two millennia, and occasional archaeological finds were dated against the sub-fossil chronologies.

In this chapter we will look at some archaeological results, from the Belfast work, which have accumulated during the last decade and review some of the lessons which have come out of the dendrochronological studies. In particular we can look at some archaeological lessons from those sites, with preserved wood, which may help in the interpretation of dryland archaeological sites. While it may seem parochial to study only those dating examples with which the author has been involved, the nature of dendrochronology is such that the lessons learned are applicable wherever oak dendrochronology is being practised. Moreover, while many of the examples are primarily archaeological, they serve to demonstrate the absolute limits of chronology available to any discipline which

requires tight chronological control in the later Holocene; archaeological dating inevitably takes us to the very limits of chronological resolution. Everything else is *worse* than this.

Turning prehistory into history?

Let's start with an apparently preposterous assertion, that it is possible to turn prehistory into history. We are all happy with the concept of those key dates which split history neatly into pre- and post- something. The arrival of a literate Julius Caesar on the shores of Britain marks 55 BC indelibly in the history books. Similarly the arrival of the Normans in England, or indeed Ireland, draws a sharp dividing line between the Norman period and everything which went before. Unfortunately, historical documentation is not universally available and by and large the quality and the quantity of available history declines rapidly as we go back into the distant past. As a result, in trying to understand the past, archaeological information becomes increasingly important the further back we go. Immediately we have to recognize that normal archaeological dating information is seldom of the same precise character as historical information – the exception being where tree-ring dates are available. However, once tree-ring dates *are* available, they do allow us to make statements of a surprisingly 'historical' character.

To give but one instance, we now know that the great oak which was to become the central post of the ritual structure at Navan Fort, Co. Armagh – the ancient capital of Ulster – last grew in the year 95 BC (Baillie 1988a). The timber was recovered during excavation of the structure and was dated by dendrochronology. The near-miraculous survival of complete sapwood, in a natural indentation on the trunk, allowed the date of the last year of growth to be specified exactly. So this relationship, of a tree-ring date and an important archaeological monument, allows us to re-create a marker date only marginally less important than Caesar's landing in Britain. We can now say:

In 95 BC the great oak, which was to be the centre post of the Navan temple, last shed its leaves. Within about six months, and certainly before the summer of 94 BC, the tree was felled. Sharp metal tools cut two linking mortices close to the base of the trunk to take the ropes with which it was drawn into position.

The year 95 BC marks the *only* event in the first century BC which has been precisely specified in Ireland. It is one of only two 'historical' events in that century which we can be pretty sure had definite influence on Irish affairs at the time; the other was the significant dust-veil event which was recorded elsewhere around the northern hemisphere in 44–42 BC (Chapter 5). So, with this quality of dating, we seem to be in a position to produce 'historical' quality statements in an otherwise prehistoric period; this in turn raises the question whether it is possible to turn prehistory into history. Perhaps we require a better

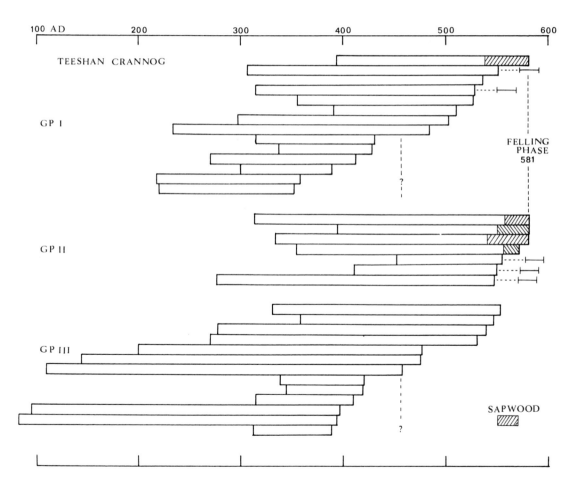

4.1 The phantom 'phase' in the samples from Teeshan crannog, Co. Antrim. Is the apparent phase around 460 real or an artefact of timber working (Eckstein et al. 1984)?

definition of what constitutes a historical statement. Which is better: an ancient written reference to a king in a year which cannot in reality be exactly specified (a typical annalistic reference) or the precise date of an archaeological or environmental event at a known location (a typical tree-ring dating)? In reality, of course, only a small number of prehistoric archaeological sites provide timbers which are suitable for dendrochronology and where such quasi-historical inferences can be drawn; so the question probably just has to remain open. However, it is a nice idea that the historical record is not constrained entirely by written records; some historical quality information is 'written' in the tree-ring records as well.

Information from wet sites

In *TRDA* a provisional list of construction dates for crannogs suggested that, in Ireland, at least some of these artificial-island structures had Dark Age foundations, between AD 550 and 650. There is now a considerable body of information about crannogs and the results of several excavations in Ireland which confirm this Early Christian building horizon. The situation is rather different in Scotland, for example, where crannogs are well known from the mid-first millennium BC, as well as from Dark Age and medieval times. For the purposes of this chapter, the wet wood well-preserved in Irish crannogs offers an excellent opportunity to study the effects, on archaeological interpretation, of intrinsic dating; i.e. with dendrochronology we can take the guesswork out of interpretation and demonstrate the difficulties which archaeologists working with post-holes (rather than the posts) might have faced.

The dendrochronological excursions into Irish crannogs had originally been aimed at the acquisition of timbers for chronology building. This interest had waned as more and more sites produced dates in the sixth and seventh centuries AD. However, in the mid-1980s several factors created a renewed interest in crannogs. These factors included the excavation of the crannog at Moynagh Lough, Co. Meath (Bradley 1985) together with the re-excavation of the Island

MacHugh crannog in Lough Catherine, Co. Tyrone (Ivens *et al.* 1986), and two centennial conferences in Edinburgh and Dublin to honour the work of Colonel W.G. Wood Martin whose books *Ancient Scottish Lake Dwellings or Crannogs* (1882) and *The Lake Dwellings of Ireland* (1886) had so thoroughly covered the subject.

The renewed excavation activity, and associated accumulation of results for conference papers, uncovered a number of intriguing results some of which have a bearing on archaeological interpretation generally. Let us start with a longstanding interpretive problem. One of the earliest of the 'oak bearing' Early Christian crannogs was Teeshan, Co. Antrim, which dated to AD 581. The timbers, used in the tree-ring work, were recovered from the spoil, following complete destruction of the site by heavy machinery. The timbers provided a useful chronology of 494 years which spanned AD 88–581 (Baillie 1982). The problem was that the distribution of end-years of the first batch of timbers showed an apparent earlier clustering around AD 460 (**Fig. 4.1a**). Was it possible that there actually had been an earlier building phase on the site a century or more before AD 581? The question was posed because such an early date for a crannog would tend to be out of line with the archaeological material associated with north Irish crannogs. In order to try a resolution of this question a larger group of samples was processed. This showed that timbers with sapwood, or with clear evidence for heartwood/sapwood boundaries, all supported the AD 581 phase. However, as the batch included samples without sapwood, it was clear from this second group that the 'phantom' earlier phase was still present (**Fig. 4.1b**). Various attempts were made to interpret what this might mean. One suggestion involved the secondary use of old timbers, possibly from a standing structure, in the make-up of the crannog. That suggestion would still leave the crannog dating to AD 581 and it might also have explained the absence of sapwood on all the older timbers: they could have been around long enough for their sapwood to deteriorate.

A second argument centred around the overall length of the ring patterns. This suggested that it was unlikely that all the timbers were felled in AD 581; the reason being that if felled at that date some of the timbers would have come from trees which had grown for 494 years. Essentially no other oaks of this sort of length are recorded in Ireland at any period in the last seven millennia. Moreover, if all were felled in AD 581 then ten of the shortest ring patterns would have had more growth rings *missing* than they actually retain. Obviously all such arguments are subjective but the conclusion from this original analysis was: 'The most likely solution . . . is that we are dealing with a crannog constructed in AD 581 incorporating timbers from at least one earlier structure' (Eckstein *et al.* 1984).

Before looking at some fresh tree-ring evidence it is perhaps worth considering the dating of this site from a purely archaeological point of view. As the crannog was destroyed (as opposed to excavated), the archaeologist would have been faced, at best, with a random selection of material culture from the site. In the case of Teeshan the earliest identifiable finds were sherds of E-ware – Continental pottery whose earliest appearance could be 'dated' to either the seventh or just possibly the sixth century AD (see Chapter 6 and Warner 1985). Other objects included fragments of bone combs, glass beads and souterrain ware, all of which could be dated no closer than 'the Early Christian period'. So an archaeologist looking at this material would have been unable

to suggest a date-range for the construction better than perhaps two to three centuries. Given this information the actual foundation date would of course be of considerable interest.

The new information on crannog activity and indeed on timber interpretation came from Island MacHugh in Co. Tyrone. This crannog was extensively excavated in the late 1930s and 1940s (Davies 1950) in the days before any scientific dating methods were available. The crannog had been visited in 1977 to ascertain if any of the extensive timbering recorded by Davies still survived. On that visit some of the trenches were found to be still open and oak timbers directly assignable to Davies' plans were recovered for dating. Two samples with sapwood were dated: Q2936, with complete sapwood, had a felling date of AD 612 and this was backed up by a felling estimate of AD 620±9 for Q2937 (Baillie 1982). So even this minor dating excursion put the main timbering phase on MacHugh into the mainstream of Irish crannog construction. In 1985 and 1986 the site was partially re-excavated by Ivens and Simpson to exploit the chronological possibilities offered by dendrochronology.

Fig. 4.2 summarizes the results of an extensive dating campaign carried out on samples from the two seasons of excavation. Two things were immediately apparent: all the substantial oak

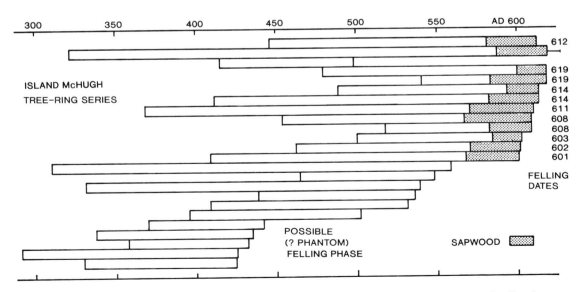

4.2 Apparent phantom phase(s) in timbers from Island MacHugh, Co. Tyrone, mimic the earlier Teeshan phase in Fig. 4.1

timbers recovered related to the first millennium AD and all the timbers with sapwood represented a phase of activity spread over the interval from AD 601 to 619. As these timbers were all complete to the underbark surface, the dates given are actual 'felling' dates, i.e. the dates of the years in which the timbers last grew. This was surprising because it would normally have been assumed that the main activity would be in a single year or in a period of a few years. Activity over 19 years is difficult to interpret. Was wood gradually stockpiled and then used in a single building operation? Was activity really sustained over almost two decades – a human generation?

Various hypotheses were suggested but the cur-rently preferred scenario is as follows. The pristine condition of the sapwood effectively rules out cutting over a period and storage. This leaves continuous activity and a plausible explanation for this might relate to the fact that the crannog was built on a natural peat-covered ridge in the lake. In the early seventh century posts were inserted in a circle and massive amounts of stones and earth were brought to make up the crannog. It is likely that this mass on top of the peat would have tended to spread outwards. It can be imagined that more or less continuous efforts might have been necessary to consolidate the crannog by adding more and more vertical timbers around the edge (Baillie 1993). Returning to **Fig. 4.2**, it

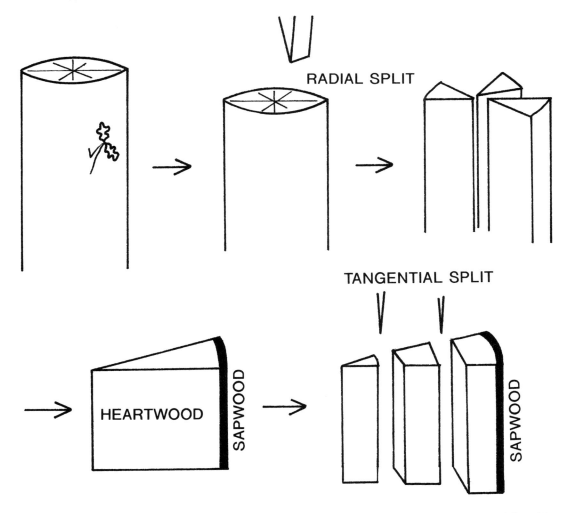

4.3 How the Island MacHugh posts were made by tangential splitting of wedges of riven oak. Using this technique, only the outer sections will retain sapwood

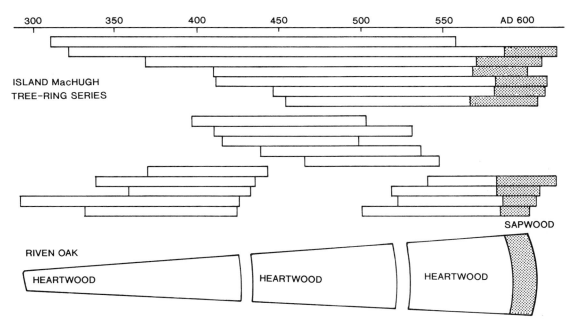

4.4 Fig. 4.2 redrawn to illustrate how the ring patterns of the timbers from Island MacHugh conform to the riven-oak hypothesis. Note how only the outer sections exhibit sapwood

is clear that at Island MacHugh we have one or possibly two phantom earlier phases as at Teeshan. Indeed, as at Teeshan, it is possible to see in these timbers a clustering of end-years which might be consistent with a felling phase around AD 460. Was there some widespread, but previously unrecognized, phase of crannog activity in Ulster in the mid-fifth century? It became increasingly important to know.

The difference in the case of Island MacHugh was that the timbers were removed from dense waterlogged peat and were in exactly the condition in which they were originally inserted. This allowed the timbers to be examined in detail. It was noteworthy that those timbers which had sapwood tended to have complete sapwood, the 'earlier' timbers had no traces of sapwood whatsoever. This observation could be coupled with the fact that several of the sapwood timbers were truncated – the centre of the tree was missing and the ring patterns started after AD 460. Was it possible that the 'earlier' timbers were in reality simply the inner portions of the truncated sapwood-bearing timbers? In this case the woodworking on the samples showed clearly how the posts had been made and explained the tree-ring observations. The Early Christian

woodworkers had exploited the radial character of oak to split the trees into thick wedge-shaped sections (**Fig. 4.3**). In order to make posts they had then sub-divided some of the wedges into two or three consecutive pieces. This process could be detected in the working details on the timbers. It was now clear that such a process would naturally tend to produce the phantom early phases. It also served to explain why the timbers with sapwood had *complete* sapwood – in excellent condition – while the 'early' timbers had *none*. **Fig. 4.4** shows the distribution of timbers redrawn to demonstrate the splitting-into-three.

Now, while this is interesting and does suggest an explanation for the previous observations on the Teeshan timbers, perhaps the most salutary point relates to the implications when sampling for radiocarbon dating. Some of the small posts, split from the centre of large timbers, look to the unwary (indeed look to anyone) like ideal samples for radiocarbon analysis. They appear to be short-lived material with all that implies for high-integrity samples. If dated by radiocarbon they would tend to give dates *too old* by around two–three centuries. Warner has written on exactly such an age-lapse phenomenon involving

4.5 Where tangential splitting of riven oak has been employed to produce building timbers, the danger is that different elements within a structure will be of intrinsically different dates. This is a particular danger if the structure is to be dated by radiocarbon

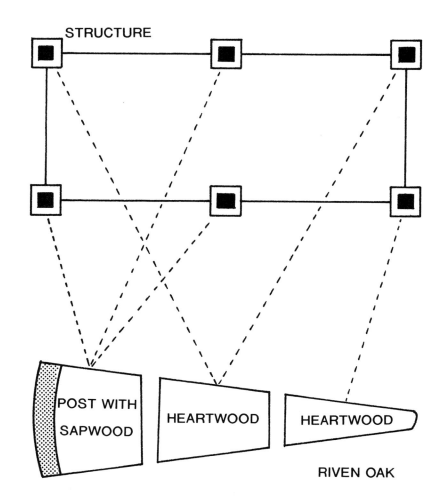

STRUCTURE

POST WITH SAPWOOD

HEARTWOOD

HEARTWOOD

RIVEN OAK

Lake

4.6 Although every post in this group from Island MacHugh was precisely dated by dendrochronology, truncation (T) and different felling dates (F) make it impossible to interpret the post configuration

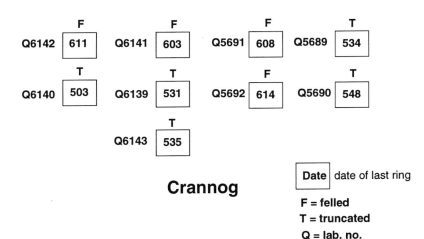

	F		F		F		T
Q6142	611	Q6141	603	Q5691	608	Q5689	534

	T		T		F		T
Q6140	503	Q6139	531	Q5692	614	Q5690	548

	T
Q6143	535

Crannog

Date	date of last ring

F = felled
T = truncated
Q = lab. no.

63

radiocarbon dates from known-age structures and has pointed out that in dating unidentified 'charcoal', i.e. charcoal other than twigs, there is a tendency for the dates to be too old by 150–200 years (Warner 1990a).

You might say that it is a major leap from an Irish crannog to a general age-lapse phenomenon; however, it has to be remembered that the technology of splitting large oak trees into radial planks goes back to the beginning of the Neolithic. The Sweet Track was made of riven oaks which were 400 years old when felled and split (Morgan 1988)! The Ballynagilly Neolithic house – with some of the earliest Neolithic radiocarbon dates in the British Isles (on 'charcoal') – was constructed using riven oak planks (Apsimon 1976). Put simply, on sites where people were using this type of split-oak technology, pieces of very old wood may be intimately mixed with contemporary remains. Perhaps more thought has to be given to the provenance of oak samples when radiocarbon dating is contemplated. **Fig. 4.5** illustrates the general problem for any structure where the split-oak technique is employed. If some posts are age-lapsed, because of their position within the tree, sampling for radiocarbon dating becomes a lottery depending on which post-hole is sampled.

To appreciate fully the dangers we need go no further than a recent paper by Williams (1989) on the early Neolithic in the British Isles. In 'selecting' radiocarbon dates from the literature she states: 'Dates on planks which might have come from large oak trees were not accepted because the "old wood effect" may make the date too old.' Apparently laudable; however, she ends up rejecting dates around 5200 BP, for the structure of the Ballynagilly plank-built house, and *retaining* dates as old as 5700 BP, on 'charcoal' from pits at the site. Ironically, the oak planks were at least recognizable as oak planks and may have been correctly sampled: the loose charcoal from the various (and anomalously old) pits has, in relative terms, no integrity whatsoever.

Finally, before leaving Island MacHugh, there is one further group of observations which may be worth recording. Along one stretch of the edge of the crannog there were a series of substantial oak posts driven down about one metre into the peat. Their configuration is shown in **Fig. 4.6**. It

was clear that the posts had been used for reinforcing and one would have assumed that there was an original row with later additions. In this case, of course, we could date the posts intrinsically, and the dates of the last growth rings are given in Fig. 4.6. Here we run right up against the limits of chronology. Some of the posts had complete sapwood, others were truncated. It is not possible from the distribution of dates to make any sense of the order of post insertion, yet this is with the actual wood of the posts intrinsically dated. If we can observe this level of difficulty under such ideal circumstances, how wise is it to infer order from post-hole configurations on dryland sites?

Prehistoric dating I

From 1982, with the Belfast oak chronology complete back to 5289 BC, the capability was on hand to date prehistoric archaeological sites. The tying down of the chronology had already provided dates for the ritual 'temple' at Navan Fort, Co. Armagh and for at least one phase of the Dorsey earthwork also in Armagh (Baillie 1988a). These dates, at 95 BC and c. 95 BC respectively, demonstrated a notable phase of building activity and showed the power of precise dating to focus attention. Previously these sites had simply been individual Iron Age constructions. Once it was realized that they were effectively contemporary, they could be seen as manifestations of a major phase of activity involving massive earthmoving and intensive tree-felling. We will return to these sites and to this episode presently. The dating of the chronology had also specified the dates of two rather enigmatic lake-edge dwellings at Cullyhanna, Co. Armagh (Hillam 1976) and Imeroo, Co. Fermanagh (Baillie 1985). The Cullyhanna 'hunting lodge', as it was called, was believed to have been a seasonal hunting camp in the Bronze Age and could now be specified to 1526 BC. Imeroo, which was almost certainly another lakeside settlement could be dated to 1478±9 BC. The similarity between these two dates, plucked from the vast timespan of prehistory, was rather surprising. Was this another phase of activity?

With the capability to date oak structures thus

established, it was necessary to cast around for sites which preserved oak timbers. One area of study had to be trackways ('toghers' as they are termed in Ireland). Over the years a lot of these structures, varying from narrow tracks to major roadways, had been uncovered in Irish bogs. Some had been studied but almost no dating evidence existed and they often tended to be loosely assigned to the 'Bronze Age'. One reason for wanting to date bog trackways had to be the possible environmental overtones associated with their construction. Obviously there could be many possible factors, either socio-economic or environmental, which might account for people wanting to build a track across a boggy area. The interpretive difficulty is well summed up by the general question, 'Do you build a track across a bog because conditions are becoming wetter or is it because the bog has dried out sufficiently to support a track, i.e. are conditions getting drier?' Irrespective of such problems it was decided that it would be interesting to see if the trackways tended to cluster in time or whether they were randomly distributed. If there were clusters then their dates could ultimately be compared with British and Continental examples, to see if there were common patterns which might again be environmentally linked. The obvious way forward was to date a series of examples. So from 1982 we let it be known that we were interested in dating trackways anywhere in Ireland.

Samples began to trickle in. At Timahoe, Co. Kildare, two clear phases of timber felling could be identified, c. 1470 BC and c. 1380 BC, for a track stratified beneath 2.5m of peat. It was clear that the lifetime of this track had been at least one century and the proximity of its primary date to those from Cullyhanna and Imeroo was certainly interesting. A remarkably similar date, 1492±9 BC, was obtained for another substantial trackway at Corlona, Co. Leitrim. This track had originally been dated by radiocarbon to 3395±170 BP (Lucas 1985). That date, which calibrates to the range 2150–1250 BC at 95% confidence, could not be realistically compared with available tree-ring dates. However, with the more refined tree-ring date it can be seen that Corlona falls neatly in with a quite tight building episode between 1526 BC and c. 1470 BC.

The big breakthrough in trackway studies came quite unexpectedly in 1985. Richard Bradshaw, at that time a palynologist at Trinity College Dublin, was supervising pollen work in Co. Longford in a bog not far from a major oak trackway. He was interested in whether the environmental impact of the 'Bronze Age' trackway might be discernible in the pollen record. A single oak sample which he supplied failed to date – an example of the difficulty often noted with individual timbers in geographical isolation (see Chapter 3). As the trackway was due to be destroyed by peat cutting, an expedition was mounted in May 1985 to acquire better tree-ring samples. Arriving at Corlea Bog, the magnitude of the trackway was staggering. Where it was exposed by peat cutting or in drainage ditches it was over 3m wide and clearly ran for at least one kilometre. It was made up of split oak trunks laid transversely, side by side, across longitudinal poles. The amount of work involved in its manufacture – the number of trees felled, split and transported – immediately raised questions of social organization and indeed environmental impact. It was also noted in passing that the tool marks on the trunks were more suggestive of iron rather than bronze technology.

For dating purposes, samples were selected which had long ring patterns and complete sapwood. Thus on two counts it was no surprise when a master of as few as four ring patterns dated directly against the Belfast chronology with an end-year of 148 BC. The Corlea trackway was indeed Iron Age; however, more than that, at that time it was the only *known* second-century BC archaeological site in Ireland! This information was relayed to colleagues in Dublin with the suggestion that a stretch of the track, now that its age was known, should be properly surveyed and recorded. As a result Barry Raftery, a leading Iron Age specialist, was commissioned to undertake a pilot study. It is interesting to chart the course of what happened next, not least to give a hint as to the number of tracks in Ireland. To quote Raftery:

> Initially the work was envisaged as limited rescue excavation . . . [however] during the following two seasons further excavations were carried out on the Corlea Track. In

addition, four other trackways . . . were investigated . . . no fewer than 16 new tracks were encountered . . . field survey in 1988 and 1989 discovered no fewer than 38 new trackways. (Raftery 1990)

The heightened interest in wetland archaeology was beginning to reveal the scale of the problem. There are large numbers of tracks, some very substantial, some ephemeral, and survey and dating becomes a major undertaking. To give an example, in 1988 a pilot survey of Bord na Mona bogland uncovered 120 new trackways in a matter of a few weeks. The culmination of this work, with European Community support in 1988 and 1989, was the setting up of an Irish wetland 'unit' in 1990.

One can't help regarding this episode as an example of the power of the dendrochronological method. The specification of a date to within a matter of months – 'the timbers were felled either late in 148 BC or early in 147 BC' – serves to concentrate the mind wonderfully. The date lifted the Corlea track out of the ordinary and gave it an importance which was fully justified in the light of the information subsequently available from its excavation. However, returning to the general question of prehistoric dating, a number of new dates have stemmed directly from this new trackway initiative. An extension of the Corlea 'road' was uncovered at Derraghan More. As Raftery describes it:

> The great Corlea 1 road extended for approximately 1km in a north-west/south-east direction across the townlands of Corlea and Cloonbreany, linking the uplands in the east with a small island of dryland in the west. Extending from the western end of the latter island . . . across a second expanse of bog was the second mighty roadway which originally ran through the townland of Derraghan More . . . for an additional kilometre. (op. cit. 37)

The timbers from this roadway consistently lacked sapwood – a possible clue that they had been exposed for longer than the Corlea timbers. The felling date could therefore only be given as 156±9 BC. Although this date is not sig-

nificantly different from that of Corlea 1, its slight tendency to be older, coupled with the lack of sapwood, may indicate that Derraghan More was constructed first. In a sense, the order of construction is not important because it is clear that in Ireland between 150 BC and 95 BC we have evidence for massive building enterprises. This has subsequently been reinforced by the discovery that the northern portion of the Dorsey, mentioned above, may actually be part of the famous Black Pig's Dyke – Ireland's foremost linear earthwork – and recent excavations have turned up timbers which date, again without sapwood, to around 150 BC. Five sites with dates between 150 and 95 BC suggest something significant going on at that time – just how significant will be seen more clearly when the dates of all the prehistoric sites are accumulated below.

Before leaving the Corlea 1 road – as Raftery says, structures of this size are too massive to be called tracks – it is worth repeating some information uncovered by a scholar at the Ulster Museum. In an early Irish tale 'The wooing of Étaín' Richard Warner noted a reference to the construction of a huge trackway:

> in the reign of Eochaid Airem the folk of the síd of Brí Léith constructed a massive causeway across the Bog of Lamrach: 'not in all the world could a road have been found that should be better than the road that they made'. (Warner 1990b)

In a nutshell, Warner believes that the places mentioned – Eochaid and Brí Léith – lie east and west respectively of our Corlea bog. Moreover, he believes that the name of the ancient bog of Lamrach is preserved to the present day in the townland name Laragh, close to Corlea. The story sounds intriguing, but becomes even more bizarre. Warner was also interested in the pre-Christian section of the Annals of the Four Masters. This is a prehistoric Irish 'history' which has become widely regarded as pure mythology, and as such is largely disregarded – as Warner states, they are 'regarded as absolutely worthless as historical evidence of events, people or chronology'. However, these annals give 'dates' to a long list of prehistoric Irish Kings.

According to the Four Masters, Eochaid Airem and his namesake brother ruled between AM (Anno Mundi) 5058 (*c*. 142 BC) and AM 5084 (*c*. 116 BC). (Warner op. cit.)

So here we have a pre-existing reference to a massive causeway, in the right part of Ireland, built for a king Eochaid Airem who reigned (on dates supplied by annals which no-one believes) between *c*. 142 BC and *c*. 116 BC. Is it possible that this causeway was and is the Corlea 1 track built in 148–147 BC? If it is, then someone is going to have to take a long hard look at those 'prehistoric' annals. As Warner points out, by the time these stories were finally written down – probably around AD 700 – there would have been no trace of the road which by then was deeply buried under peat. For people to know of its existence by that time implies an active and fairly accurate oral history!

Apart from the mid-second-century BC roadways, another half-dozen oak tracks have been successfully dated by tree-rings. While these have the advantage of being precise dates, they do expose, yet again, the limitations of dendrochronology. In the five years since the dating of Corlea 1 only a handful of further tracks have been tree-ring dated; in the same period Raftery can refer to '57 tracks [which] have been investigated, some extensively, some on a limited scale . . . radiocarbon age determinations are either already available, or are pending, for all the excavated tracks' (Raftery 1990). It will be interesting to see a complete list of the calibrated radiocarbon ages for these sites, when it becomes available. This is where the question of significant clustering will be answered for the first time. It will also be interesting to see if the apparent clusters of building activity, suggested by tree-rings, around 1500 BC, 900 BC and 150 BC are supported by the accumulated radiocarbon evidence. However, it should be noted that, irrespective of what the radiocarbon evidence suggests for periods of trackway construction, the tree-ring dates undoubtedly specify phases of activity for substantial *oak* tracks. Currently *all* the Irish trackways which have included substantial oak timbers have been successfully tree-ring dated.

Prehistoric dating II

A fairly obvious assumption, by someone setting out to date prehistoric archaeological sites, might be that the sites, as found, would be randomly distributed in time. In practice, as we have seen, as datable prehistoric sites have turned up in Ireland the pattern has been anything but random. By 1993 the number of Irish prehistoric sites dated by dendrochronology, including separate phases on two sites, stands at 26. All fall in the first 2400 years BC (**Fig. 4.7**). The dates tend to occur in discrete clusters – which is most surprising. What is going on? Why do the sites cluster? Why were people felling oaks and putting them into contexts in which they would survive at these particular times? Is there something special about the levels of human activity or is there something special about environmental conditions or is it survival which is the critical factor?

Obviously no-one knows for certain the answer to any of these questions, but it is possible to speculate. Could it be that there is some tendency – inherent in these sites – for survival to be intimately connected to environmental change? If you build a settlement close to a lake, that does not, in itself, guarantee survival of the timbers. But if you build beside a lake whose level subsequently rises and submerges the site then survival and environmental change become linked. The prehistoric sites from which timbers have survived include trackways, lakeside settlements, a dug-out canoe, a lake dwelling, a linear earthwork and a ritual temple. This range of site types would seem to preclude the clustering being an artefact of biased sampling. With the exception of the somewhat accidental survival of the timbers from the Navan temple – where again the raising of an artificial mound over the site may have caused a rise in the local water-table – all the surviving datable timbers belong to sites constructed in wet environments where survival might be expected. This still leaves us with the question why these three short episodes seem so well represented in the first two millennia BC. Can we infer that these episodes represent increased human activity or are they something superimposed on the normal activity?

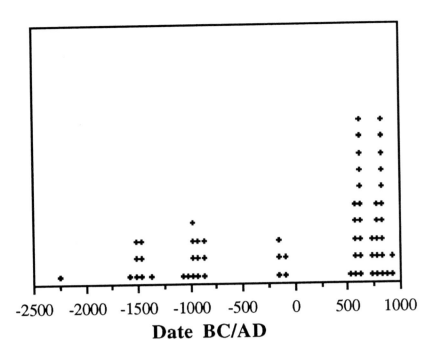

4.7 The non-random distribution of oak-bearing Irish archaeological sites dated by dendrochronology

Summary

The dendrochronological dating of archaeological timbers is rapidly becoming routine for all periods back to the Neolithic. As time goes on, more and more sites will be precisely dated across northern Europe. The impact of this dendrochronological revolution will be to firm up all aspects of chronology; overall pictures will begin to emerge. It seems fair to say that those sites with precise dates will be intrinsically more important, in any overall archaeological understanding, than those dated by other means. As the corpus of sites increases, more and more patterns of human activity should be revealed. The first excursions into prehistoric dating may appear to raise as many questions as they solve; however, with more dates, spatial patterns should begin to emerge. Perhaps the most important factor will be the interplay between the precise dates for archaeological sites and those for environmental events, also deriving from the tree-ring record. Since the two chronologies will be fully compatible, it should be possible to infer past human responses to environmental change more clearly than ever before. Some preliminary steps along this road are presented in later chapters where the Irish dates, cited above, are related to the apparently catastrophic effects of large volcanic dust-veils.

This chapter has also introduced the issue of interpretation in the light of intrinsic dating. The lessons there are that things are not always as they seem. That posts are found in a logical configuration does not automatically imply that these posts will be of exactly the same date. With the lessons from Island MacHugh we can now safely speculate that, where oak is involved, there is a range of possible relationships between any given configuration of posts; even where the posts were inserted at the same time the wood itself can be intrinsically different in date. So, any archaeologist submitting a single radiocarbon sample from a multiple post configuration may well be indulging in a lottery as to whether the sample will truly date the construction.

It should also be remembered that the dendrochronological dating of post configurations is the ultimate dating refinement. Yet, the examples given show that even with tree-ring dating many questions cannot be answered, i.e. there are questions of date and relationship which can *never* be answered. If there are questions which cannot be answered when the posts exist in their post-holes, how much worse is the situation when only the post-holes survive?

Radiocarbon high-precision wiggle matching

Any discussion of dating refinement has to take account of advances in radiocarbon dating. Indeed, the original stimulus, behind the construction of the Belfast long oak chronology, was the recalibration of the radiocarbon timescale, and we have looked at the completion of the tree-ring standard in Chapters 1 and 2. The radiocarbon calibration measurements, on precisely dated blocks of oak tree-rings, were performed by Gordon Pearson and his team in the Radiocarbon Laboratory at Belfast. The results were presented at the 1985 Trondheim radiocarbon conference and published in *Radiocarbon* in 1986 (Pearson *et al.* 1986). The Belfast results were so similar to the parallel measurements on German oak performed by Minze Stuiver, at Seattle, that the combined curves were accepted as an agreed international standard for the calibration of conventional radiocarbon dates (Stuiver and Pearson 1986; Pearson and Stuiver 1986).

One important outcome of this high-precision calibration work was the proving of the distinctive short-term wiggles in the calibration relationship which had originally been proposed by Hans Suess (1970). These wiggles appear to be solar induced, in that variations in solar activity affect the production rate of carbon-14 in the earth's upper atmosphere. Thus, as a bonus from the calibration work – aimed at improving the interpretation of radiocarbon dates for archaeologists and others – the scientific community was presented with their best record of past variations in solar activity; of obvious interest to astrophysicists and climatologists.

One key factor in this calibration work was the development of so called 'high-precision' radiocarbon measurements. These were measurements which aimed at realistic precisions of around ±20 years. This can be compared with most conventional (or commercial) radiocarbon measurements which often have realistic precisions of around ±80 years. The research-standard high-precision dates allow an additional radiocarbon dating refinement. Because of the shape of the calibration curve, with its wiggles, it is possible to date pieces of wood (or indeed any regularly stratified organic deposit) by measuring the radiocarbon age of consecutive blocks of tree-rings and fitting this new mini-section of calibration to the calibration curve. The procedure is illustrated in **Fig. 4.8** where five samples from a timber from Ardnagross horizontal mill

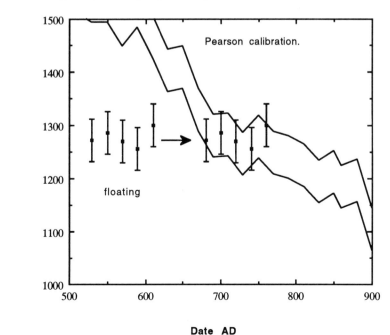

4.8 High-precision radiocarbon dates on five consecutive 20-year blocks of rings, from Ardnagross horizontal mill, wiggle matched against the Belfast calibration curve, date the mill to the later eighth century (Pearson 1986)

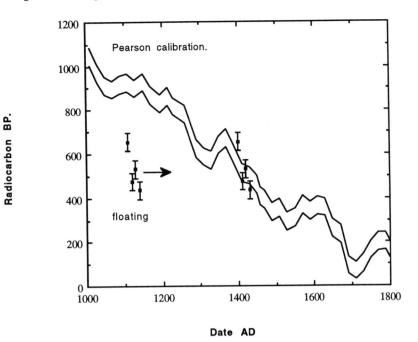

(undatable by dendrochronology) must fit the flat portion of the calibration curve in the eighth century AD. Although Fig. 4.8 shows a visual representation of a wiggle match, there are mathematical procedures for obtaining a best-fit of the sample dates to the calibration curve and these have been published by Kruse *et al.* (1980), Clark and Morgan (1983) and Pearson (1986), among others.

Such a procedure can allow astonishingly accurate dating estimates to be made: e.g. the Sweet Track was estimated to date to 'within 10 years of 3800 BC' (Baillie and Pilcher 1988); a dating which was confirmed when the Sweet Track was dated by dendrochronology to 3807 BC (Hillam *et al.* 1990). The following examples demonstrate how high-precision wiggle matching can answer some dating questions almost as precisely as dendrochronology itself.

Caerlaverock Castle revisited

In the moat of the late thirteenth-century castle at Caerlaverock, near Dumfries, a series of timber bridge foundations were uncovered during excavations in the late 1960s. Subsequent tree-ring dating allowed three clear felling phases to be established, associated with the excavator's Phase 1 and Phase 2 bridges (Rigold 1975). The

dates were *c.* 1277, 1333 and *c.* 1371 (Baillie 1982). The timbers of the excavator's Phase 3 bridge were massive but extremely short-lived – the maximum number of rings being 59. Inevitably these short ring sequences could not be dendrochronologically dated. However, from the architectural history of the castle, it could be inferred that the use of bridges may have been rendered obsolete by the insertion of a long draw-bridge, probably in the mid-fifteenth century (Watson 1922). Did the Phase 3 bridge therefore fall between 1371 and *c.* 1450? As a test of the high-precision wiggle-matching technique this seemed like a good example. In fact, the example was aimed not just at dating the Phase 3 bridge but at assessing if it would work successfully with only four consecutive decade samples. The result is shown in **Fig. 4.9** (Pearson 1983). The four related dates are constrained to fit the calibration curve consistent with an end-date in the second quarter of the fifteenth century. QED.

Deerpark Farms: the door-frame

In the late 1980s, excavations were conducted at a raised rath at Deerpark Farms, Co. Antrim. Although there are tens of thousands of Dark Age raths (or ringforts as they are also known) in

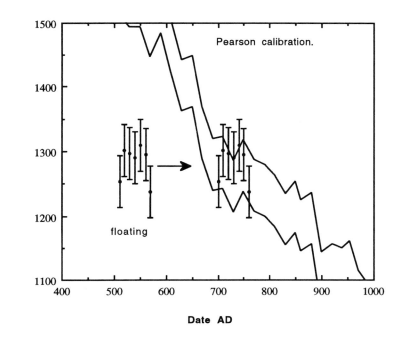

4.10 High-precision radiocarbon dating of stratified wicker houses at Deerpark Farms, Co. Antrim, indicate that construction starts after 680 (dates courtesy of Dr Chris Lynn, N.I. Environment Service)

Ireland, there are only comparatively small numbers of raised raths. These sites contain stratified 'tell-like' deposits and those which have been excavated previously suggest periods of occupation between the seventh and the twelfth century AD (Lynn 1981). The example at Deerpark Farms was the first to produce substantial organic remains from a dryland site. Apparently at some stage in the eighth century the level of the site had been raised and this, combined with the topography of the site, raised the water-table within the site. As a result, the lower portions of several wicker houses were found in an excellent state of preservation (Lynn 1987, 1988). Our interest lies in the fact that one of these houses retained its oak door-frame intact and *in situ*. Both uprights retained total sapwood and had last grown in AD 648; so this phase represented one of the very few precise dates associated with raths in Ireland.

However, it is possible to extract additional chronological information. Because the construction of the individual houses could be placed in order, on grounds of archaeological stratigraphy, it is possible to consider samples of wicker from the *consecutive* buildings as 'stratified organic samples'. High-precision radiocarbon dates, for the consecutive phases, all fall between 1237±20 BP and 1309±20 BP (Chris Lynn pers. comm.). Reference to **Fig. 4.10** shows the high-precision calibration curve across this period with the wicker house dates plotted. It is clear from these dates that all the wicker constructions, surviving on the site, relate to the century *after* AD 670. Since the house with door-posts was by no means the earliest in the sequence, here was an oak door-frame of AD 648 in a house likely to have been constructed well after AD 670. While at first sight this may appear to represent some tension between a tree-ring date and dates derived from high-precision radiocarbon dating, there are several relevant factors to be considered.

First, it was apparent that, as found, the door-frame was *already* in a re-used position. Second, it is historically recorded that substantial items like door-frames were re-used – in some cases numerous times – in wicker houses. Third, on a more circumstantial level, it is notable that the dates AD 648 and AD 720 bracket a clear building

71

hiatus in Early Christian Ireland (see Chapter 8). So the interval between felling and final context is not only *not* a problem, it is in retrospect to be fully expected. The corollary is again, as with the timbers from Island MacHugh and Ballynagilly above, the need for vigilance by archaeologists dating sites where only charcoal or other dendrochronologically undatable samples are available for radiocarbon analysis; in such cases there is a serious danger of selecting samples which will suffer from a marked age-lapse effect. Oak timbers are doubly suspect both because of the split-oak problem (above) and because as substantial timbers they are *most likely to be re-used*. A good rule of thumb would be to date only wicker elements and to avoid any substantial timbers. Overall, the concept of high-precision wiggle matching can be applied to any closely stratified, short-life, archaeological samples, or even peat (see Clymo *et al.* 1990).

Note of caution on high-precision wiggle matching

Unfortunately, the whole business of radiocarbon wiggle matching depends on the multiple radiocarbon measurements being fully *compatible* with the original calibration measurements; if a laboratory with a dating off-set attempts wiggle matching there is a real danger of 'missing the right wiggle' and producing the wrong date range. The whole issue also assumes that the Pearson/Stuiver calibration curve is truly definitive, something now called into question by these authors having slightly revised the original 1986 internationally agreed calibration curve (Pearson and Stuiver 1993; Stuiver and Pearson 1993). In principle it would still seem best if wiggle matches were performed in laboratories which carried out the original calibration measurements. Unfortunately, even under this condition, one wiggle-match exercise, carried out in Belfast, with timbers from the Late Bronze Age site at Flag Fen, produced a wiggle-match date two centuries from the date eventually specified by tree-ring dating – despite the wiggle-match dates being performed on the same radiocarbon set-up as the calibration measurements. In this particular case there may be grounds for asking if the true calibration relationship is represented by the existing calibration curves, for the period around 1200–1000 BC. So even wiggle matching, the 'state-of-the-art' radiocarbon technique, has to be treated with a degree of caution.

5 Volcanoes and tree-rings

Background

In the late 1960s Ferguson completed the construction of the long bristlecone pine chronology back to 5142 BC, the material for the chronology being drawn from the White Mountains of California (Ferguson 1969). Although regarded as extremely robust, its position as the world's first really long chronology meant that there was little to check it against. With the known ability of the bristlecone to miss rings, there could obviously be questions as to its internal consistency. It was very useful therefore when LaMarche and Harlan (1973) produced an independent upper-tree-line bristlecone chronology back to 3435 BC. This chronology used material solely from Campito Mountain in the southern part of the White Mountains. Apart from two missing rings, at 2142 BC and 2681 BC in the Campito chronology, the two chronologies were in perfect agreement over more than five millennia.

While LaMarche's work was important in the overall story of world chronology – in particular since it checked Ferguson's chronology which had provided the precisely dated wood samples used in the original Suess radiocarbon calibration – it also turned out to be important for some direct environmental reasons (LaMarche 1974). LaMarche noted that in the long bristlecone records there were some rings which exhibited frost damage. Frost rings in these high altitude trees are apparently caused by 'temperatures well below freezing at some time during the growing season . . . extra-cellular ice formation causes dehydration and physical disruption of immature xylem cells, leaving a permanent record in the wood' (LaMarche and Harlan 1973). Of particular interest was the widespread occurrence of frost damage in the growth ring for AD 1884, a year known to have been unusually cool in the western United States. Because of the coincidence between the dates of several frost rings and large volcanic eruptions – e.g. Krakatoa 1883 (bristle-

cone 1884), Katmai 1912 (bristlecone 1912), Agung 1963 (bristlecone 1965) – by the early 1970s LaMarche suspected that his trees were recording the climatic effects of at least some large volcanic eruptions (LaMarche 1970).

LaMarche's original paper on the subject of frost-ring events caused few ripples; so the volcano story, as it was to become, was upstaged by the definitive ice-core paper by Hammer et al. in 1980. Long ice-cores from Greenland provide an essentially annual record of compressed snowfall. Within the layers of ice, stable isotopes, dust and acid, all derived from the atmosphere, provide a record of past variation down to seasonal resolution (note seasonal but not necessarily precisely dated). In particular, layers of sulphuric acid are definitive markers of sulphur put out by large volcanoes. The Hammer et al. paper, using results from the short Crête core, provided a list of dates for major volcanic eruptions back to the sixth century AD. The dating resolution for this period was estimated to be 'within a few years'. For example, they placed the Icelandic Edjkla eruption c. AD 934, at around the time of the first colonization of Iceland. A much longer core (approximately 1400m) from Camp Century provided a record from around the time of Christ back to beyond 100,000 years ago. For the period 2000–10,000 BP the dating resolution was estimated to be of the order of ±2% (Hammer et al. 1980).

The Hammer et al. observations were of a relatively small number of significant acidity peaks in the first six millennia BC. These are listed in **Table 5.1.** Of particular interest was the peak at 1390±50 BC. It was suggested that this might record the Bronze Age eruption of Santorini in the Aegean. Archaeologically this was an extremely important eruption as it represented a major caldera-forming event in an area of high civilization. Everyone would like to know just what the effects of the eruption were and exactly *when* it took place!

Table 5.1

50 ±30 BC
210 ±30 BC
260 ±30 BC
1120 ±50 BC
1390 ±50 BC
2690 ±80 BC
3150 ±90 BC
4400 ±100 BC
5400 ±100 BC

The principal ice-core acidity layers observed in the Camp Century core in the first six millennia BC (Hammer *et al.* 1980)

The suggested ice-core date for Thera fell into a somewhat controversial archaeological area involving various strands of argument (see Chapter 7 for a detailed discussion). In brief, the Minoan civilization was based on Crete (which lies some 100km to the south of Santorini) with outposts on other islands, including Santorini itself. It was generally believed, by archaeologists working with pottery sequences, conventional typologies and finds of Aegean objects in Egyptian contexts (and vice versa), that the civilization ended around 1450–1500 BC – 'dated' against the Egyptian historical timescale (Hankey and Warren 1974). However, some radiocarbon dates from the buried Minoan settlement on Thera (Thera is one of the islands which make up the remaining rim of the Santorini complex) seemed to suggest an earlier date – perhaps as early as the seventeenth century BC (Michael 1976). While the 1390±50 BC ice-core date was too recent to fit with radiocarbon evidence for the eruption, it did fit quite well with the beliefs of those archaeologists who favoured a 'low' chronology. In fact, for someone who was happy with the end of the Minoan civilization around 1450 BC, the ice-core date merely confirmed their chronology. It has, of course, to be noted that Hammer *et al.* had no way of relating the Greenland acid layer directly to the Santorini eruption: Santorini was simply the most famous large volcano known to have occurred in the mid-second millennium BC.

Being in line with conventional wisdom, the date proposed by Hammer *et al.* was accepted at face value; anyone unhappy about the apparent clash with the rather old radiocarbon dates would have been confounded with arguments such as 'sample dilution with radioactively dead carbon from the volcano'. This argument – always a bit of special pleading – says that because volcanoes leak carbon dioxide which contains no radioactive carbon-14, it might be expected that plants growing close to the volcano would incorporate 'more' inert carbon and hence 'less' radioactive carbon. If such samples are radiocarbon dated 'less' carbon-14 is detected and the date comes out *older* than a sample of the same age from a non-volcanic source. These arguments are backed up by some rarefied results from plants growing very close to active volcanoes. It would seem unlikely that they would apply to cereals or other food crops growing over large areas on an island where – to put it no more strongly – the wind blows.

So the scene was set for LaMarche to introduce his frost-ring results. In their 1984 paper LaMarche and Hirschboeck pointed out the strong link between bristlecone frost rings and large volcanic eruptions. They also noted that there was only one frost event in the second millennium BC, that it was severe, and that – at 1626 BC – it fitted well with the radiocarbon evidence for the Santorini eruption. It is fair to say that this perfectly reasonable suggestion – '. . . it offers the intriguing possibility of dating precisely the cataclysmic eruption on Santorini . . .' (op. cit. 125) – was greeted with less than enthusiasm by the archaeological traditionalists.

Warren, a firm believer in the low chronology, replied to LaMarche and Hirschboeck by restating the conventional archaeological case for a *c.* 1500 BC dating and by criticizing the reliability of the frost-ring record (Warren 1984). In fact Warren concluded that the frost rings were 'proxy data – they could be caused by volcanic eruptions; but they could equally well be caused by other influences on climate'. He saw 'little support for linking the . . . event at 1626 BC specifically with the eruption of Thera' and pointed out that 'the link is not substantiated by archaeological data nor strongly supported by radiocarbon evidence' (op. cit. 493). So, according to Warren, suggestions of a seventeenth-century BC date for the Thera eruption could safely be discarded.

Interestingly, there is a fundamental flaw in this

quite famous Warren paper which is worth pointing out. Discussing the 1626 BC tree-ring suggestion and the 1390±50 BC ice-core suggestion, Warren says: 'For either date to be correct it needs to be compatible with the archaeological dating of the eruption' (op. cit. 492). Here I would disagree with Warren. Back around the sixteenth and seventeenth centuries BC the Egyptian historical chronology is *not* absolute. Warren himself admits, for example, that the eighteenth-dynasty pharaoh Tuthmosis III can be variously dated from 1504–1450 BC through to 1479–1425 BC and the earlier Hyksos pharaoh Khyan ruled 'within about 1660–1580 BC'. It is well known that there are perpetual arguments about the detail of the Egyptian chronology and it is technically possible for the errors to be greater than those cited by Warren and believed by Egyptologists – for example, see Kitchen (1991). In strict chronological research terms it is *not* true that 'for either date to be correct it needs to be compatible with the archaeological dating of the eruption'! The ultimate role of the scientist in this debate is to provide some *fixed points* on which to hang the Egyptian chronology. If, as LaMarche and Hirschboeck suggested, Thera did erupt around 1626 BC then we would know that there was some fundamental flaw in either Warren's links from the Aegean to Egypt or in the Egyptian chronology itself. So here was an ongoing debate about the date of the Santorini eruption which quickly resolved itself into two extremes – the earlier *c*. 1626 BC 'scientific' camp and the conventional *c*. 1500 BC archaeological camp.

(At this point, for the sake of consistency hereafter, it should be noted that the computerized tree-ring date 1626 BC actually referred to the calendar year 1627 BC. LaMarche, for computer convenience, had used a year 'zero' which does not occur in the historical calendar (Hughes 1988). From here on LaMarche and Hirschboeck's date will be discussed as 1627 BC.)

The role of the Irish tree-rings

It is at this point that the Irish tree-rings come into the story. In 1984 agreement had been reached with the German workers that the Irish chronology was complete back to 5289 BC

(Pilcher *et al.* 1984 and see Chapter 2). By 1985 the basic data – the individual ring patterns used in the 7272 year chronology – had been archived as a permanent record. It was therefore possible to look at what happened to Irish trees at any point in time within the last seven millennia. So, with no particular vested interest in the result, the graphs were extracted for a selection of trees which had grown across 1627 BC. Obviously there was no certainty as to what to expect: would 1627 BC be a narrow ring? – would there be anything out of the ordinary? It was impossible to predict and so, as is usual with dendrochronology, an empirical approach was adopted: go, look and see.

The first batch of trees to be examined came from Garry Bog, Co. Antrim which is one of the most northerly raised bogs in Ireland. It was immediately noticeable that some of the Garry Bog trees showed narrow bands of rings in the 1620s BC – not specifically in 1627 BC (**Fig. 5.1a**). Perhaps most impressive, at this early stage, was the graph for tree Q1863. This ring pattern stopped at 1630 BC and there, on the graph, originally plotted by Jennifer Hillam around 1975, was the note 'impossible'. It should perhaps be explained what this meant. When the original Garry Bog chronology was being pieced together, trees were sometimes encountered where the pattern of rings became so narrow or distorted that (a) they were impossible to measure or (b) there was some serious doubt about the ring *count*. Such sections of ring pattern could easily prove difficult to cross-date and certainly did not merit inclusion in a master chronology. So, in the case of Q1863, only 164 rings were measured and, somewhat arbitrarily, measurement was stopped at the ring for 1630 BC (of course when originally measured the date of the tree was unknown, its true date only becoming available after 1984). When this tree was repolished and remeasured it was found that the growth rings, while extremely narrow, were clearly discernible down to 1626 BC, thereafter the pattern broke down and measurement was absolutely impossible.

This is the sort of circumstantial evidence of which I am fond. Here, at a date specified by LaMarche and Hirschboeck on the basis of trauma in bristlecone pines, we had, in Ireland, trees registering a downturn in growing conditions with the extreme case of Q1863. Trees from other sites showed similar effects and one, Q5392 from Sentry Hill, exhibited a clear colour change at the beginning of a band of narrow rings which started in 1628 BC. It was clear that even these initial observations supported LaMarche's case. The event in the 1620s was not just a local Californian event. The problem was, could it simply be coincidence? Some of my colleagues thought so – or rather thought that it would be impossible

to convince anyone that the finding was significant. However, other strands of evidence lent support to the idea that there was something in the story. For example, it was noticeable that some English and German chronologies also showed narrow rings at the same time; see **Fig. 5.1b.**

In 1986 the opportunity of a six-month visiting professorship in the Tree-Ring Laboratory in Tucson helped to provide the answer. I had with me the newly archived Irish prehistoric data. For

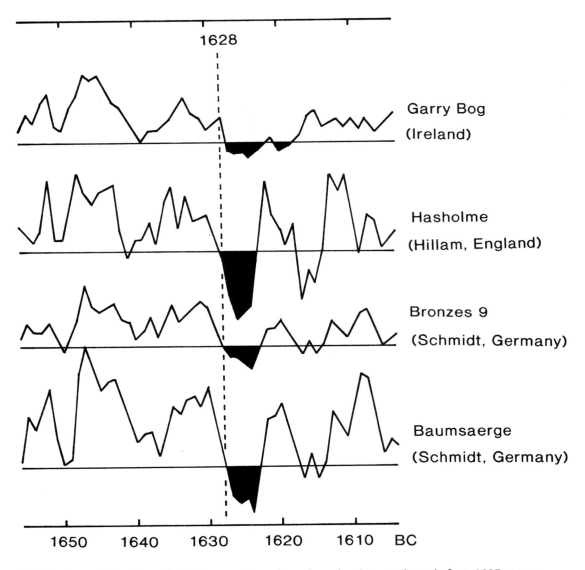

5.1 LaMarche and Hirschboeck's 1984 suggestion of a major volcanic event in, or before, 1627 BC confirmed by reduced growth in (a) Irish and (b) English and German oak chronologies

some weeks I played around with the ring patterns across the 1620s BC. In particular I was interested in trying to quantify the effect in some way. I looked at various configurations: how many trees had narrow rings in any given year? – how great was the magnitude of the change? – did the ring widths drop below some given percentage of the widths of the previous rings? – did they drop below the average of the previous decade? etc., etc. Eventually I was struck by the fact that several of the trees had their *narrowest* rings in the 1620s BC. Now there was something which might be significant; it could certainly be quantified! Obviously every tree has to have a narrowest ring or rings; however, because there are many effects on trees, any of which could be sufficiently detrimental to produce a narrowest ring, it might be expected that a narrowest ring could be produced at any time in the life of a tree. So, overall, given the long lives of oak trees, we might expect the narrowest rings to be fairly randomly distributed in time; it might be significant when a number of trees produced their narrowest rings at the same time.

One snag with that approach was the obvious thought that a lot of trees on a single bog could be effected by some entirely local factor. This suggested that a simple sum of trees with narrowest rings would not necessarily be significant; some measure of the effect on different sites had to be included. For the oaks crossing the sixteenth and seventeenth centuries BC the question was posed: what percentage of trees put on their narrowest rings in each decade and how many *sites* were involved? This approach showed that the decade of the 1620s – with eight trees from four sites showing narrowest rings – was fairly easily picked out from those two centuries (if the percentage of trees with narrowest rings was multiplied by the number of sites then the 1620s 'scored' some 120 'units'). The next thing was to check through a lot more decades and see how common such scores were. The first major test was to look at all the decades in the second millennium BC. The high scores were the 1940s (109), the 1840s (100) and the 1140s (143). This immediately showed that scores as high as that in the 1620s were rare. However, the really interesting point was the high score in the 1140s BC. The decade of the 1150s also had a high score (95).

Here was an 'event' which was possibly more impressive than that in the 1620s. A quick search of the dates listed by Hammer *et al.* showed that the 1150s/1140s fell within the error limits of their 1120±50 BC acidity peak – one which they attributed to an eruption of the Icelandic volcano Hekla. Clearly it was essential to search the rest of the record.

The result was *astonishing*. In the whole of the prehistoric Irish record – from 95 BC to 5200 BC – there were only three decades with scores higher than the 1620s. These were the 4370s BC (220), the 3190s BC (144) and the 1140s BC (143). As noted above, Hammer *et al.* had cited major volcanic eruptions at 4400±100 BC, 3150±90 BC and 1120±50 BC. The procedure might be simple, but it appeared to produce the answer straightaway. What were the chances, I asked, of someone, looking for support for a volcanic eruption postulated by a tree-ring worker, finding a series of dates which coincided with the dates of volcanic eruptions postulated independently by ice-core workers? The implication had to be that the Irish trees were recording the climatic downturns associated with the dust-veils which were recorded as significant acid layers in the Greenland ice-cap. **Table 5.2** lists the synchronizations which existed, by 1987, on the basis of a first survey of the Irish material for 'narrowest-ring events'.

Table 5.2

Ice Cores (1980)	Tree-Rings (1986)	Ice Cores (1987)
AD 540±10	AD 540	
BC 210±30	BC 207	
BC 1120±50	BC 1159	
BC 1390±50	–	
–	BC 1628	BC 1645±20
–	BC 2345	
BC 2690±80	–	
BC 3250±80	BC 3195	
BC 4400±100	BC 4370	

Coincident events in the Greenland ice record and the Irish tree-ring record

In order to check these results, Martin Munro set

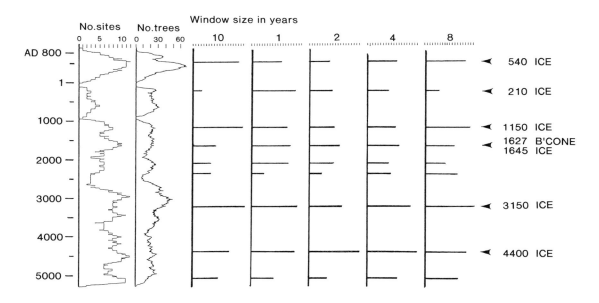

5.2 A simplified diagram showing coincidence between major volcanic acid layers in Greenland ice-cores and narrowest-ring events in Irish bog oaks (Baillie and Munro 1988)

up a computer program to duplicate the analysis using a different statistical approach. The results, now including an assessment of the probability associated with clusters of narrowest rings, were run for different windows of time from single years to blocks of 16 years. The results were essentially identical to the original analysis and were published in 1988 (Baillie and Munro 1988). **Fig. 5.2** shows a simplified diagram of the synchronizations between the Irish oak narrowest rings and the ice-acidity layers from the Greenland ice-cores.

One obvious question related to the volcanoes which were responsible for these effects. The starting point here had to be the 1627 BC event for which LaMarche and Hirschboeck had *suggested* Santorini. This began to look very interesting. Something was showing up in two sets of tree-rings (three if the German chronologies were included). Meanwhile, Sturt Manning was reassessing the radiocarbon dates associated with Akrotiri – the town on Thera buried by the Santorini eruption – and concluding not only that a date for the eruption in the seventeenth century BC was most likely but that such a solution was not precluded by the archaeological evidence (Manning 1988, 1990). Clearly Santorini had to be a good possible candidate for the 1628 BC vol-

cano. The event starting in 1159 BC might, as Hammer *et al.* had suggested, be Hekla 3 in Iceland. The event in the 3190s BC could have been an earlier Hekla eruption – Hekla 4. This suggestion would rely on the 4500±120 BP radiocarbon date cited by Hammer *et al.* (1980). That date would calibrate out to something like 3000–3400 BC at 1-sigma (2900–3600 BC at 2-sigma). However, more recently new radiocarbon dates for Hekla 4 began to suggest a considerably younger age, and a high-precision wiggle match on stratified peat associated with the Hekla 4 layer (identified in Irish peat by Jon Pilcher and Valerie Hall) suggests that the true date of Hekla 4 should be in the range 2310±20 BC, close to another narrowest-ring event at 2345 BC (Hall *et al.* 1994). Thus the identity of the volcano responsible for the 3195 BC narrowest-ring event remains unknown.

The question of the volcano associated with the 4370s BC event turned out to be very interesting from a chronological viewpoint. In 1980, Hammer *et al.* had attributed their 4400±100 BC acidity layer to Mt. Mazama – the hypothetical volcano which stood on the site of what is now Crater Lake, Oregon. The massive, caldera-forming, Mt. Mazama eruption has been extensively dated by radiocarbon to around 6400 radiocarbon years BP. Hammer *et al.*, using an *uncalibrated* radiocarbon date of *c.* 4400 bc (*c.* 6400 BP) for Mazama, associated Mazama with their 4400±100 BC acidity layer. This was, of course, wrong. Calibrating a radiocarbon age of 6400 BP would give a calendar date somewhere around 5400 BC, a full millennium older than the 4400±100 BC ice-core (tree-ring 4375 BC) date. Interestingly in their 1980 paper Hammer *et al.* also noted an ice signal at 5400±120 BC! With Mt. Mazama thus removed as a candidate for the 4375 BC event, the responsible volcano again remains unknown.

In a sense it was not all that important, in the first instance, to identify the volcanoes responsible for the effects in the trees. What was important was the specification of the precise dates for some potentially major environmental events. That specification would be the first step towards a better understanding of those effects. (In fact these early signs of difficulty in attributing specific volcanoes to specific effects have subsequently been borne out; it is apparent that it is almost impossible to date any prehistoric volcanoes exactly and thus it is essentially impossible to prove which volcano or volcanoes were responsible for which environmental effects.)

This initial survey of the main 'narrowest-ring' events in the Irish oaks had also thrown up the dates 207 BC and AD 540. 207 BC stood out, not because it had a 'score' in the same league as the 1620s BC, but because it had the highest score in the whole of the first millennium BC and the narrowest rings were all in the same year. The date AD 540 simply represented the highest score in the chronology for the first millennium AD. One obvious question relates to the position with the last millennium: what happens in recent times? Here one runs into a philosophical problem. Most, indeed the vast majority, of the prehistoric oaks in the 1985 archive of Irish trees, had grown on peat bogs. It has to be imagined that such trees would be more sensitive indicators of environmental conditions than trees rooted on mineral soils. In the first millennium AD the population is mixed between bog oaks and archaeological timbers, so it was felt reasonable at least to investigate the data set. However, in the last millennium essentially all the oaks were land-grown. This poses the problem: what is a site? While it is clear that oaks on different bogs can be specified as coming from different sites, it is much more difficult with land-grown timbers. With most medieval timbers the source is unknown. Timbers from different buildings could have come from the same source, etc. As a result of the imponderables associated with the timbers of the last millennium, this period was left out of the study.

It is now necessary to backtrack slightly to pick up some of the other threads of this story. There are two issues which need to be put into a temporal context because their relationship to the story is quite different depending upon when the information surfaces. These relate to a 'new' ice-core dating for Santorini on the one hand and the involvement of Chinese 'history' on the other. This is a case where tracing the story in real time gives it quite a different perspective from simply following the dates of the various published articles.

The 'new' ice-core date

In 1987 Hammer *et al.* published a new suggested date for the Santorini eruption, based on identification of a significant acid layer at 1645±20 BC, in the Dye 3 ice-core from Greenland. This replaced their previous suggested identification of a layer at 1390±50 BC in the Camp Century core. From a tree-ring viewpoint this was good news, because all the lines of evidence for a major volcanic event now pointed at the seventeenth century BC. However, the new date also gave rise to some puzzlement.

It was clear from the Irish tree-rings that LaMarche and Hirschboeck were seeing a non-local, probably hemispheric, volcano-related event before any of the dendrochronologists knew of the new ice-core date. It is for this reason that dendrochronologists would maintain that the new seventeenth-century ice-core date *supports the tree-ring date*, until proven otherwise. Given that the published 1645±20 BC range actually *brackets* the 1620s tree-ring dates, and given the other synchronizations listed in Table 5.2, intuitively both the seventeenth-century tree-ring and the ice-core observations should relate to the same date (see Chapter 6). It therefore came as a surprise when the ice-core workers claimed that 1645±20 BC was in some way *distinct* from 1628/7 BC. Of course, it could be a different and distinct date but this seems inherently unlikely given that there is no error in the tree-ring dating and an acknowledged error in the ice-core date. Indeed, since it is the tie-up between the ice-core events and the tree-ring events which form the very basis for saying that Irish trees are recording dust-veils, it would seem illogical to assume that in the seventeenth-century case we are seeing different events!

So, from a dendrochronologist's perspective, until proven otherwise it should be assumed that there was one major, dust-veil-related, environmental event in the seventeenth century BC and that it took place at, or just before, 1628 BC.

Ancient Chinese records

It is also necessary to backtrack slightly in order to pick up one of the other threads of the story. While still in Tucson, I had communicated some of the results to a colleague, Peter Kuniholm at Cornell, and as a result called on him on the way back to Ireland. One of his colleagues had asked to meet me because of a particular interest in the AD 540 date. Apparently, it turned out, there was some evidence to suggest that the Chinese had records of a catastrophic event at that time. China? Where did China fit in?

Kuniholm passed on to me a copy of a paper by Pang and Chou (1985). Basically Pang, working at Caltech, was interested in using astronomical references in early Chinese texts, including the Bamboo Annals, to tie down the dates of the early Chinese dynasties – in particular the Shang (which again is not definitively dated). There are some very elegant interpretations of solar and planetary configurations which can be fixed in time by 'back computation'. The first notable example is the identification of a five-planet conjunction in the reign of King Yu, the founder of the Hsia dynasty (the semi-mythical dynasty before the Shang). Apparently Chinese records state that 'at the time of [King] Yu the five planets were strung together like a string of beads'. Pang and his colleagues were able to find that 'in late February 1953 BC Mercury, Venus, Mars, Jupiter and Saturn came within only 5 degrees of one another. So close that they could be blocked out by a thumb held at an arm's length! Furthermore on 23 February 1953 BC they appeared to be indeed strung up in a nearly straight line . . .' (Pang 1987). With this information the beginning of the Hsia dynasty could be placed in the twentieth century BC. Secondly, the Bamboo Annals state that 'in the first month of spring of the first year in the reign of King Yi of the Western Zhou dynasty the day dawned twice . . .'. Pang identifies this event with a solar eclipse which occurred at daybreak on 21 April 899 BC, an event which would very adequately explain the observation (Pang *et al.* 1989; and pers. comm.).

So into the somewhat shaky chronology of early China Pang was able to inject a series of precise dates. This ongoing work places the start of the important Bronze Age Shang dynasty *close* to 1600 BC and the end *close* to 1100 BC. Our particular interest in this work derives from some other related references in the Chinese records. Pang and Chou (1985) had noted that there were references associated with the last Hsia king (immediately before the Shang) and with the last Shang king, both of which suggested first-hand observations of the effects of volcanic dust-veil events at those times. Although all the information was not initially available it is now possible to abstract the case that Pang and Chou were making.

As noted above, the Shang is bracketed by the approximate dates *c.* 1600 BC and *c.* 1100 BC. Pang *et al.* (1989) list that at the time of the last Hsia king, King Chieh, 'the earth emitted yellow fog . . . the sun was dimmed . . . three suns appeared . . . frosts in July . . . the five cereals withered . . . therefore famine occurred'. Similarly close to the end of the Shang 'in the fifth year of Chou (last king of the Shang dynasty) it rained dust at Bo. For 10 days it rained ashes, the rain was gray . . . it snowed in July . . . frosts killed the five cereals . . .' (Pang *et al.* 1988). Although these details were published later, as early as 1985 Pang and Chou had drawn attention to the possibility that three putative dust-veil events in the Chinese records might be related to the Etna (44 BC historical date),

Hekla 3 (1120±50 BC ice-core date) and Santorini (1390±50 BC ice-core date/1627 BC tree-ring date) eruptions. Martin Bernal informs me (pers. comm.) that the Chinese scholars see, in the evidence for dust-veils at the start and end of the Shang dynasty, a possible explanation of the Chinese concept of 'Mandate of Heaven' which is associated with dynastic change. Certainly an interesting thought, in the light of some of the accumulating information, on events of this type, which will be discussed below.

So, whether we like it or not, there was, from 1986, a loose suggestion that dust-veil events seemed to be recorded in China around two of the dates coming out of the Irish oaks. When the Chinese work was reviewed in some detail some remarkable coincidences became apparent. These are best exemplified by the events which show up in the Irish trees at 207 BC and AD 540 and which appear to be related to the Hammer *et al.* 210±30 BC and AD 540±10 acidity dates. Note that the precise tree-ring dating specifies the actual dates for the environmental effects for the first time.

The Chinese records, by the late third century BC, are precise historical records. So, in 208 BC we have 'the stars lost from view for 3 months' and in 207–205 BC we have Chinese famines (Pang *et al.* 1987). Indeed, around 206–202 BC (depending on the source) we have another change of dynasty in China. Some similar elements occur around AD 540. In AD 536 the star Canopus, used by the Chinese to 'assure themselves of good times ahead and to demark the seasons', was not seen. In the same year there was frost and snow in July and August. From AD 536–8 there were severe famines (Weisburd 1985). Here then were two Irish tree-ring dates which tie in extremely well with dramatic events in China and which, by extension, reinforce Pang's suggestions of possible volcano-related climatic links in the seventeenth and twelfth centuries BC. This in itself is a fairly startling possibility, because, if it were proven correct, it would draw together the prehistoric chronologies of the East and West by fitting certain marker dates where both areas suffered extreme conditions and 'recorded' the same hemispheric events. We will return to these events below.

The story continues to build

With the four dates 1628 BC, 1159 BC, 207 BC and AD 540 specified by tree-rings, and with the ice-core and Chinese information in hand, it was interesting to see if other information existed relevant to these events. Moreover, the story was so intrinsically good that, as it developed, it was disseminated in a series of popular articles (Baillie 1988b, 1989a, 1989b). These in turn flushed out some interesting information from individuals around the world. The following section looks at several of these items in a little detail; they range from the purely factual to the outright speculative. They suggest to me that, in the last few millennia, there were major volcanic dust-veil events whose environmental consequences had profound effects on human populations; that these events were recorded in various archives – both natural and human – because they were inherently catastrophic, and that it is for this very reason that we might (with hindsight) expect them to have been recorded. It is also worth noting that, assuming the overall hypothesis to be true, i.e. that the narrowest-ring events in the Irish trees are recording the effects of large volcanoes, this was the first time that the true dates of these events were known. With the dates specified it is possible to begin to see what else was going on at the same time as these events. So tightening chronology, by bringing together differing strands of evidence, makes some important events visible which previously were invisible due to the chronological *smearing* of the dates of the various phenomena which seem to be involved.

Related tree-ring information

It was already known that some German oak chronologies showed narrow rings – reduced growth – following 1628 BC. Then, as the prehistoric English bog-oak chronology was being pieced together, it was found that two long chronologies, which both started around 3200 BC, both ended in the mid-seventeenth century BC (see Chapter 2). In fact the only English material to span the 1620s BC was provided by Jennifer Hillam at Sheffield (pers. comm.). This

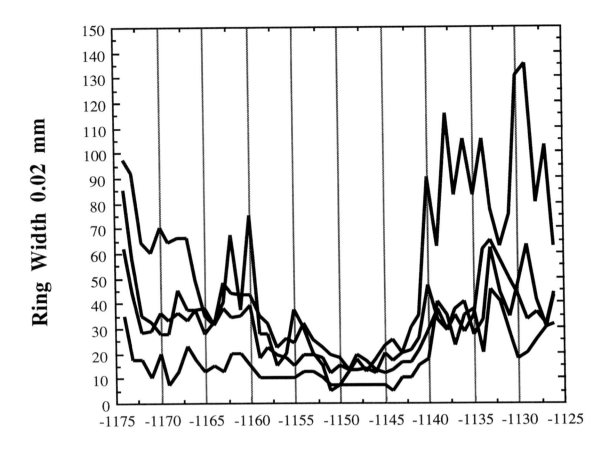

Date BC

5.3 Oak-ring patterns from four different north Irish bogs showing the 1159–1141 BC reduced growth event with its remarkably synchronous recovery

chronology, from Hasholme, shows a distinctly narrow band of rings beginning at exactly 1628 BC (Fig. 5.1b). So, the effects of the 1620s volcano-related environmental event show up widely as reduced tree-growth in northern Europe.

Moving to the third century BC, Hollstein's master chronology showed a dramatic narrow event from 208 to 204 BC (Hollstein 1980), and a major erosion phase in German river valleys appears to have started c. 200 BC (see Chapter 9). From the other side of the Atlantic, Val LaMarche wrote in 1987 to say: 'We've just finished up tabulations of frost-ring dates from . . . recent collections. *Re* the Chinese famine date of 207 BC, we have a significant frost ring on both Sheep and Campito Mtn sites in California at

206 BC' (pers. comm.).

At this early stage it was interesting that there appeared to be very little tree-ring back-up for the 1159 BC event. This seemed a little strange because it was clear from the Irish ring records that this was by far the most traumatic of the volcano-related events. Virtually all the bog oaks showed an extremely narrow band of rings at this time and it was noticeable that, in a number of specimens from different bogs, the duration of the event was exactly the same – lasting from 1159 BC to 1141 BC, see **Fig. 5.3.** For the effects to *end* at the same time implied the release of some environmental 'pressure' around 1141 BC. However, the concept of such a release from environmental pressure carried with it the implication that the pressure had lasted for almost two decades. Obviously this could be due to something like raised water-tables which subsided on different bogs at the same time (though that in itself sounded like special pleading). Intuitively the event felt like a very long-drawn-out episode of changed conditions and it seemed logical to ask what the effects – sufficiently unpleasant for oak trees to suffer as they obviously did – might have been on human populations inhabiting Ireland at that time.

So colleagues were asked: 'Did anything significant happen in the middle of the twelfth century BC?' The answers were interesting. Somewhere around the twelfth century BC, allowing as always for the flexibility in archaeological and even ancient historical evidence, the whole fabric of ancient society appeared to have crumbled. In most of Britain there was upland abandonment, particularly severe in Scotland, followed by an upsurge in the construction of defensive sites (John Barber pers. comm.; Keys 1989). At around this time Burgess observed a major change in Bronze Age material culture (Burgess 1985; and see below). Around the Mediterranean there was an endless list of movements and collapses (Bryson *et al.* 1974). Most interesting was the demise of the Mycenaean civilization in Greece with the ensuing four-century 'Greek Dark Age' which descended on the Mediterranean region. Here was an extremely dramatic decline, at around the right time, where people had already argued for some sort of environmental 'event'. In 1974, Bryson *et al.* had given support to an idea, originally proposed by Carpenter (1966), that the Mycenaean decline might have been due to a prolonged and highly regionalized drought. Here was an observation of something unpleasant in at least two regions at around the same time. With the tree-ring effects precisely dated and all the other human effects flexibly dated, the next obvious question was: 'Are these effects related?', indeed 'Are these events one and the same?' Given the pieces of evidence cited here, one could be forgiven for the following mental flight. What if the following list all relates to the same event?

Volcano affects hemispheric climate pattern
Irish trees suffer 1159–1141 BC

Twelfth century BC people abandon
    upland Britain
Twelfth century BC Mediterranean
    civilization collapses
Twelfth century BC Chinese observe
    volcanic effects
Twelfth century BC replacement of the
    Shang dynasty

If they did so relate, then we would know the date of the event from the Irish tree-rings! We will consider some of the additional information which has become available below.

Irish Annals I

Asking around, it was also pointed out that in the Irish Annals there were two rare and cryptic references to 'failure of bread' in AD 536 and AD 539 (Warner 1990b). Given that these are the early years of the annals, and that previously they had not been regarded as very reliable, it is very interesting that they record hardship in Ireland at the same time as severe famines are recorded in China. It also didn't escape notice that the Justinian plague begins in AD 542 and is in fact recorded as arriving in Ireland in AD 544/5 (suggesting that the annals are in fact not a bad record). Any doubts about a volcanic link with the AD 540 event were dispelled by the observation that 'the densest and most persistent dry fog on record was observed in Europe and the Middle East during AD 536–537' (Stothers 1984; Stothers and Rampino 1983; see Chapter 6).

The Anglo-Saxon Chronicle

The way that some of the evidence accumulated is interesting in itself. In 1988 I pointed out to Heinrich Härke, a Dark Age specialist, the body of firm evidence for an event around AD 536–45 and suggested that its effects might be looked for in the archaeological record. As a specialist in the period his first reaction was to reach for a copy of *The Anglo-Saxon Chronicle*. A quick search revealed that there was no direct reference to anything related to a dust-veil. In fact for dates between 534 and 544 there were no references at all with the exception of solar eclipses in AD 538 – 'This year, fourteen days before the kalends of March [15th Feb] the sun was eclipsed from early morning till nine in the forenoon', and in AD 540 – 'This year the sun was eclipsed on the 12th of the kalends of July [20th June] and the stars showed themselves fullnigh half an hour after nine in the forenoon' (Garmonsway 1962). This seemed a little strange: two solar eclipses seen from England within two years? Fortunately John Tate, a member of the Ulster Archaeological Society, works at the Armagh Planetarium and was able to check the accuracy of the references. Interestingly the eclipses did occur, just as recorded, but they were not total eclipses as seen from England! They would have been total in the Near East or the Mediterranean and it is likely that they were recorded in Byzantine annals. As the descriptions infer totality, it seems reasonable to ask why might two Byzantine eclipses be recorded in *The Anglo-Saxon Chronicle?*

It is important to realize that *The Anglo-Saxon Chronicle* is not a strictly contemporary document. The early sections were 'compiled' around the ninth century presumably drawing on earlier records (Härke 1991). It seems that there are only three possible explanations for the eclipses being there. Either the references were taken from available Byzantine sources, by the later compilers, to pad out the thin existing records; or they were inserted because the compiler was interested in things astronomical; or they were put in as interpretation or clarification of some pre-existing references in available English sources.

Clearly this is highly speculative, but the following explanation does suggest itself. It does not seem likely that the eclipses were used as padding. At this early stage in the *Chronicle* many years have no references at all. Again, if the explanation were simply some scholarly interest in astronomical events, then it is strange that no other astronomical phenomenon is referred to between the start of the record and AD 664 when we have the cryptic 'In this year there was an eclipse of the sun'. This does leave the third and tantalizing possibility, namely that the references were elucidatory. Is it possible that the compiler(s) were confronted with some pre-existing English sources which said something like 'the

sun was dim this year' or 'the sun gave no heat this year'? The eclipses, appearing to clarify the situation, were then copied from Byzantine annals? The reason for raising this is the known, significant, dimming of the sun in AD 536 and 537, as discussed by Stothers and Rampino (1983). Was the dimming also recorded in England and why twice? It is of course impossible to take this any further but the following question can be raised. Given the dates of the eclipses cited in *The Anglo-Saxon Chronicle*, and the suggested explanation for their presence there, and given the known evidence for a severe dust-veil in AD 536, could there have been more than one dust-veil between AD 536 and AD 540? Is it concievable that there were three?

Now the reason for bothering to record this unbelievably circumstantial case of the *Chronicle* eclipses is because of something which had been raised by Stothers and Rampino (1983) and elucidated by Horgan (1987). At 44 BC we have another dust-veil event similar in every respect to those in 208 BC and AD 536, with the exception that, at that time, we have no available Irish trees. The list contains:

50±30 BC	Greenland ice-core acidity peak (Hammer *et al.* 1980)
43 BC	Bristlecone pine frost-ring event (LaMarche and Hirschboeck 1984)
44 BC	After Caesar's death 'there were earthquakes and the obscuration of the sun's rays: for during all that year its orb rose pale and without radiance' (Plutarch)
44 BC	Chinese histories record a red daylight comet in May and June 44 BC. The comet's colour can be attributed to volcanic dust (Horgan 1987)
44–42 BC	In China, six consecutive grain harvests (3 years) failed (op. cit. 84)
43 BC	China: April it snowed and frost killed the mulberries. The sun was pale blue and cast no shadows (op. cit. 84)
43–42 BC	China: evidence for several dis-

tinct eruptions. By October 43 BC the sun seemed to have recovered, but in spring 42 BC the sun, moon and stars again appeared 'veiled and indistinct'. Ice-core workers, in attempting to match historical records with acidity peaks note that 'the ice-cores show no record of a summer [i.e. no summerlike change in chemical composition of the atmosphere] between acid peaks representing two of the eruptions which, according to histories, were about a year apart in May 43 BC and March 42 BC' (Horgan after Herron 1982)

If we plug in Virgil – 'after the death of Caesar . . . how often we saw Etna flooding out from her burst furnaces, boiling over the Cyclopean fields, and whirling forth balls of flame and molten stones' – who is definitely citing Etna (Forsyth 1988), we may be looking at up to *three* volcanic events between 44 BC and 42 BC.

As has already been noted, 20 years of accumulating oak timbers from Ireland failed to uncover any oaks which spanned 95 BC to 13 BC. This gap in the chronology was bridged using Roman oaks from Carlisle (see Chapter 2). As a result it was not possible to see if Irish oaks recorded a narrowest-ring event around 44 BC. However, virtually every timber from Carlisle shows very narrow rings at 40 and 39 BC. This is a time delay very reminiscent of that between AD 536 and AD 540. Interestingly, Scuderi in a recent paper on volcanic signals in a 3000-year foxtail pine chronology from Cirque Peak, in the Sierra Nevada, also finds 'a large decrease between 44 and 43 BC and continued decreased ringwidth values in both 42 and 41 BC' (Scuderi 1990). So here are two definite dust-veil events, at 44 BC and AD 536, where there is either direct evidence or circumstantial evidence to suggest more than one dust-veil within a few years with effects lasting over a number of years. This evidence alone raises the question of multiple eruptions: could this be the factor which singles out some of these events? We will return to this issue in Chapter 6.

Irish Annals II

Another unexpected twist to the tale was provided by information contained in the ancient Irish king list. It was noted above that in Ireland the *Annals of the Four Masters* record 'failure of bread' in AD 536 and AD 539. These annals also have a 'prehistoric' section where early Irish scholars pieced together an Irish world history; the final version being written down in the seventeenth century AD. It has become accepted that all the early references, pre-AD 500, are mythological. However, Warner (1990b) has pointed out that if we take these annals at face value and look for references to catastrophes, we find that such events are relatively few in number. The few severe events which do occur are assigned 'dates' which bear some remarkable similarities to the tree-ring dates. Apart from the AD 536/539 examples, it will suffice to quote the following:

> AM 3580–3656 i.e. 1620–1544 'BC'
> Tigernmas died, with three-quarters of the men of Ireland . . . This reign was followed by seven years without a king

> AM 4020–4169 i.e. 1180–1031 'BC'
> plague . . . in which . . . perished . . . a countless number of the men of Ireland

> AM 4991–4001 i.e. 209–199 'BC'
> There was a great mortality of cattle in the reign of Bressal . . . (op. cit. 31)

Other scholars have great difficulty with the concept of these annals being meaningful in any way and suggest that Warner is overstating his case (James Mallory pers. comm.), while Warner himself points out that there are grave difficulties associated with postulating mechanisms for the transmission of such early annals. However, he also points out that early scholars may have had access to oral king lists which might just retain an approximate chronology on the one hand and which would, almost by definition, carry an epithet, a key word or statement as an aid to memory, for each reign. What better mechanism than to record the most profound events? Again it is difficult to take this further, though a separate example of the apparent accuracy of this, previously disregarded, record has already been noted in Chapter 4, in association with the Corlea 1 trackway. The least we can say is that the coincidences involved are 'interesting'.

The Venus Tablets

Something very similar can be said about the next piece of 'evidence'. Let us start by posing a question: is there any pre-existing reference to anything which might be volcano-related in the narrow window of time 1630–1628 BC? Surprisingly there just might be. The 'evidence' relates to the so-called Venus Tablets and was drawn to my attention by a Mr Leroy Ellenburger of St Louis who wrote: 'In year 9 of the Venus Tablets of Ammisaduqa there is a nine-month, four-day invisibility that . . . could have been produced by Thera's dust veil, in which case [it] would date these tablets without the fuzz of statistical fitting. But this suggestion is too speculative for the Venus Tablet scholars.' When you look up what a reviewer has previously said about this dating you find that there are a list of what appear to be 'observations' of the planet Venus in the reign of King Ammizaduga of Babylon. In year nine there appears to be a nine-month and four-day 'invisibility' cited as a predictive formula, namely, 'If . . . Venus disappears in the west, remaining absent in the sky 9 months 4 days . . . [then] . . . king shall send greetings to king.'

Since the Venus records are believed to be astronomical observations, it should be possible to back-compute and find out which period the observations actually refer to. This, with lots of provisos, has been attempted. So, what dates have been suggested for year nine of Ammizaduga? On the basis of the configurations of the actual observations on the tablets, Huber (1977) has suggested that 'only four solutions are thought to be more or less compatible with both history and astronomy. These are: year 1 of Ammizaduga began in 1701, 1645, 1637 or 1581 BC.' If we correct for year nine, we see a pre-existing suggestion that there was a nine-month four-day invisibility of Venus in either 1693, 1637, 1629 or 1573 BC. Huber performed various tests on the data and concluded that the middle two dates are least likely. However, irrespective of that, we are confronted with a possible, pre-existing, suggestion that something may have obscured the Babylonian skies in 1629 BC. Given the circumstantial nature of much of this evidence, it is still astonishing that in a narrow specified date range of 1630–1628 BC it is possible to find even the remotest suggestion of a pre-existing reference to obscured skies.

Call for Cybele

In a speculative short article on the volcanic story entitled 'Do Irish bog oaks date the Shang dynasty?' (Baillie 1989b) some statements were made which were taken as a challenge by one ancient historian. Referring to the 208 BC event I had written: 'If this is indeed Laki in Iceland, then archaeologists in Britain and Ireland should be looking for signs in the record here, and classicists should start searching the classical authors.' Almost by return, an article appeared in *The Ancient History Bulletin*. Forsyth (1990) pointed out that indeed there were possibly relevant things going on in the Mediterranean area in this decade. In 206, 204 and 203 BC Livy mentions various 'portents seen in the sky', including double suns and haloes around the sun which sound like classic dust-veil-related phenomena. Epidemics are recorded around Rome in 208 and 205 BC. Interestingly in 205 BC things were sufficiently bad for the Romans to consult the Sibylline books and 'to bring the image of Cybele, the Magna Mater, to Rome from Asia Minor'. As Forsyth summarizes: 'We conclude, therefore, that there is evidence in the ancient sources of several phenomena that could be associated with a major event creating a dust-veil: unusual atmospheric apparitions, epidemics and a disruption of the food supply' (op. cit. 78).

The Gordion chronology

While all this was going on it was becoming apparent that the worst event in the Irish tree-rings – the mid-twelfth-century BC potential catastrophe – was in fact the least well-substantiated 'event'. There was no supportive bristlecone pine frost-ring evidence. The ice-core date 1120±50 BC was too loose to help significantly and the Chinese references at the end of the Shang were poorly placed at 'c. 1100 BC'. There was, however, one tantalizing piece of information. During the 1980s Peter Kuniholm had been putting together long tree-ring chronologies in Greece and Turkey. One source was the Midas Mound Tumulus at Gordion, Turkey, which provided an enormous, 806-year, juniper chronology which was known to span the approximate period from the eighth to the sixteenth centuries BC (Kuniholm and Striker 1983). Kuniholm noted that in this chronology there was one 20-year period 'where annual growth was abnormally large, accompanied by abnormal fluctuations both up and down'. Given the likely archaeological age of the chronology Kuniholm knew that this anomaly probably fell in the twelfth century BC. As the chronology is not yet dated by dendrochronology, in order to tighten the dating of the chronology, Kuniholm commissioned a radiocarbon wiggle match. In 1990 he was able to report: 'Now that Bernd Kromer . . . has successfully wiggle matched 18 sets of specifically numbered rings from the Gordion chronology with the high-precision oak curve from Europe, we also see that this 20-year anomaly is centred on 1159 BC and the two decades following' (Kuniholm 1990). So here was some serious tree-ring support for a long-drawn-out environmental effect in the mid-twelfth century BC.

Burgess and catastrophism

In 1985 Colin Burgess, a long-standing catastrophist, wrote an article on population, climate and upland settlement. In it he reviewed some ideas about what he saw as population collapse in Britain at two points in time: in the sixth century AD and in the twelfth century BC. His thesis was that 'since population disasters are well known in British history, [shouldn't we] expect them in prehistory'. His starting point was the known population collapse in the fourteenth century AD, associated with the Black Death. He pointed out that the expanded population of the thirteenth century was ripe for reduction by disease, starvation and strife and asked, 'Is overcrowding the principal factor, the prerequisite from which disease, famine and warfare spring?' Interestingly he added: 'The state of overpopulation may itself be triggered by climatic change. A level of population that may comfortably be supported in one period may become unsupportable when the environment becomes less favourable . . . . Britain, with so much of its land marginal, was particularly sensitive to the pressures which lead to population disasters, especially climatic deterioration' (op. cit. 196–7). In a nutshell, with kind climate the population expands; with deteriorating climate the population contracts. The rate of the contraction would presumably depend on particular circumstances. The vector, as above, could be any combination of famine or disease or warfare.

The fourteenth-century Black Death and its consequences are comparatively well documented; the collapse in the sixth century AD less so. However, Burgess argued that all the right conditions prevailed to make the events of the AD 540s a dry-run for the events of the Black Death. The Justinian plague arrived after AD 542 and 'appears to have been as savage and far reaching in its consequences as the Black Death'. So, just at the time of one of the dust-veil events, Burgess believed that there had been a significant population collapse and not just in Britain. Just as important from the point of view of this discourse, was the population collapse which Burgess believed he could see in the archaeological record in the later second millennium BC. In 'the mild climatic episode [which] came to an end . . . . c. 1250–1000 BC' Burgess saw all the ingredients for yet another, similar, population decline. Specifically, he saw in the abandoned upland settlements, in the development of defensible hill-top enclosures and in the observed drop in the amount of metal in everyday use, all the signs that somewhere at the end of the second millennium BC a deterioration in climate and a population collapse had taken place. 'The proposition therefore is that the population of Britain, after reaching its maximum around 1300 BC, perhaps as high as the Domesday figure, collapsed during the next century or two, and by the end of the millennium had been halved' (op. cit. 213). **Fig. 5.4** shows his prior

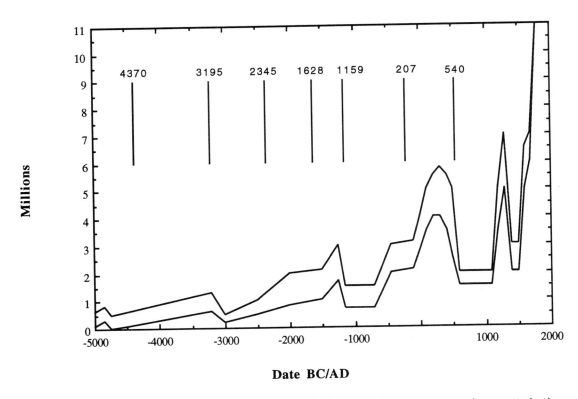

5.4 Burgess' 1985 population graph for Britain plotted with the dates of the narrowest-ring events in the Irish oaks, suggesting a link between the population collapses in the twelfth century BC and the sixth century AD and major dust-veil events (Burgess 1989)

ideas of dramatic collapse both around the twelfth century BC and the sixth century AD.

Here we see an interesting phenomenon. Among the six coincident tree-ring/ice-core events we have examples at 1159 BC and AD 540, just at times when Burgess has already postulated severe effects on human populations. Is this a further coincidence or is there some causal connection? Another question suggests itself: could the twelfth-century decline be abrupt rather than long-drawn-out? Could Burgess have been reading slow climatic deterioration when an abrupt short-term downturn in conditions would suffice? Some thoughts on this type of problem are presented below. One striking aspect of Burgess's arguments relate to plague as a possible vector in the collapse, see Chapter 8.

Overall, it appears that by putting a dust-veil event into the twelfth century BC we may be providing an explanation, a mechanism, a contributory factor, which can be added into the existing framework. Burgess points out that it wasn't just in Britain that systems collapsed: 'The breakdown of the existing order in the East Mediterranean c. 1250–1150 BC has long been a familiar concept. The Aegean world, Mycenae, the Hittite empire and the great Late Bronze Age cities of Cyprus and Syria all came to an inglorious end, and even Egypt was so exhausted by the struggle as to be finished as a world power.' So what was the role of the dust-veil? Was it the prime mover in collapse or was it simply superimposed on a pre-existing deterioration? Burgess clearly thinks so: 'It is clear then that the late second millennium climatic downturn had already started in the Mediterranean by the early thirteenth century. In this case Baillie's volcanic event of the 1150s and 1140s will have had an exacerbating effect' (Burgess 1989).

Conclusion

Up to here the surprise factor had still been at work. None of this was expected, so each new piece of evidence, circumstantial or otherwise, came as a bit of a shock: why should it work? – why should these dates keep coming out of different lines of evidence? At some point the surprise begins to fade and is replaced by a feeling that the phenomenon is real – that there was something about these particular events which made them stand out, i.e. at some point one actually begins to believe in the reality of the events.

Of the six coincident events in the tree-ring/ice-core records, additional information has quickly accumulated for the last four – at 1628, 1159 and 207 BC and at AD 540. While the case is still circumstantial for 1628 BC and 1159 BC, the close ties with historical information make the case for significant events at 207 BC and AD 540 incontestable. To summarize (the order is purely chronological and does not imply degree of integrity of the evidence), the events currently look like this:

1628 BC

1645±20 BC	Ice-core acidity layer
1629 BC	Venus Tablets 1 in 4 chance sky obscured
1628 BC	Irish trees go narrow
1628 BC	English trees go narrow
1628 BC	German trees go narrow
1627 BC	Bristlecone frost ring
1620–1544 'BC'	Irish 'king list' catastrophe
1600±30 BC	Chinese dust-veil record
1600±30 BC	Chinese dynastic change

1159 BC

1180–1031 'BC'	Irish 'king list' catastrophe
1159 BC	Irish trees go narrow
1153 BC	Egyptian famine
1150±10 BC	Turkish tree-ring anomaly
1120±50 BC	Ice-core acidity layer
c. 3200 BP	Antarctic acidity layer
c. 1100 BC	Chinese record dust-veil
c. 1100 BC	Chinese dynastic change
c. 12th c. BC	British upland abandonment
c. 12th c. BC	Collapse Mediterranean civilizations

208 BC

210±30 BC	Ice-core acidity peak
210–200 BC	Irish murrain of cattle
208 BC	Stars invisible in China
208–204 BC	Hollstein narrow rings in German oaks
207–204 BC	Chinese famines
207 BC	Irish narrowest-ring event
206 BC	Bristlecone pine frost-ring event
205 BC	Roman apparitions, epidemics and famine
204–202 BC	Chinese dynastic change
200 BC	German river-gravel deposition phase
197±9 BC	End of Irish bog-oak chronologies

AD 536

AD 535, 536, 541	Sierra Nevada cold years
AD 536–537	European dry fogs
AD 536	Cold summer Fennoscandinavia
AD 536	Irish failure of bread
AD 536–538	Chinese famines
AD 536	Star Canopis not seen in China
AD 537	Mortality in Ireland and Britain
AD 538	Anomalous Anglo-Saxon 'eclipse'
AD 539	Irish failure of bread
AD 540	Anomalous Anglo-Saxon 'eclipse'
AD 540±10	Ice-core acidity peak
AD 540–542	Irish narrowest-ring event
AD 542	Start Justinian plague

There are many difficulties with a story of this sort. Not least are the difficulties in assessing which volcanoes were responsible for particular effects or, indeed, how many volcanoes were involved, and we will look at some of these factors in Chapters 6 and 7. However, it seems inescapable that at least some of these events are real. If that is the case then we might reasonably expect some of them to show up in various other records as they become available. Archaeologists, for example, might expect to come across evidence relating to these dates. This occasioned me to christen them marker dates, i.e. dates which we might *expect* to show up in various records (Baillie 1991a).

We can't leave this chapter without superimposing these environmental events on the distribution of Irish archaeological tree-ring dates discussed in Chapter 4 and illustrated in Fig. 4.7. When we do this, we find the situation as in **Fig. 5.5.** Given that the two sets of infor-

mation should be completely independent (the dating of sites is an independent operation from the identification of narrowest rings in the master chronology), the diagram smacks of some non-random process being in operation (environmental determinism perhaps?). What is particularly striking is the way the two data sets appear to respect one another.

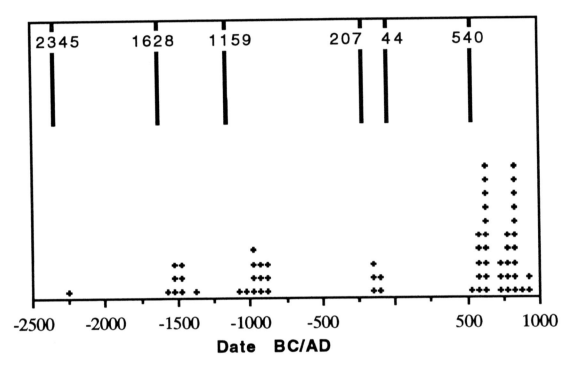

5.5 The non-random distribution of Irish archaeological dates from Fig. 4.7 plotted with the dates of the narrowest-ring events in the Irish oaks. Although the two sets of dates are independently derived, this diagram suggests that the archaeological dates respect the narrowest-ring dates

6 Volcanoes and chronology: the AD 540 story

Introduction

In Chapter 5 we saw how the volcano story, triggered by LaMarche and Hirschboeck's 1984 suggestion that a 1627 BC frost-ring event might relate to the eruption of Santorini, took on a life of its own. Large ancient volcanoes appear to have had wide-ranging effects. Unfortunately, this expanding body of evidence exposes an apparent tension between the environmental consequences of these ancient dust-veil events compared with recent volcanological experience. This raises the question: are the volcanoes of the last few centuries, viewed by volcanologists as a yardstick for volcanoes generally, a truly representative sample or have volcanologists been lulled into complacency by the relative *lack* of effect of the massive Tambora eruption of AD 1815, the largest explosive eruption in recent times?

We have now observed that Irish bog oaks may be affected for 5 or 8, or even 18 years – at times which should, because of the ice-core links, be related to volcanic dust-veils – but apparently such durations for volcanic effects are regarded as unlikely by volcanologists. As a result there is a clear tension between the lines of evidence. What is going on? Are the environmental effects genuinely short but the bog oaks suffer for years afterwards? Are the volcanoes simply superimposed on some ongoing environmental change? Are they an additional 'kick' to already teetering systems? Is there something different about these ancient events in comparison with recent dust-veils? – were they in some way bigger or more effective? This chapter looks at some of these issues. However, its real purpose is to look at just how difficult it is to date, and interpret, some natural events. Even large volcanic eruptions tend to be effectively instantaneous; attempts to date the year of an ancient eruption typify the problems involved in attempting to date past events generally.

Volcanoes and climate

Confronted with the various questions outlined above, it becomes necessary to find out something about the known environmental effects of recent volcanic eruptions. This is, it turns out, part of a major and extremely complex international research field (see, for example, Handler 1989; Chester 1988; Rampino *et al.* 1988). To start at the beginning, there is a straightforward reason why volcanoes show up in the Greenland icecap. Sulphur dioxide thrown into the stratosphere arrives on the surface of the ice as sulphuric acid and is incorporated into the ice record. There are several areas of research which suggest reasons why we might also see the effects of major dust-veil events in less immediate recorders such as Irish trees, bristlecone pines and indeed Chinese records. The basic mechanism appears to be cooling of the northern hemisphere (Sear *et al.* 1987) with resultant disruption of the normal climate circulation patterns leading to local extremes of weather including wetness, cold and/or storminess (Kelly and Sear 1985).

Surprisingly, the 'dust' in a dust-veil is not now regarded as a significant contributor to the hemispheric cooling. Current wisdom suggests that the dust washes out very quickly and makes little contribution to the effect a volcano has on climate. However, it would not be surprising if dust were to make a re-appearance in the arguments at some stage, given the observation that, as with radioactive residues from bomb tests, the higher it is injected into the stratosphere the longer its residence time is likely to be (D. Harkness pers. comm.). The reason for making this comment is that modern studies have been restricted to what, judging from their environmental effects, have been medium-range volcanoes. As always, the exception is Tambora which was very large but where the effects seem to have been rather limited, for whatever reason.

As a result, volcanologists have only a small temporal assemblage of volcanoes for study and these may not be fully representative of the range of possibilities likely to be encountered in the course of thousands of years. (A cynic might say that a 200-year study period for a phenomenon which has been going on for billions of years, might leave something to be desired.) It is possible therefore that dust may, in some explosive superplinian or ultraplinian eruptions, be injected so far into the stratosphere that its residence time increases from months to years. Be that as it may, current wisdom blames the climatic effects on sulphuric acid droplets which have a relatively long residence time and which cause surface cooling. Currently attention is focused on these acid aerosols and they dictate thinking on the duration of environmental effects: 'for significant eruptions the stratospheric aerosol depth can be perturbed for several years' (Rampino et al. 1988). Two factors conspire to limit the perceived duration of the effects. One is the instrumental record explored by Sear et al. (1987) which suggests that the effects are limited to about three years, the other is Tambora (AD 1815), whose effects, while severe in 1816 (the 'year without a summer') appear to have been over by about 1818. So modern eruptions suggest that volcanoes are not a cause for significant environmental concern.

Overall, the study of the effects of large eruptions highlights a particular chronological problem for volcanologists – only precise dating allows a particular volcano to be related to its effects. The difficulty, noted above, of knowing which ancient volcano caused which effect is currently a limiting research factor. Indeed

Stothers and Rampino (1983) implicitly recognize this when they note that the ice-core record can be best understood when the contributions of local and global eruptions can be separated on the basis of *historical* information.

However we look at it, the volcanoes of the last few centuries have singularly failed to produce effects anything like those we seem to be seeing in the accumulated lists in Chapter 5. Where are we going wrong? Are we misreading the past environmental evidence in some way? Is there something wrong with our current understanding of the effects of large volcanic eruptions?

Perhaps the easiest way to address these problems is to look at case studies, to see the various lines of argument involved and to try to assess the relative quality of the various strands of evidence used by volcanologists. It becomes apparent, when we do so, that chronology is a highly important and a much neglected facet of the study of ancient volcanoes. Volcanoes have largely been studied in isolation and dating has been regarded as a completely secondary consideration. To cite just one example, Simkin *et al.* in their *Volcanoes of the World* (1981), which is virtually a bible to volcanologists, give a 'chronological' list of volcanic eruptions which *mixes* calibrated and uncalibrated radiocarbon dates. In archaeology such arbitrary mixing would not be acceptable. However, it seems that volcanologists – studying some of the greatest natural hazards on earth – have not, as yet, given chronology adequate consideration. (See also the comments on the treatment of Mt. Mazama by Hammer *et al.* (1980) in Chapter 5, and other points below.)

So, in the remainder of this chapter we will look at one case study from the early historic period when we can see reasonably well what is going on, due to the availability of detailed and precisely dated historical and tree-ring information. Then in Chapter 7 we will review an example from prehistory where the case becomes particularly complicated and where the lack of tight chronological control defeats all current attempts to specify either the date or the effects of the major Bronze Age eruption of Santorini (Thera).

The case of AD 536–45

Was it Rabaul?

Essentially all the relevant information on this Dark Age event is from the 1980s and it is quite possible that the event could not have been properly discerned prior to 1980. The date is AD 540 and it springs almost from nowhere in a footnote in Hammer *et al.* (1980). In a note added in proof they stated

> In a new ice core from South Greenland (Dye 3), a strong acidity signal was found and preliminarily dated at AD 540±10. This might be the Yukon eruption . . . if so, the global acid fall-out was of the order of 70 million tons.

Since, according to the ice-core researchers, the amount of acid deposited on Greenland depends on the latitude of the volcano concerned, and since for a low-latitude eruption there is a scaling factor of three (op. cit. 232), had they assumed an Indonesian volcano as the source of their acid layer they would have estimated something like 200 million tons of sulphuric acid fallout. So this acid layer at AD 540±10 in Dye 3 represented somewhere between a large and a very large amount of sulphur injected into the atmosphere. This example shows nicely the dilemma facing volcanologists and ice-core workers, i.e. the difficulty of linking volcanoes to effects when radiocarbon is the only dating tool available. It is worth noting how Hammer *et al.* arrived at their suggested identification of the volcano involved with the 540 acid layer. Reference to Simkin *et al.* (1981: 112) shows that in their list of volcanoes the only really large eruptions (volcanoes with a volcanic explosivity index (VEI) of 6 or greater) around AD 540 were the White River eruption, Alaska (uncalibrated radiocarbon date 525 ad), and Rabaul, New Britain (uncalibrated radiocarbon date 540 ad). Hammer *et al.*, for whatever reason, opted for the White River eruption. In 1983 Stothers and Rampino opted for Rabaul as the most likely cause of the dry fogs recorded in the Mediterranean in AD 536 and 537 (presumably the same event as the AD 540±10 ice acidity). Their suggestion was based on another radiocarbon date for the White River eruption, at 700±100 ad (op. cit. 6363).

Here we see the typical chronological dilemma for the volcanologists. With the original radiocarbon dates, whether calibrated or not, either (or both) the eruptions could date to AD 536. Indeed, given that Simkin *et al.* acknowledged the early parts of their list to be highly incomplete, *neither* eruption need be constrained to AD 536 (the effects could have been due to some unknown eruption). The new radiocarbon date for White River only partially resolves the issue. Further, it is reported that there are new radiocarbon dates for Rabaul, around 1300 BP, suggesting that that eruption may be somewhat later than originally supposed (C. McKee pers. comm.). So it appears that volcanologists are very much at the mercy of radiocarbon evidence and can, on occasion, be forced into subjective judgements when they attempt to relate poorly dated volcanoes to historically dated environmental effects. When the environmental evidence is itself flexible, as was the case with all the prehistoric ice-core evidence, volcanological attributions necessarily take on the form of a lottery.

Ignoring for the present which volcano (or volcanoes) caused them, let us return to the effects of the AD 536–45 events and what they may have meant for people living at the time. Here volcanologists and environmentalists have done the basic groundwork. Stothers and Rampino (1983) supply quite thorough documentation on what happened in AD 536 and thereafter. They quote Procopius: 'during this year a most dread portent took place. For the sun gave forth its light without brightness . . . and it seemed exceedingly like the sun in eclipse, for the beams it shed were not clear'; and John Lydus: 'The sun became dim . . . for nearly the whole year . . . so that the fruits were killed at an unseasonable time.' Reports from Constantinople suggested climatic upset for more than a year and a late chronicler, Michael the Syrian, apparently elaborated that 'the sun became dark and its darkness lasted for eighteen months. Each day it shone for about four hours, and still this light was only a feeble shadow . . . the fruits did not ripen and the wine tasted like sour grapes.'

So around AD 540 there is evidence for a major volcanic event recorded indelibly in Greenland (but see below) while in the Mediterranean the sun was dim in AD 536–7. This episode is regarded as the densest and most persistent dry fog in recorded history. From the dimmed-sun records, Stothers (1984) estimated that, for up to eighteen months in AD 536–7, the sun must have appeared up to ten times fainter than usual. Rampino *et al.* (1988) amplify further when they report a contemporary Italian record by Cassiodorus: 'The sun . . . seems to have lost its wonted light, and appears of a bluish colour. We marvel to see no shadows of our bodies at noon, to feel the mighty vigour of the sun's heat wasted into feebleness, and the phenomena which accompany an eclipse prolonged through almost a whole year. We have had . . . a summer without heat . . . the crops have been chilled by north winds . . . the rain is denied . . . .' As Rampino *et al.* paraphrase: 'Cold and drought finally succeeded in killing off the crops in Italy and Mesopotamia and led to a terrible famine in the immediately following years' (op. cit. 87).

The effects do not end there. In China the years AD 536–8 were marked by summer snows and frosts, drought and severe famine (Weisburd 1985). Pang and Chou, whose work is reported by Weisburd, noted that in some parts of China the weather was so severe that 70–80% of the people starved to death. In Ireland, as noted in Chapter 5, the *Annals of the Four Masters* record two references in AD 536 and 539 to 'failure of bread'. We have already noted the two aberrant solar eclipses recorded in *The Anglo-Saxon Chronicle* which *may* have been an attempt by a later compiler to 'explain' some pre-existing English references of 'the sun was dim this year' type? Also in the British *Annales Cambriae* there is a reference to 'mortalitas in Brittania et Hibernia', in AD 537.

Now what may we be seeing here? A significant dust-veil blots out a lot of sunlight, presumably around the whole northern hemisphere. The resultant cooling and climatic upset causes famine in areas from China to Europe. Potentially a large number of people die on a hemispheric scale. Burgess (1985) has already voiced the opinion that the Justinian plague of the sixth century AD may have been as severe as the Black Death of the fourteenth century. By that he implies the demise of between one-third and one-half of the population in some areas. The Justinian plague 'starts' in AD 542. That is, it is first recorded in the Mediterranean area in AD 542, having almost certainly travelled from somewhere further east or south. By 544/5 it has reached areas as remote as Ireland. All of this is hardly coincidence. It is highly likely that the Justinian plague 'breaks out' at this time as a direct result of the famine, death and population disruption brought on by the dust-veil event of AD 536–7.

So, it seems obvious that the effects of this eruption (or eruptions) were greater than anything experienced in the last two centuries. This is borne out by Stothers' estimate that the excess visual atmospheric optical depth of 2.5 in AD 536 is approximately twice that associated with our largest recent eruption, Tambora, which scored only 1.3 by comparison (Stothers 1984). This point, on its own, tells us that our suite of modern eruptions is not fully representative. However, because of the tight chronological control offered by both historical and tree-ring information, we can see that in the case of the AD 536 eruption the effects certainly lasted through until at least AD 542.

Additional tree-ring evidence

In the original Belfast work, the sixth-century event showed up very clearly in essentially all the site chronologies in northern Ireland; **Fig. 6.1a** shows the master chronology for northern Ireland across the relevant period. It is clearly there in an oak chronology from Carlisle in northern England. More recently a new chronology from Whithorn in southern Scotland shows identical effects (A. Crone pers. comm.) (**Fig. 6.1b**). Chronologies from Germany show less extreme effects but do show reduced growth nevertheless. Perhaps it was the lack of extreme effects in Germany which temporarily threw us off the scent. Perhaps, we thought, the effects on trees were only severe in northern Britain and Ireland and much less so elsewhere, irrespective of the evidence for

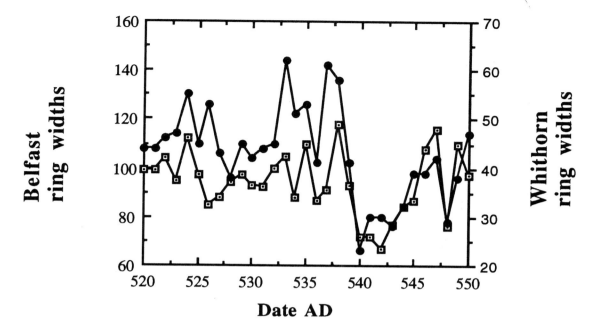

6.1 Restricted growth in oaks from (a) Ireland (solid dots) and (b) Whithorn, Scotland (squares), at AD 540 (Whithorn data courtesy A. Crone)

famines from the Mediterranean and China at the time.

What started to turn the tree-ring picture around was the discovery that the Fennoscandinavian temperature reconstruction by Briffa *et al.* (1990, 1992) showed AD 536 to be the second coldest summer in the last 1500 years. Keith Briffa kindly supplied the annual values of the reconstruction which allowed us to plot the data across the sixth century. The resulting **Fig. 6.2** was clarification of the fact that AD 536 was associated with a period of reduced temperature lasting until 550. This caused us to take another look at the European oak chronologies. It was clear that different chronologies responded differently through time. In particular, the Göttingen chronology showed clear signs of dropping into a narrow band *before* AD 536, in fact as early as 531. Did this mean that the effects had started before the documented 536 dust-veil? If this were the case did it mean that the 536 event was superimposed on an already deteriorating environmental regime?

These are obviously questions which one would like to be able to answer. However, returning to the original Irish masters there was little or no sign of such an early start. This caused us to think about the nature of trying to assess environ-mental change from tree-ring chronologies. When you have a number of chronologies from different areas do you expect them all to do the same thing? The answer is, of course, that you shouldn't! It would be quite possible for a particular area chronology to be responding to some entirely local effect. So, if there are lots of chronologies available, it would seem sensible to see how they are responding as a group. For the sixth century AD it was possible to isolate some 15 site or regional oak chronologies from Ireland, Scotland, England and Germany. **Fig. 6.3** shows a mean chronology containing the information from all 15. (To make the chronology, each site or regional chronology had a straight line fitted and the yearly values converted to percentages; this was done in order to get over the problem of different units and formats used by different workers.) It is clear that the European oaks show a strong negative departure in AD 536, dropping on average to 85% of the width in 535. They then recover in 537 and 538 before plunging to less than 75% of their pre-536 width in 540 and 541. The overall

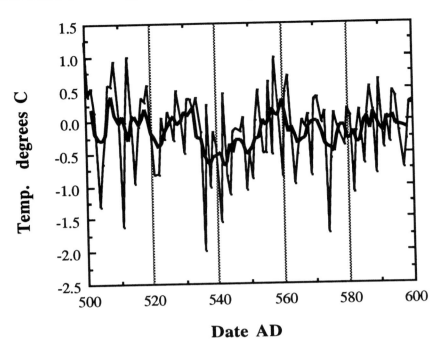

6.2 Raw and five-point smoothed Fennoscandinavian summer temperatures reconstructed from pine ring widths and densities (Briffa et al. 1990: 1992) showing reduced temperatures across AD 540 and notable cold summers in 536 and 541

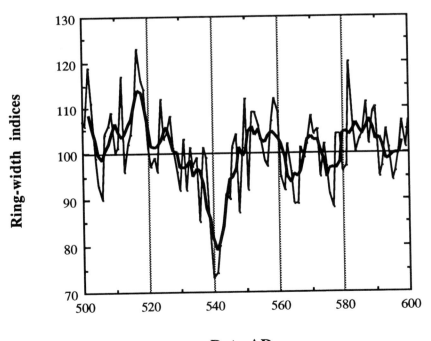

6.3 Raw and five-point smoothed mean growth indices for fifteen European oak chronologies showing the dramatic growth reduction at AD 540

chronology does not return to pre-536 values until 546. The year 536 also stands out because it is a clear negative signature with 14 out of the 15 chronologies showing reduced growth in that year. So, overall, European oaks show an abrupt effect in AD 536, a recovery and reduced growth for some years thereafter.

Fig. 6.4 shows five-point smoothed curves for Fennoscandinavian temperature and European oak growth, together with smoothed ring widths

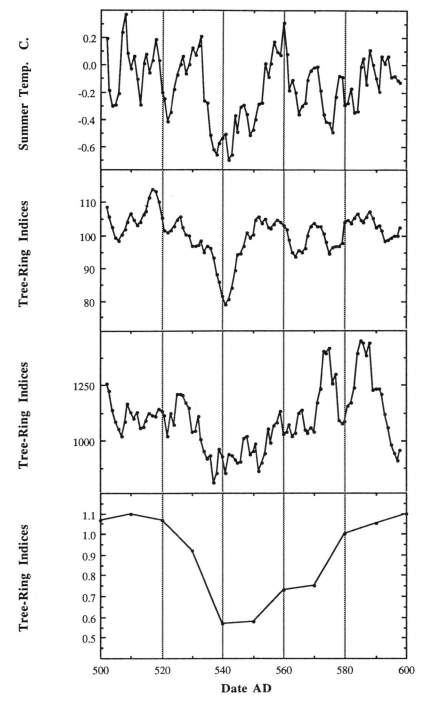

6.4 Comparison of tree-ring effects at the AD 536–45 event. (Top to bottom) smoothed Fennoscandinavian temperatures, European oak width indices, American bristlecone ring widths and American foxtail ring widths (Scuderi 1990)

for bristlecone pine and foxtail pine from the western United States. It is clear that the decade-long downturn, associated with the 536 event, is very widespread. What is particularly interesting is that in the case of the bristlecone pine we know that LaMarche (1974) had attributed reduced growth to lower temperatures. The same is true for Scuderi's foxtail pine record from the Sierra Nevada (Scuderi 1990). In this latter case, Scuderi specifically suggested that reduced

97

growth was due to lower temperatures brought on by volcanic dust-veils. So in many ways that suggestion has come full circle; Scuderi's observation of volcano-related reduced growth in the sixth century is entirely in line with volcano-related reduced growth in Europe, suggested independently by the Irish narrowest-ring work. More recently, Scuderi has published a temperature reconstruction for the Sierra Nevada in which he cites 535, 536 and 541 as his second, third and fourth coldest years in the last two millennia (Scuderi 1993).

Even though it makes perfect sense – that a hemispheric dust-veil could affect tree-growth everywhere around the northern hemisphere – it is still rather a surprise to discover such a consistent effect. The surprise is partly due to the fact that dendrochronologists are conditioned to think in regional terms. Dendrochronology, in terms of pattern matching, does not work right round the northern hemisphere; no-one would expect to be able to *match* Irish oak ring patterns to those of bristlecone or foxtail pine. The difference here is that we are not matching patterns in any overall sense, instead we are looking at growth records in specific years and, clearly, in some highly constrained years there can be hemispheric response. In fact, if we go to Douglass' original work, on pine from the American southwest, we see that the growth ring for AD 536 is 'often microscopic and sometimes absent' (Douglass 1938). The same applies to more recent chronologies from Wetherill Mesa, in the same area, on Pinyon pine, Douglas fir and juniper; all show extremely narrow growth rings in AD 536 (Nichols and Harlan 1967).

The remarkable consistency with which trees record reduced growth in this dust-veil year raises some interesting questions with respect to reduced biomass in the northern hemisphere (we don't have any available information from the southern hemisphere). What would the implications be for the carbon cycle if all trees produced, say, 10% (or 20% or 30%) less growth in a particular year? Can we extrapolate from trees to the whole biomass? Would crop yields right round the northern hemisphere have been reduced by the same amount? In such a situation do we expect trees or domesticated cereals to suffer more? We don't know the answers to these questions but we do know that human populations suffered widespread famine in 536 and succeeding years. Perhaps in this case, the real message from the trees and the famines is that, when the biomass is sufficiently reduced, humans are merely one part of the biomass reduction. This latter point takes us rather neatly to the question of related archaeological evidence.

Archaeological evidence relating to the AD 536–45 event

All the discussion, so far, about the AD 540 event has been derived from historical sources and tree-rings. If the effects, in the broadest sense, of this volcanic dust-veil event were even half as widespread and half as severe as seems possible from the available records, then we might reasonably expect the event to show up in the archaeological record – perhaps as a building hiatus, perhaps in increased burials, perhaps as population movement. Unfortunately, archaeological chronologies based on artefacts normally lack the resolution to see decades rather than centuries. However, despite this, some workers do see change around this time. For example, Härke (1987) notes changes in weapon burials around the mid-sixth century. Fulford (1989) sees trade stopping between the Mediterranean and Britain. Such evidence gets us close to concluding that we may be dealing with an archaeological marker date; but can the case be proven? It seems that now, with the availability of tree-ring dates, we may be able to discern real change in the archaeological record within a decade of the traumatic AD 536–45 events.

During the 1970s, while piecing together an oak chronology in Germany, Becker dated a large selection of Dark Age oak coffins (Becker 1974). Although originally a floating chronology, these coffins have been absolutely dated since 1980 (Hollstein 1980; Becker 1981); the distribution is shown in **Fig. 6.5a**. During the 1960s and 1970s Hollstein had also been accumulating tree-ring dates for sites and timbers (op. cit.); their distribution is shown in **Fig. 6.5b**. It is clear that, despite widespread sam-

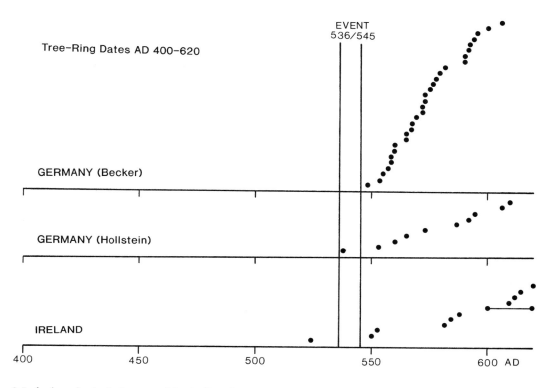

6.5 Archaeological change evident after the AD 540 event in Germany; (a) after Becker (1974), (b) after Hollstein (1980) and (c) in Ireland after Baillie (1991a)

pling, German archaeologists have had little luck in turning up substantial oak timbers from the period AD 400–540.

In Ireland, as discussed above, twenty years of site accumulation yielded the distribution of tree-ring dated sites shown in Figs. 4.7 and **6.5c.** Essentially no archaeological sites have produced datable oak timbers between 95 BC and AD 550, while from AD 550 we see the steady accumulation of sites, mostly crannogs. (The one dated object pre-550, the Oxford Island dug-out, can be ignored for the purposes of this discussion, though see below.) In England a very similar picture emerges (Tyers, Hillam and Groves pers. comm.), so that, if we plot out the total numbers of sites dated by dendrochronology in Europe across this period we obtain the distribution in **Fig. 6.6a.** The appearance of increased numbers of tree-ring dated sites just after AD 540 is striking. What does this mean? For a considerable period of time, dendrochronologists have been acquiring oak timbers in an essentially random fashion – taking whatever is

excavated, accidentally discovered, or is available in museum collections. That random sampling turned up almost no datable oak timbers of the fifth and early sixth centuries AD but successfully produced timbers, in quantity, from the mid-sixth century onwards. Irrespective of any considerations of the significance of the sites or objects involved, the clear implication is that, once we can date things closely, we see evidence for archaeological 'change' in Europe around AD 536–45.

Since all the evidence points to the effects of the dust-veil being seen in trees in both the Old and the New World, can we see any sign of the effects in the archaeological record in America to round out the story? Here we run into one of those areas where caution is necessary. It is easy to find suggestions of change in the archaeological record in the Americas 'about AD 500', or 'about 600', or even 'about 550'. For example, McGhee talking about the High Arctic says: 'After about 700 BC there is another gap in the archaeological record, with little evidence of

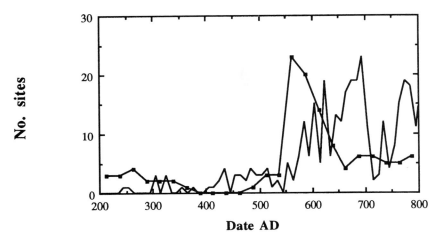

6.6 Archaeological change in (a) Europe (dots) and (b) America (Robinson and Cameron 1991) at AD 536–45 as indicated by the notable increase in dendrochronologically dated sites and objects in both regions immediately after that time

occupation until after about AD 500' (McGhee 1983: 173). Or again: 'Adaption to drier conditions may have occurred in the Great Basin, and a drier climate is also suggested for the west coast of South America, beginning about AD 600' (op. cit. 176). Or yet again, talking specifically of Peru: '. . . Pampa Grande perched in the strategic neck of the Lambayeque valley . . . was the largest Moche complex some 1400 years ago . . . some scholars think that a prolonged drought *about* [my italics] AD 550 displaced large groups of Moche living to the south . . .' (Long and Benn 1990).

But is 'about' good enough to link these observations with the precisely dated events around AD 540? This is where the danger of sucking in evidence is at its strongest. It would be nice if these various strands of evidence could be used to confirm the picture, but it is unfortunately true that they are not sufficiently well dated. If we fall into the trap of using such loosely dated material we may end up by creating an *artificial* horizon simply by sucking everything into the precisely dated horizon. No, what we need is some archaeological evidence from America which is precisely dated. Fortunately some suitably dated evidence has now become available. In 1991 Robinson and Cameron published a directory of *Tree-Ring Dated Prehistoric Sites in the American Southwest* which, according to the authors, 'lists more than 1300 dated sites' and 'contains all dated prehistoric sites' in the south west. This precisely dated data set is ideal to look for signs of archaeological change. **Fig. 6.6b** shows the number of

dated south-western sites (or phases) per decade from AD 200 to 800 (plotted with the number of sites per quarter-century from Ireland, England and Germany for comparison). It is clear that there is a major increase in the numbers of sites, being dated by American dendrochronologists, immediately after the AD 536–45 event. Given that dendrochronologists tend to date whatever becomes available, this is evidence for 'change' in the nature of the archaeological record at that time. It is also worth noting in **Fig. 6.6b** that there are *no* building dates from the American south-west in the decade of the 540s. This is the only decade in the period AD 440–1500 for which no felling dates exist; probably a significant observation in itself.

So, everywhere that annual resolution data is available, it appears to be possible to see the effects of this event. This still leaves the question whether the other loosely dated evidence for change relates to the same time. Unfortunately there are no easy answers. As noted above, it would be nice if we could relate some of the other evidence to the event, particularly the Peruvian evidence. Evidence for prolonged drought in that area might just give some clues to links between El Niño and the 536 dust-veil. Adequately dated evidence of the timing of the drought might allow a remote test of Handler's idea that El Niño is triggered by surface cooling brought on by dust-veils in recent times (Handler 1989).

The involvement of trade

One interesting sidelight on the AD 536–45 event is the way in which largely independent workers develop ideas which eventually come together to make, what appears to be, a real story. Post-Roman trade between Byzantium and the British Isles is one case in point. Warner, who had excavated an important royal ringfort at Clogher, Co. Tyrone, had noted a 'stratigraphical horizon . . . called the "Yellow Layer" which . . . from a gamut of non-circular evidence should date to around AD 600' (Warner 1985). The key point about the yellow layer was that it separated material assemblages containing two distinct types of imported pottery. Below the yellow layer were 'fine red table wares of late Roman Mediterranean origin, and amphorae from the same general area' – so-called 'B-ware'; while above the layer were found examples of the distinctive 'E-ware' whose origins were probably in Gaul. So, in the west of Ulster sometime 'around AD 600' (on archaeology chronology) there is a notable change giving rise to two mutually exclusive imported pottery assemblages.

Imported pottery is, by definition, international in character, so it is interesting to see a recent paper on the subject from a Mediterranean perspective. Fulford, accepting that 'there is now general agreement and understanding of the area of origin of the [Mediterranean] imported wares', turns his attention to the nature of the underlying trade which must account for the presence of the pottery in places like Britain and Ireland (Fulford 1989). On balance he sees a case for the Mediterranean wares in the British Isles having derived from the eastern Mediterranean, i.e. from Byzantium, and he suggests: 'From western Britain and Ireland as a whole the tableware can be fitted within a period of about 75 years, between c. 475 and c. 550' (op. cit. 4). So, having postulated a scenario of Byzantine trade up to the mid-sixth century, he rounds out the story with reference to Procopius who appears to be the last Byzantine historian who actually seemed to have direct knowledge of Britain. From our point of view the critical aspect is that, according to Fulford, before the mid-sixth

century there was a regular trade in Mediterranean pottery to the British Isles, thereafter none. As Warner pointed out, the Mediterranean wares are replaced by wares from a completely different European theatre. So here is a categoric 'change' in the close vicinity of our independently derived environmental trauma of AD 536–45. Surely this is not just a coincidence. The question is: can we now date Warner's yellow layer to AD 550 rather than his 'around AD 600'?

The use of strange pieces of ancient history

The point made above about extrapolation from Peruvian droughts to dust-veils causing El Niño events is an example of how ancient records can be used as possible hints regarding the understanding of past environmental change. This type of information is interesting because it is inherently *soft* in character. It can hardly ever be used to prove anything but it can nevertheless sometimes act as a clue to what to look for in order to prove what actually did happen.

As an example of how this can come about, we can look at the case of tephrochronology. In the later 1980s Andy Dugmore and Anthony Newton were researching into layers of Icelandic tephra in Scottish bog deposits. The layers are present and can be traced back by elemental analysis to specific eruptions in Iceland (Dugmore and Newton 1992). The idea of this work is to use identified layers of tephra to allow better time control of other micro- and macroscopic studies on peat; in effect to create a tephrochronology. The discovery of volcano-related environmental downturns in Irish bog oaks coupled with the Scottish tephrochronology work led to a research programme to produce a tephrochronology in north Irish bogs (Pilcher and Hall 1992). This work has successfully demonstrated replication of Icelandic tephras in different peat bogs in Ireland. (Not to put too fine a point on it, even though the particles are normally less than 100 microns in size, north Irish bogs are *full* of Icelandic tephra.)

The observation of the effects of eruptions, albeit indirectly, in tree-rings and as tephra lay-

101

ers in peat, does raise the profile of volcanoes in the Irish consciousness. Ireland has not suffered much from volcanic activity in the last 50 million years – or has it? The concept of Icelandic tephra in Ireland raises the issue of some strange references in the Irish annals. For example 'Cathal O'Conor . . . died in 1224; and his death was accompanied by strange portents . . . . An awful and strange shower fell this year in Connacht . . . and other districts, followed by terrible diseases and distempers amongst the cattle which grazed the lands where the shower fell; and their milk produced extraordinary internal diseases on the persons who drank it.' Also: 'A frightful shower fell in Connaught, which injured the grass and herbage' (Wilde 1851); the Icelandic volcano Hekla is reported to have erupted in AD 1222. Similarly: 'AD 932; Fire from heaven burnt the mountains of Connaught – the streams and lakes dried up and many people were burned by the fire'; the Icelandic volcano Edjkla erupted in AD 934±2 (Hammer *et al.* 1980). So, these appear to be direct descriptions of something like the fluorine poisoning known in Iceland to be associated with volcanic eruptions (Sigurdsson and Pálsson 1957). It is known from Icelandic studies that 'the soluble fluorine [can] be chemically adsorbed on the surface of tephra particles' (Oskarsson 1980). Animals ingesting the fluorine suffer a variety of symptoms, which would not be at odds with the ancient Irish descriptions, resulting in substantial mortality. These dated examples are not the only ones: an earlier description occurs in the sixth-century *Life of St Columba*:

> One day while the saint was living in Iona, he saw a heavy rain cloud that had arisen from the sea in the north . . . [he said] this cloud will be very hurtful to men and beasts and . . . [will] drop pestiferous rain upon some part of Ireland . . . and it will cause severe festering sores to form on human bodies and the udders of animals. Men and cattle who suffer from them, afflicted with that poisonous disease, will be sick even to death.

It is not known whether this is a first-hand observation or part of a miracle attributed to the saint (who is credited with miraculously curing the afflicted); however, there is little doubt that it has all the flavour of a description of a chemical cloud from the north, i.e. towards Iceland.

Once a possible rational explanation has been advanced for what were previously seen as 'strange' references, one is forced to look at some others which might make sense in the same vein. For example, in the prehistoric section of the same annals there is a reference in the year Anno Mundi 5001, i.e. *c.* 199 BC (Warner [1990b] suggests a range 210–199 BC) to 'a great murrain of kine in the reign of Breasel Bodhiobadh; only one bull and heifer was left alive' (Wilde 1851). In Chapter 5 we saw that there was a significant dust-veil event at 208 BC which Hammer *et al.* (1980) suggested might be due to the Younger Laxar-lava in Iceland. Putting this information together, a murrain of cattle might not be such a strange reference after all.

I would hasten to stress again that this type of information doesn't prove anything, but it may provide clues as to what might be looked for in suitable archaeological, or other, deposits. As ever, it is the bringing together of dates which begins to shed light on what have previously been largely incomprehensible statements in ancient records. Perhaps the most interesting aspect of these annal references is that, if we begin to believe that the ancient annalists were genuinely trying to describe real events, we should do them justice by having a closer look at some of the other things they mention. To give one last example: 'AD 1178; The river at Galway was dried up for a day' (Wilde 1851). What does one make of this? It is very odd for a river to dry up for only one day, especially the river at Galway. Could it be, for example, that the river didn't dry up so much as the sea retreated? Might we be seeing a faint reference here to some sort of tectonic effect? This seems far-fetched until one discovers that there was a significant eruption of the Icelandic volcano Katla in 1179!

Having introduced some 'strange' evidence from the annals, which was previously difficult to interpret, but which now begins to make some sense, this is a fitting place to review that unfinished dug-out canoe from Lough Neagh, referred to above and in Baillie (1982).

The unfinished dug-out from Lough Neagh

The point was made above that very few archaeological sites in Ireland appeared to date to the period between 95 BC and AD 536 (see **Fig 6.5c**). The one exception relates to an *unfinished* dug-out boat from Oxford Island on the southern shore of Lough Neagh, the major body of water in the centre of Ulster. This dug-out, sample Q3911, retained no sapwood and was estimated to have been felled in the range AD 524±9 (AD 524±18 for 95% confidence) (Baillie 1982: 241). Since dug-outs are essentially random objects this date was not originally considered to be significant. In fact, referring back to the description of this boat in 1982, it was stated: 'The terrible thing about this date is

its extreme over-refinement. There is no need to know the date of a dug-out to this level of precision . . . .' Indeed in 1982 that was the case. However, somewhat ironically, once a traumatic event is postulated between AD 536–45, an interesting possibility becomes apparent. The number of sapwood rings in Irish oak is highly variable and the 95% confidence range does allow the possibility that the dug-out could represent a tree felled somewhere between AD 506 and 542. It therefore becomes technically possible that the unfinished dug-out was abandoned around the time of the AD 536–45 trauma.

This in turn raises the question why a partly finished dug-out might be abandoned. We can assume that an unfinished oak dug-out wasn't the intended end product (as it wouldn't float). So, presumably, whoever was making it abandoned it for a reason. In 1982 this didn't seem important. Now, one obvious possibility would be a sudden rise in the level of Lough Neagh (submerging the boat which was not sufficiently

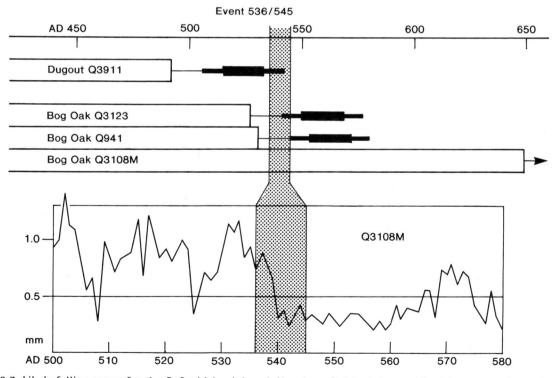

6.7 Likely felling range for the Oxford Island, Lough Neagh, unfinished dug-out boat intersects the period of the 536–45 event. Bog oaks from close to Lough Neagh die or show reduced growth at the same time, implying raised water levels

hollow to float). While this logic may seem stretched, we do have a partial check on the level of Lough Neagh at around this time. Some naturally preserved oaks were recovered from deposits at the north-west corner of the lough in the 1970s. Of a group of eight trees belonging to this Dark Age period, two ceased growing in the ranges AD 541–77 and AD 545–80 respectively, while the only tree to grow across the period, Q3108M, exhibits an extremely narrow band of rings starting in AD 540 (**Fig. 6.7**). Since these trees were apparently growing below the normal pre-nineteenth-century level of the lough it is quite likely that this extreme narrowing of the growth rings could have been induced by rising lough level. So, although without sapwood none of this can be proven, the previously anomalous existence of this unfinished dug-out could be explained by the events associated with AD 536–45. In case this sounds like special pleading a remarkably similar, though undated, example of abandoned canoes can be quoted. 'At Lough Gara . . . the canoes found were lying on what had been the shore of a smaller lake. They were under 5 to 6 ft. of water' (Dobbs 1956: 114). One moral seems to be that one should never be casually dismissive of dendrochronological dates

The ice-core anomaly at AD 540

Depressingly, there is one chronological aspect of all this which appears to be inexplicable. The starting point of this discussion, the original specification of a significant acidity layer in the Dye 3 core at AD 540±10 (Hammer et al. 1980), was abandoned in favour of a layer dated AD 516±4 (Hammer 1984: 56)! As it is clear that there was a major dry-fog event in AD 536, with effects lasting for years afterwards, this movement of the ice acidity layer to AD 516 casts serious doubt on the ice-core chronology in the sixth century AD. If we ask what happens in the wider ice-core record around this critical time, we find that in Hammer et al. 1980, the original Crête core *stopped* at AD 553±3 and the Camp Century core turned out to be *unusable* down to the first century AD. So, until recently, the ice-core information for the sixth century AD relied solely on the Dye 3 core. By moving the 540±10

acid layer by 24 years, Hammer cast doubt on the integrity of that core in the sixth century AD. It had become obvious, as Rampino et al. (1988) have pointed out, that this sixth-century section was 'still in need of revision'; certainly, using tree-ring terminology, it was in need of *replication*.

With this situation in mind, the results of the recent GISP2 and GRIP cores, from Summit, Greenland, were awaited with interest. Unfortunately, preliminary results from the GISP2 core indicate no significantly enhanced acidity in the annual layers attributed to the years around AD 536–40 (Zielinski pers. comm.). Indeed Zielinski says that the closest acid signal is 'a modest signal at AD 529'. While the overall error limits associated with the dating of this section of the GISP2 core (conservatively stated to be ±2% (Alley et al. 1993) but believed realistically to be less than ±1%, i.e. less than ±15 years in the sixth century AD) would allow AD 529±15 to bracket AD 536, the size of the signal is apparently not in keeping with the strong acid signal which would be expected if sulphur is the principal driving force behind significant environmental effects. So, we seem to be seeing severe environmental effects but no relatively large sulphur signal in the case of AD 536. However, it has to be pointed out that the GISP2 core has a missing 14-metre section (believed to be equivalent to some 70 annual layers) between c. AD 614 (±15) and c. AD 545 (±15). In fact, the section of core is not missing but came up as 'trash', i.e. shattered ice. So, as this introduces an imponderable into the dating of the core below the missing section, it is not beyond the bounds of possibility that the existing GISP2 core does not cover the AD 536–45 period at all. This issue will only be resolved when the section of core below the 14-metre gap is precisely dated by links to known-age events such as Vesuvius in AD 79 (or just possibly Taupo which erupted close to AD 180).

The coincidence of 'problems' with no less than three ice-core records in the sixth century is hard to swallow. The GISP2 core is 3km in total length yet the missing section falls just where questions had already been posed! Perhaps there is a separate story in these observations alone.

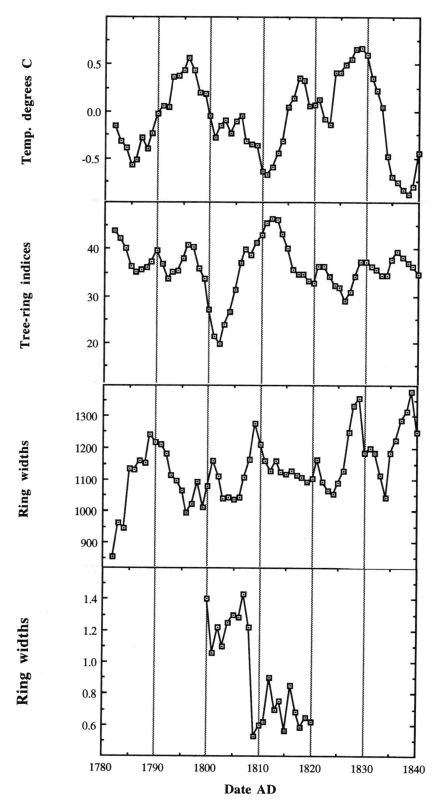

6.8 Unlike Fig. 6.4, comparison of tree-rings across the AD 1815 Tambora event show no obvious signs of common response. (Top to bottom) smoothed Fennoscandinavian temperatures, European oak width indices, American bristlecone ring widths and American foxtail ring widths (Scuderi 1990)

However, fortunately, there is a fallback situation. The Danish GRIP core (also 3km long and from a site just 30km from the GISP2 location) may provide the answers when the results of its analysis become available.

Given the scale of effects after AD 536, there will be a lot of questions to be asked (indeed answered) if there is *no* significant ice signal at this time. Härke has picked up on this issue in the context of those anomalous eclipse records in *The Anglo-Saxon Chronicle* in AD 538 and 540 and spells out two possibilities as follows:

> . . . the entire northern hemisphere was affected in the late 530s by a sudden climatic deterioration caused either by a major volcanic eruption (Baillie's suggestion) or by dust-veils from a cometary impact (Victor Clube['s suggestion]). (Härke 1991)

If the ice-core evidence is correct and there is *no* significant acidity layer in the Greenland ice around 536 then Clube's suggestions will have to be taken seriously (see Clube and Napier 1990) and we will have to decide how we might separate ancient descriptions of the effects of volcanoes from those of cometary impacts; or (we could add) from those of the solar system passing through an interstellar cloud; or indeed from a major undersea outgassing event. In every case, whether it is the dating of volcanoes, or the dating of ice-cores, or the dating of Peruvian droughts, the only answer is the tightening of chronology to allow direct association (or disassociation) between the various strands of evidence. In this case, dendrochronology, in combination with historical evidence, has provided the focus (Baillie 1994).

A comparison with Tambora

Before leaving this AD 536 event, it is worth comparing its effects with those of the largest explosive eruption of recent times – Tambora, 1815 (Harington 1992). Because we have looked at 536 at annual resolution we have been able to see the synchronous effects across the northern hemisphere. We can of course look at 1815 in the same way: there are plenty of tree-ring chronologies around for the period. What is most striking is the lack of effect in chronologies from the same areas as those which showed the AD 536 event so clearly. **Fig. 6.8** shows smoothed curves for Fennoscandinavian temperature (Briffa *et al.* 1992); bristlecone pine (LaMarche and Ferguson pers comm.); European oak and foxtail pine (Scuderi 1990). It is clear that there is no consistent effect, again suggesting the qualitative difference with AD 536. Tambora may have caused various environmental problems but they appear to have been much more regional than the seemingly hemispheric effects of the sixth-century dust-veil. One interesting fact about the various data sets around AD 1815 relates to the noticeable troughs which *don't* occur at the time of Tambora but in the 15 years before. We know that these dramatic downturns are *not* synchronous in real time because the tree-ring patterns are all precisely dated. (Imagine the situation if we had sloppy time-control on this data, as is normal with most other types of evidence; given the historical references to things happening in 1815–17, there would be a strong temptation to 'see' each of the flexibly dated troughs as 'evidence' for the widespread effects of the 1815 event – the suck-in effect again.) So, there is an enormous gulf between knowing the true date of pieces of evidence and having flexibility to accommodate evidence.

Conclusion

There can be no doubt that some momentous happening took place in the mid-sixth century AD; the information is summarized in **Fig. 6.9**. It is also clear that we do not definitively know the cause (or causes). However, the sixth century is as yesterday in geological time; something which could happen then could happen now. It is important that this event be fully understood, whether it be volcanic, or meteoric, or indeed something we simply haven't thought of.

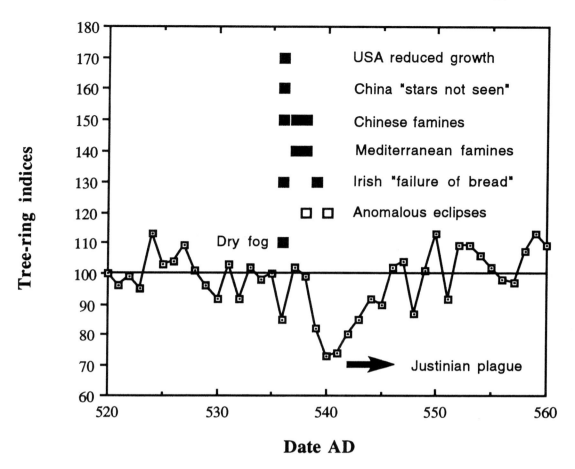

6.9 Summary of phenomena related to the AD 536–45 event, plotted with the annual resolution curve for European oak

7 Volcanoes and chronology: the Bronze Age eruption of Santorini (Thera)

As was noted in Chapter 5, the dating of the Bronze Age eruption of Santorini is important. Here was a large eruption, in an area of high civilization, which must have had effects on human populations both locally and in neighbouring areas. Obviously we would like to know just what those effects were. If precisely specified, it would act as a chronological marker horizon throughout much of the Aegean. Santorini is also important volcanologically because, involving a sea-level caldera collapse – with many questions about the interactions between water and magma – it is an eruption type not well represented in the recent repertoire. So here is an eruption with strong interest for both archaeologists and volcanologists; indeed, because it is one of the few prehistoric eruptions which have been intensively studied, it is a major testbed for volcanological theory.

In this respect Santorini is quite different from Vesuvius. When Vesuvius buried Pompeii and Herculaneum on 25 August AD 79, it left few questions to be answered. The date was known, the archaeology was completely preserved and the eruption, while locally important, seems not to have been of global significance; overall there are no doubts about those relationships. Santorini, only some 16 or 17 centuries earlier, was a major caldera-forming eruption, possibly of a specialized type, and its environmental consequences may be intimately tied up with its archaeological consequences. Chronologically it is immensely important because, if the combined might of the archaeological and volcanological worlds cannot date an event of this magnitude, what chance is there of ever truly refining either archaeological or volcanological chronology, outside those sites amenable to dendrochronology or high-precision wiggle matching? So progress on the dating of Santorini is symptomatic of progress in prehistoric dating generally. One could also venture that progress in the understanding of the Santorini eruption, and its environmental effects, may be symptomatic of progress in the understanding of ancient volcanoes generally.

Having stumbled accidentally into this maelstrom, purely through some very narrow growth rings in Irish oaks, it has been possible to bring a dendrochronologist's perspective to the problem (Baillie 1990b). For example, it is particularly interesting to see the way in which the attempts to date the eruption of Santorini highlight the inherent weaknesses in archaeological interpretation, ancient history, volcanology, ice-core studies and routine radiocarbon analysis. The whole story serves to demonstrate the remarkable dating resolution offered by dendrochronology. In the whole debate the only *fixed points* are 1628 BC and 1627 BC, both derived from tree-ring studies (see Chapter 5); everything else gives every appearance of being flexible. In fact, if Santorini didn't erupt in 1628 BC (or one or two years earlier) then no-one knows when it did erupt because there are *no* other specific candidate dates! So, in this chapter we can review some of the chronological problems presented by Santorini. I hope it will become clear that chronology is the key to ever fully understanding the event.

The archaeological evidence

The conventional archaeological dating of the Thera eruption is at the end of the period termed Late Minoan 1A. For many years confusion between the destruction of Akrotiri, on Santorini, at the end of LM1A, and the collapse of the Minoan civilization on Crete, some 100km to the south, at the end of LM1B had presented a chronological red herring. Since the Minoan collapse was conventionally placed around 1450 BC, the apparent link with Santorini had the effect of pulling down the date of the eruption. To some extent this explains Warren's position of extreme opposition to an early – i.e. seventeenth-century – dating for the eruption (Warren 1984); while Santorini was linked to the end of the Minoans the huge jump back to the seventeenth-century was 'impossible'. The situation has now been partly resolved by the discovery of ash, from the Santorini eruption, stratified before the end of the Minoan period. So now the Minoan civilization ends at the end of LM1B, conventionally c. 1450 BC, but this is *separate* from the Santorini event at the end of LM1A (Manning 1990; Renfrew 1990). The only remaining archaeological question is: how long was the LM1B period? More recently, Warren has conceded that the Santorini eruption could be as old as 1520 BC (possibly even 1550 BC); however, he still cannot countenance a date as early as the seventeenth century because of the constraints imposed by various Aegean archaeological links with Egyptian chronology (Warren 1991).

Not surprisingly, given the nature of much archaeological dating based on stylistic considerations, disputed stratigraphy, etc., opinion is divided on whether the archaeological evidence for the date of the eruption is actually constrained to the later sixteenth century BC or whether it could be compatible with a seventeenth-century date for the eruption. It has to be noted that workers other than Warren and the traditional school could satisfactorily re-interpret the archaeological evidence to fit with a seventeenth-century date for the end of LM1A (Manning 1988; Betancourt 1987). Thus it is fair to say that archaeological opinion is split on the matter and no amount of conventional archaeological endeavour can currently establish a precise date for the Santorini eruption.

In fact, an outsider could again raise the issue, as noted above, as to whether the dating of the eruption should be regarded as a *test* of the Egyptian chronology, rather than relying upon that chronology. This is where the independent dating of the environmental effects of an eruption in 1628 BC become significant. To repeat the main issue: if the 1628 BC effects were caused by Santorini, this would call into doubt either Warren's links with the Egyptian chronology or the Egyptian chronology itself.

The scientific methods

If the archaeological world is divided on the Santorini issue, then the scientific world is equally divided on many of the issues, though in ways unrelated to the archaeology. Radiocarbon, tree-rings and ice-cores have all been brought to bear on the dating question. Radiocarbon by direct attempts to date the burial of the town of Akrotiri; tree-rings and ice-cores, indirectly, via the question of remote environmental effects.

Radiocarbon

The main direct dating thrust has been the measurement of short-life samples, mostly seeds, from the site of Akrotiri which was buried by the eruption. Large numbers of radiocarbon measurements have been made on samples which, it is hoped, relate closely to the date of the eruption (**Fig. 7.1**). This spread of dates makes it very difficult to arrive at a specific radiocarbon age for the eruption. Since any radiocarbon age has to be calibrated, it becomes inevitable that radiocarbon cannot resolve satisfactorily between the seventeenth- and the sixteenth-century archaeological options. Despite all the effort, Housley *et al.* (1990: 213) are forced to state 'the probability that the result lies in the seventeenth-century BC age range is *c.* 70% against a *c.* 30% probability that it lies in the sixteenth century'.

In fact, the situation is substantially worse than that statement suggests. If one looks seriously at the calibration curve – the measured relationship between residual radiocarbon activity and known-age tree-ring samples – it is clear that it is not technically possible to differentiate between a 1628 BC and a 1530 BC option. Reference to **Fig. 7.2**, where Pearson's high-precision results are plotted with 2-sigma errors, shows that the calibration is essentially flat across the critical period. Only if the calendar date of the eruption had been younger than 1520 BC, or older than

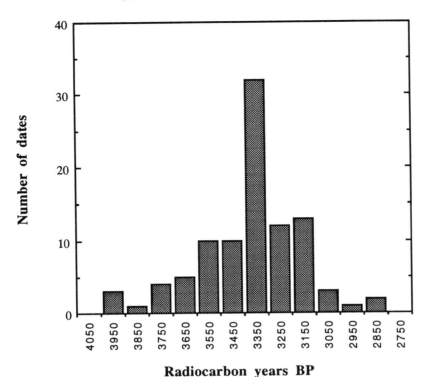

7.1 A frequency diagram of 96 radiocarbon dates associated with the instantaneous Bronze Age eruption of Thera (Santorini)

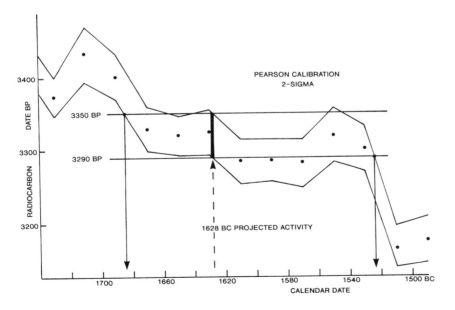

7.2 The radiocarbon calibration curve is essentially flat across the seventeenth and sixteenth centuries BC making it impossible to accurately date the eruption of Thera by this method. The radiocarbon date for an actual 1628 BC sample could not be interpreted to better than c. 1680–1530 BC.

1670 BC, might it have been possible to see the true date from the radiocarbon evidence; had the radiocarbon dates from Akrotiri clustered around any radiocarbon age younger than 3250 BP, then Warren would have been shown to be broadly correct. Since every discussion of the radiocarbon evidence, with the exception of the self-confessed 'confusing' results from the Simon-Frazer group (Nelson *et al.* 1990), centres around radiocarbon ages of 3330 BP, it is most unlikely that the eruption was as late as 1520 BC.

One fact that emerges from this discussion is that, when it comes to critical dating questions, simply acquiring more and more radiocarbon dates for a 'point' sample may be a waste of time. All the radiocarbon evidence has done, in this case, is suggest that Warren's *c.* 1500 BC date for the eruption is unlikely. In the absence of a high-precision wiggle-match date, radiocarbon simply cannot answer the question. It also has to be mentioned that at least some doubt has been cast on the Akrotiri samples themselves. This doubt relates to the issue of a possible 'old carbon' effect which might be inherent in samples that grew close to an outgassing volcano. This issue is now largely discounted by the scientific community but is still laboured by revisionist scholars who wish to shorten ancient chronology (James 1991). The principal reason that the proposed effect is discounted is the fact that other Late Minoan sites in the Aegean, not associated with the volcano, appear to yield similar radiocarbon ages (Sturt Manning pers. comm.).

Ice-cores and tree-rings

Ever since LaMarche and Hirschboeck's announcement of a seventeenth-century BC frost-ring event, it has been obvious that remote environmental effects cannot specify which volcano might be involved. Everyone accepts that the ice-core acidity layer at 1645±20 BC and the tree-ring effects at 1628 and 1627 BC cannot be directly attributed to the eruption of Santorini. This fact, while self-evident, has been laboured by several authors, most notably Pyle (1989, 1990a). However, all the environmental effects can, in some measure, be related to the effects of volcanic eruptions and the dates all fall within the possible range of the Santorini eruption, on the basis of the radiocarbon and archaeological evidence. So the occurrence of these environmental effects in the seventeenth century, proximate to the Santorini eruption, makes it possible that they do in fact date that eruption. Put another way, there has to be a finite possibility that Santorini erupted in 1628 BC or one or two years earlier. Most people would have to agree with that last statement because, in scien-

tific terms, it is self-evident. (Even in the worst case, Santorini erupted somewhere in a window of 140 years – 1670 BC to 1530 BC – so, since *any* large eruption between 1630 BC and 1624 BC would have been involved in the environmental effects, Santorini must have at least a 1 in 20 chance of being involved. This in itself precludes anyone from using Pyle's arguments to simply dismiss the 1628 BC scenario.)

Unfortunately, there is virtually no glimmer of agreement, even on this last point. There is controversy about every possible aspect of the various relationships between the Santorini eruption, the radiocarbon evidence, the date of the acidity layer, the amount of sulphuric acid recorded in the ice-core, the amount of acid produced by the eruption and, indeed, about which eruption produced the acid. Most of the rest of this chapter will involve an attempt to unravel this complex set of arguments.

Disentangling Santorini

Let us start with an apparently simple disagreement – the relationship between the 1645±20 BC ice-core acidity layer and the 1628/1627 BC tree-ring effects. As a dendrochronologist I always found it strange that Hammer *et al.* (1987) failed to give precedence to LaMarche and Hirschboeck's 1627 BC frost-ring date. If 1627 BC is in print (as it was) as a suggested date for a large volcanic event, and other workers find evidence for a large volcanic event in a range which brackets 1627 BC (as 1645±20 BC clearly does), then one would normally assume that the latter date was tending to confirm the former. Obviously Hammer *et al.* did not see things in that light and one has to assume that their citing 1645±20, rather than 1627, reflected the confidence which they had in the precision of the ice-core record at that time. Indeed, Hammer and Clausen (1990: 177) state: 'The error limit quoted for the ice-core date is certainly not the most probable error [*sic*], even though the error might be as high as ±20 years.'

So, although at first sight one would assume that the 1645±20 ice-core date and the 1628/7 tree-ring dates should represent the *same* event, in reality, or at least in the view of the ice-core workers, they could be different events. One problem which surfaces here is the different perspective of workers in different fields. The dendrochronologists feel that their work, with its extreme accuracy, deserves priority. The ice-core workers, with their definite links to volcanic activity (by way of the acid layers), feel that theirs is the hard information. We certainly shouldn't be surprised at this. The danger only comes if such sentiments colour judgements. So, perhaps a consensus statement would help to clarify the position; perhaps something along the following lines:

> It looks as though something volcanic and environmental is going on in the later seventeenth century BC. The tree-rings specify some environmental effects at 1628 BC and it is not impossible that the 1645±20 BC acidity layer represents the same event. Given the radiocarbon evidence Santorini has to be a possible candidate.

While such a statement is heavily qualified, it does at least provide a hypothesis for testing. The alternative is to take Pyle's line that 'there seems no strong reason at this time for attributing a date of 1645 BC or 1626–1628 BC to the Minoan eruption . . .' (Pyle 1990a: 172). Such a statement is technically just as correct but it is extremely negative where the former is at least optimistic. One approach recognizes the subtlety of factors such as circumstantial evidence and coincidence, the other does not. Perhaps Pyle provides us with the perspective of the geologists who study the volcanoes themselves. Only workers not familiar with the dating methods involved could give 1645±20 equal weight to *two* tree-ring dates at 1628/7 BC.

The volcanological evidence

Volcanologists have studied Santorini intensively. Their findings clearly relate to the ice-core, tree-ring and radiocarbon debates by way of (i) the amount of sulphur outgassed by Santorini, (ii) the amount of sulphur registered in the 1645±20 ice-core layer, (iii) the frequency of large eruptions and (iv) the related question of the occurrence of other candidate eruptions around the seventeenth century BC.

Volcanologists attempt to estimate the amount of sulphur put out by a volcano by estimating the difference between the amount of sulphur in the original magma and the amount remaining in the degassed magma. This is done by 'estimation of pre-eruption volatile content by analysis of glass inclusions in phenocrysts' and comparison of the results with measurements on the degassed magma (Sigurdsson *et al.* 1985). Obviously, to calculate the total outgassed sulphur, it is also necessary to know how much magma was produced. Unfortunately, finding out just how much magma came from an ancient eruption is not an exact science. For a start, no-one in the volcanological field appears to talk in the same units: it is possible to report recent estimates such as 'the total volume of collapse . . . is of the order of 27–30 cubic km' (Pyle 1990b) or 'The total Minoan tephra fall is now estimated at 42 cubic km' (Sigurdsson *et al.* 1990) or 'The erupted mass from the Minoan event therefore consists of . . . a total of 39 cubic km DRE (dense rock equivalent)' (op. cit. 100). The total volume estimates depend on isopach maps of the dispersed ash (Pyle 1990b) and, indeed, the recent volume estimates have had to take account of new observations of the Santorini ash in Turkey (Sullivan 1988). So it is unlikely that we have the final volume figure for Santorini. What is not in doubt is that it was a large eruption. If we put this fact together with the following statement, 'Probably any explosive eruption bigger than Krakatau's in 1883 can be detected in one or both of the polar ice-sheets, because so much magma is erupted that the sulphur release is bound to be fairly large in any case' (Rampino *et al.* 1988), it seems quite plausible that Santorini might show up as a Greenland acidity layer. Unfortunately Rampino was making a general statement. When we come to Santorini the volcanologists tell us that it appears to have been a low-sulphur eruption and 'judging from the petrological estimate, the acidity signal from Santorini was probably so low that it may not be detectable in the Greenland ice-sheet' (Sigurdsson *et al.* 1985).

The question of the sulphur

So, how much sulphur was put out during the Santorini eruption and how much is recorded in the Greenland ice at 1645±20 BC? This appears to be the crucial question of the entire debate. After the discussions at the 1989 Thera III Congress, Manning came away believing, quite correctly, that 'on petrological grounds the sulphuric acid production of the Thera eruption was eight to twenty, or ten to twenty times *too small* [my italics] to have accounted for the large 1644 BC [*sic*] acidity spike' (Manning 1990). So, at face value, the 1645±20 BC acidity layer appears *not* to line up with Santorini. If, as the dendrochronologists believe, the ice-core and tree-ring events are the same, then the trees also would not line up with Santorini; something which would be very unfortunate from a dating point of view.

If one wants to retain 1628 BC as a possible date for Santorini, one's first reaction is to contest this volcanological conclusion and, indeed, there are some areas of uncertainty in the volcanology of Thera (see for example Sparks and Wilson 1990). Not least are the recent changes in the sulphur estimates. Just a few years ago Sigurdsson *et al.* (1985) wrote: 'We have estimated a volcanic volatile yield of 3.86 x 10^{12} g H_2SO_4 from this explosive eruption' – this can be thought of as 4 million tons of sulphuric acid. Currently, Sigurdsson *et al.* (1990) are of the opinion: 'When scaled to the total erupted mass of magma, these figures give an estimate of the sulphur output to the atmosphere from the Minoan eruption as . . . equivalent to a 1.7 x 10^{10} kg volcanic aerosol composed of H_2SO_4.' They also state: 'The error in this value is ±20% due to the microprobe analysis of sulphur; the additional error due to uncertainty in the estimate of total erupted magma is believed to be of the same order' (op. cit. 105). This can be thought of as 17 million tons of sulphuric acid or maybe 20% to 40% more. So on these grounds alone, the discrepancy between the Santorini sulphur output and the ice-core acidity (which Manning reported correctly from the Thera III Conference as 8–20 times) could be squeezed down to a factor of times five or possibly even times four. If we then quote the

ice-core workers saying things like 'Magnitude estimates on several eruptions . . . [from ice acidity] . . . could easily be wrong by a factor of 2 for several reasons . . .' (Hammer *et al.* 1980), it becomes clear that, with a bit of squeezing, the discrepancy could conceivably be as low as a factor of times two. Perhaps we're getting there. So, between the 1989 Conference when Thera, according to the assembled volcanologists, *couldn't possibly* be 1645/1628 BC – because it had put out too little sulphur – and the publication of the Thera III proceedings in 1990, we have a situation where the amount of sulphur from the eruption is no longer so out of line with that in the Greenland ice (see also below).

One could also point to the fact that environmental impact may not be solely related to sulphur; after all, there must have been some 'dust', and what are the environmental consequences of the 5 *billion* tons of magmatic water stated to have been associated with the Santorini eruption (Sigurdsson *et al.* 1990)? In addition, it is not known just how much seawater may have been evaporated into the atmosphere during the eruption. Sigurdsson *et al.* also estimated that it was possible that the eruption evaporated 5 billion tons of sea-water. Had that been the case, then it could have added an additional 15 million tons of sulphuric acid output and 100 million tons of hydrochloric acid (op. cit. 107). These figures would have gone some considerable way towards explaining the apparent discrepancy between the volcanological estimate of the sulphur output of Santorini and the acid layer in Greenland. Unfortunately, that hope appeared to be frustrated by the lack of hydrochloric acid in the 1645±20 BC layer (Hammer *et al.* 1987). (To confuse things still further, it is widely believed that HCl is rapidly scavenged from the atmosphere by a complex of chemical reactions; otherwise even relatively small eruptions could wipe out the ozone layer. So perhaps the lack of HCl in the ice at 1645±20 BC does not in itself preclude the sea-water hypothesis; leaving the sea-water in could help to make Santorini more environmentally effective.) However, even to accumulate this list of components of Santorini's contribution to atmospheric aerosol is a sobering exercise. It raises the question of whether the scientific community really understand the potential effects of such a complex eruption.

One thing seems clear, any way the figures are manipulated: attempts to reconcile Santorini with the 1645±20 ice acidity, and, by association, with the tree-ring events, appear to meet with only limited success. There is still a discrepancy between the estimated sulphur output and the acid in Greenland. If the estimates of sulphuric acid from Santorini were fixed (which clearly they are not, but let's deal with one thing at a time), the one remaining ray of hope might be the reliability of the ice-core estimates of global acid fall-out. Is the ice-core record as good as everyone seems to assume? Before dealing with this area of the debate, which may in fact contain the solution to the whole problem, it is necessary to look at two of the other complicating factors, namely the frequency of eruptions and other possible candidate volcanoes.

The question of multiple eruptions

Consider for a moment the ice-core estimate of 100–200 million tons of sulphuric acid in comparison with the 'maximum' of perhaps 20 million tons generated by Santorini. The conclusion immediately jumped to is that the 1645±20 BC acidity layer in Greenland cannot therefore relate to Santorini. However, such a conclusion is not absolute. There must be a finite possibility that the discrepancy could be accounted for by the simultaneous eruption (within a year or two) of Santorini and some other, unknown volcano. In theory it is certainly possible that more than one large volcano could erupt at the same time. In fact there are several lines of relevant argument. We have already seen in Chapter 5 that the years following 44 BC may reflect an accumulating dust-veil as several eruptions occur within a few years. There is also that interesting circumstantial case in the late AD 530s. In virtually all the events discussed in Chapter 5, we are seeing very widespread effects and longer durations than those normally associated with eruptions in recent times. Could multiple eruptions be the crucial factor which

makes these events stand out?

The question of multiple eruptions is interesting because statistically they *have* to occur. One of the first criticisms of the 1628 BC suggestion for Santorini came from Pyle (1989). In essence he was arguing that large eruptions are common (3 per decade greater than VEI 4) and that neither the ice-core workers nor the dendrochronologists could say 'which' volcano caused the effects they observed. Pyle's argument was that because 'big' eruptions (VEI more than 4) are 'common', then either the ice-core acidity and/or the tree-ring effects could have been caused by any one of a potentially large number of volcanoes; thus, to pick out Santorini was, in Pyle's view, unjustified. While this is self-evidently true, nevertheless, we do know from radiocarbon evidence that Santorini erupted close to this time. It is undoubtedly the best-dated eruption of the period and the only one categorically known to fall within a century of 1628 BC. So, irrespective of frequencies, Santorini has to be a front candidate for involvement with the eruption which caused the environmental effects in 1628 BC.

However, Pyle failed to address the corollary of his own argument. If large eruptions occur at the rate of three per decade, then, on Poisson statistics alone, we could expect to have more than two (note, not two but more than two) large eruptions in a single year once every 250 years or so. So one natural consequence of 'large eruptions being common' is that from time to time several are bound to erupt simultaneously. Interestingly, although multiple eruptions are a logical consequence of frequent eruptions, the mention of such a phenomenon as a possible solution to the Santorini/ice-core conundrum is inevitably greeted as special pleading. It is useful therefore to note that in a recent review Chester (1988) cites Budyko's view that 'if four large eruptions are taken as representative of the past 100 years and this frequency of occurrence is assumed to coincide with the overall frequency throughout the Quaternary and, in addition, eruptions are considered to be independent events and subject to purely random variations in frequency, then . . . 40 large eruptions occur [in a] century, once every 10,000 years. Moreover, 130 large eruptions can be expected [in a century] once every 100,000 years and 100 large eruptions within five years once every million years.' So someone else believes in Poisson statistics and multiple eruptions.

The problem for the volcanologists is, of course, that their records are so poor that they have no good experience of multiple eruptions. One reason for this is the 'smearing' effect of radiocarbon dating – the technique most commonly employed by volcanologists to date their recent eruptions. The case is stated simply: if, for sake of argument, five large eruptions occurred in a single year, and each was dated by radiocarbon, it would be *absolutely impossible* to see that they had erupted at exactly the same time; their dates would be smeared over decades to centuries. This explains why volcanologists have never seen any sign of a simultaneous multiple eruption in the past. Put another way, because of the limitations of radiocarbon dating, potentially the greatest natural hazard on earth is effectively invisible to volcanologists.

To restate the issue: even if Santorini did not produce enough sulphur to account for the 1645±20 BC acidity layer (and there has to be a finite chance that it did) there must be a finite possibility that the discrepancy (between the estimate of the sulphur output of Santorini and the ice-core acidity) could be accounted for by the simultaneous eruption of Santorini and some other, unknown volcano.

Other candidate eruptions

This brings us to the question of other candidate eruptions. Vogel *et al.* (1990) have now suggested three other eruptions – Avellino (an earlier Vesuvius), an earlier Mt. St Helens (Y) and Aniakchak II (Alaska) – which, on the basis of radiocarbon evidence, may have taken place at about the same time [*sic*] as the Santorini eruption. In many ways this is the piece of information which introduces the maximum levels of flexibility into the whole debate. Originally Santorini was the only candidate eruption which might have caused the environmental effects at 1628 BC. Now Vogel *et al.* have raised the possibility that either

(a) one of these other eruptions caused the 1628 BC environmental effects, or
(b) some completely unknown eruption caused the 1628 BC environmental effects, or
(c) some combination of eruptions caused the 1628 BC environmental effects.

However, these new candidates should be viewed with some caution for the following reason. If Santorini, which has received massive dating effort, cannot be dated by radiocarbon to better than something like 1670-1530 BC, then it is extremely unlikely that the new candidates, on the basis of a few radiocarbon determinations, can be as well dated. Put another way, we know beyond reasonable doubt that, in dating terms, Santorini has to be considered as a candidate, but that is not necessarily the case with the new candidates. For example, if we look at the radiocarbon dates used by Vogel *et al.* to 'date' the Avellino (Vesuvius) eruption we find that their 'weighted mean date' of 3360±40 BP is based on manipulation of radiocarbon dates which actually range over 3240–4180 BP (op. cit. 535). However, one logical consequence of pushing other eruptions into the seventeenth/sixteenth centuries BC is to increase the chance that Santorini and some other large volcano erupted within a year or so. We should remember that there is at least some possibility that volcanic activity is not a purely Poisson process – look at Lamb's DVI indices for the last 500 years – and it is clear that rates of activity have altered with time. It may also be that large volcanoes have some inherent tendency to cluster because of some natural trigger (see, for example, Stothers 1989). So the case can be argued either way. More eruptions increase the possibility of simultaneous events, while non-Poisson processes might explain the apparent rarity of tree-ring/ice-core events (and presumably large eruptions) in the first few millennia BC.

Before leaving Vogel *et al.*, it is interesting to see how they have been wrong-footed by the new sulphuric acid estimates for Santorini. When they were producing their 'alternative candidates' paper they were, of necessity, using the 1985 Sigurdsson *et al.* estimate for Santorini of 4 million tons of sulphuric acid output. So at that time they could claim:

1) 'If aerosols from Avellino approximated to the very similar AD 79 eruption, they would have been predominantly sulphurous and three times more abundant than those from the larger Theran eruption', i.e. perhaps 12 million tons of sulphuric acid.

2) 'Mount St Helens Y may have yielded only half as much sulphate as Thera . . .', i.e. perhaps 2 million tons of sulphuric acid.

3) 'Aniakchak II could have produced sulphur emissions four times greater than Thera's', i.e. 16 million tons (Vogel *et al.* 1990: 536).

Now, with Santorini pushing up to perhaps 17 million tons of sulphuric acid (or maybe 20 million tons or even more?) it appears, by Vogel *et al.*'s own admission of the size of the other candidates, to be one of the biggest known sulphur-producing eruptions in the mid-second millennium BC.

Ancient history

Before attempting a solution to the Santorini puzzle, there is one last information source which needs to be assessed. With flexible archaeological, volcanological and ice-core evidence is there any chance that ancient history might help us to date Santorini? It is perhaps simplest to quote Manning's (1988) statement after Betancourt (1987):

> This significant dust-veil event . . . ought to have been reported in the Egyptian records of the earlier 18th Dynasty if it had occurred at the traditional date of ca. 1500 BC. There is no such record. This is an argument *e silentio*, but as the extant records for this period are very complete . . . the silence in the records is odd. An eruption earlier, in the Second Intermediate period, is less likely to have been recorded.

However, since that was written Davis (1990) has pointed out a description of a terrible storm in Egypt during the reign of Ahmose. If this 'storm' was a record of the effects of Santorini, then the conventional dating would be 'either between 1550 and 1528 BC or between 1539 and 1517 BC' (op. cit. 234). While this is undoubtedly a possible solution, unfortunately it would not provide a test of the Egyptian chronology. After all, if Santorini really did erupt in 1628 BC and if it were recorded in the reign of Ahmose, then Ahmose would currently be wrongly dated. In the same vein, even if some of the theories about the plague of darkness, associated with the biblical Exodus, do reflect some dim memory of the Santorini dust-veil, they supply no accurate chronology for the solution of the problem. So ancient history cannot supply the answer for the date of the Santorini eruption (though see Chapter 10).

Possible solution 1: The carefully worded statement

Given these various strands of evidence and the wide range of the arguments, it might seem that resolving the issue, in the absence of better dating of the Santorini volcano itself, is a near-impossibility. However, it has to be stressed that, just because there are many strands of argument, this does not mean that the 1628 BC possibility has been explained away; it may have been argued against, but it has certainly not been explained away. So, up to this point, had I been forced to write a conclusion, it would have been worded as follows:

> Patently no-one knows the true answer, but equally no-one can dismiss the possibility that Santorini, either alone or in combination with some other eruption, may have caused the 1628 BC environmental effects.

This would of course be the most attractive solution. It would allow the 1645±20 BC event, Santorini and the 1628 BC event to be compatible, thus wrapping up the story. Of course, part of the attraction of such a neat solution would be that it would give the dendrochronological date pre-eminence, while explaining everything with the greatest economy of argument. However, a more reasoned approach to the problem suggests a different solution.

Possible solution 2: The ice-cores and a possible solution to the Santorini problem

Since the true solution is not available, the Santorini problem has to be handled as a puzzle. Possible solutions have to be set up and tested. What follows is therefore an objective attempt to solve the problem following up on the question of the variable quality of available evidence. As discussed above, we can note how the acid yield of Santorini, based on direct physical measurement of the amount of sulphur degassed from the magma, has varied from 4 million to 17 million tons within just a few years. However, because they are based on physical measurements, it is hard to argue with these estimates beyond certain limits (though see below). In contrast, the ice-core acidity estimate *cannot* be so soundly based. So, we are entitled to ask, 'Just how good is the ice-core record?'

Let's briefly review the history of the ice-cores. The Crête core, from central Greenland, gave an excellent record of known volcanoes back to AD 553±3. The Camp Century core, from north-west Greenland, provided an extended record back, for something like 100,000 years, from AD 40; between the present and AD 40 this core was degraded. When the Irish tree-rings showed up the narrowest-ring events, listed in Table 5.2, this confirmed that the Camp Century record, for the prehistoric period in which we are interested, was indeed good within the quoted dating limits (Hughes 1988).

It was a surprise, therefore, to discover that in 1984 Hammer had published a somewhat damning revision of the Camp Century record: 'Out of the 18 highest acidity signals . . . [before AD 40] three moderately high signals had to be deleted, 4 signals had to be lowered somewhat and 7 signals could not be remeasured correctly due to bad core quality . . . one moderately high signal was higher than previously measured' (op. cit. 63). Fortunately, in this revision none of the layers which coincided with the tree-ring record was deleted. However, it was noticeable that one of the signals deleted was that at *c.* 5400 BC – a likely candidate for the Mazama

eruption when calibrated radiocarbon dates are taken into account. Yet Mazama is one eruption one really would have expected to show up in Greenland; for it to disappear is in itself sufficient reason to call the re-analysis into question. Also it was reported that, in this remeasurement attempt, the Camp Century core was found to be degraded between *c.* 1600 BC and *c.* 2300 BC – a critical point in time for anyone interested in the Santorini question. So these 'revisions' cast doubt on the Camp Century record and, as a result, everyone seems to have written off Camp Century. However, the tree-ring links, discussed in Chapter 5, suggest very strongly that Camp Century was basically sound.

This leads us to the third core, from Dye 3 in south Greenland. Dye 3 was hailed as a new and detailed record with the first important result being the AD 540±10 acidity layer reported in Hammer *et al.* 1980 (see Chapter 6). The really significant development with Dye 3 was of course the revised suggestion of Santorini at 1645±20 BC (Hammer *et al.* 1987), and, as we have seen, this acidity layer has given rise to considerable controversy. So the question about the ice-core record reduces to 'How good is the Dye 3 ice-core record?' It transpires that the Dye 3 core leaves a lot to be desired! There are no less than five worrying points about Dye 3:

1) The original AD 540±10 date was subsequently moved to AD 516±4 (Hammer 1984: 56). As discussed above, this is strange given the known occurrence of a major dry fog in AD 536.
2) In his 1984 paper, Hammer shows no significant acidity layers between 50 BC and 1645 BC which implies that this core records nothing significant at 208 BC.
3) Ditto, referring to the original 1120±50 BC acidity layer Hammer states 'no similar high signal exists in the Dye 3 core' (op. cit. 62).
4) Ditto, referring to the original 1390±50 BC acidity layer Hammer *et al.* (1987: 518) state 'no acidity peak is present in the Dye 3 ice-core at *c.* 1390 BC'.
5) With the importance of the 1645±20 BC acidity layer in the Dye 3 core, it is ironic that Hammer *et al.* (1987: 518) have to admit that 'the Camp Century acidity

record, was later found to be incomplete, in particular during the period 1600–2000 BC'.

So, from AD 550 to 2000 BC, with the exception of the acidity layer at 50 BC, there appears to be no replication of the Dye 3 ice-core record. This observation radically dents the credibility of the estimates of global acid fall-out from the Dye 3 acidity layers. How trustworthy is a particular global fall-out estimate, based on one spot on Greenland, when the same event appears not to be recorded at all at another, apparently reliable, spot? This lack of replication highlights some of the other comments associated with the ice-core work, such as '. . . the complicated depositional pattern caused by non-uniform washout by precipitation' (Hammer 1977: 482) and 'magnitude estimates . . . could easily be wrong by a factor of 2' (Hammer *et al.* 1980: 232) etc. The reason for raising these issues is to demonstrate that the ice-core record contains an element of flexibility which is well recognized by those working with that record.

Now how do we handle this information? One reaction would be to say that, because of the lack of replication, the ice-core acidity layer at 1645±20 BC should be ignored. After all, there appears to be no back-up to substantiate its existence and, on the basis of what happened to some of the original Camp Century layers, its permanence cannot be guaranteed. However, this sounds like special pleading from a dendrochronologist, so we'll drop that approach. The second reaction is to attempt to stand back from the debate and ask ourselves what we really know with any certainty about the ice-core record.

An attempt to be objective about the ice-core record

There are several things which we now know about the ice-core records which were not known until recently.

1) As above, we know that the Dye 3 record between 50 BC and 2000 BC is less 'good' than the Camp Century record for the same period.

2) We know that the acidity layers in the original

Hammer *et al.* (1980) paper were a relatively good record vis-à-vis the tree-ring record, see Table 5.2.

3) We know the petrologic acid estimate for Santorini does not agree with the ice-core acid estimate at 1645±20 BC.

4) We also know that the 1980 ice-core dating was surprisingly good. If we look at the centre points of the estimated dates of the major acidity layers and compare them with the tree-ring dates, we see that Hammer *et al.* were remarkably accurate – much more accurate than their errors would imply:

tree-rings 207 BC   ice-core 210 BC (±30)
tree-rings 1150 BC ice-core 1120 BC (±50)
tree-rings 3190 BC ice-core 3150 BC (±80)
tree-rings 4370 BC ice-core 4400 BC (±100)

The solution to this current problem may therefore offer itself as follows.

We momentarily set aside the 1645±20 BC acidity layer and pretend that Dye 3 never existed. Next, common sense, and points 1, 2 and 4 above, suggest that the original Camp Century core contained a very good acidity record. Perhaps, therefore, we should go back to a time before the Camp Century record was tampered with and downgraded. It has to be remembered that the Camp Century record was only called into question after an attempt to extract additional information from the deteriorating core in 1984. Since there is a lot of evidence which suggests that it was a good and comparatively well-dated record, the mistake may have been in abandoning it to the poorly replicated Dye 3 acidity record.

A quick search through the literature shows that the relevant section of the Camp Century record, from 1200 BC to 1850 BC, was published separately in 1980 (Hammer 1980: 369); **Fig. 7.3** shows the relevant section. In the original paper it was, of course, the 1390±50 BC layer which was highlighted. It seems to have been forgotten that there is, on this profile, a smaller acidity peak close to 1600 'BC' (ice-core date). Now, although the core was later claimed to be degraded, there is actually nothing to suggest that there was anything wrong with this original plot. Moreover, we know from (4) above that the

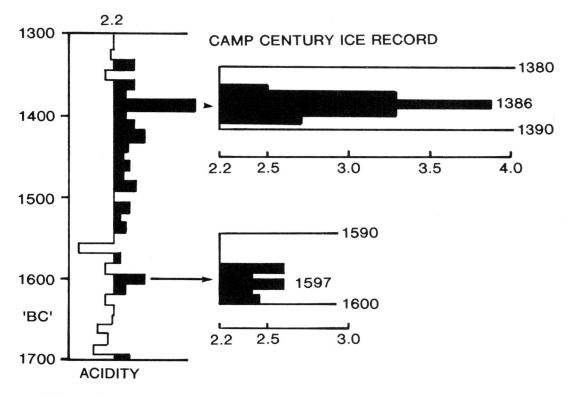

7.3 Acid record in the Camp Century core from Greenland (Hammer 1980), showing the 1597±30 BC acid peak in comparison to that at 1386±30 BC

dating was likely to be good to within about 30 years. Looking at the expanded section around 1600 'BC' it is clear that there were enhanced acidity levels for something like five years, specifically 1595–1599 'BC'. Here we have, in a proven ice-core, something which deserves at least a second look.

So how much acid fall-out is represented by this five-year enhanced signal around 1595–1599 'BC'? Here we are helped enormously by the original attention paid to the 1390±50 BC acid peak in the same core. Remember that Hammer et al. made the assumption that the 1390 spike was Santorini. They then estimated from its acidity that, if it was Santorini (applying suitable geographical factors etc.), it represented global fall-out of c. 125 million tons of acid (Hammer et al. 1980: 231; Sigurdsson et al. 1990, 106).

Again, referring to Fig. 7.3, it is clear that we can make almost direct comparisons between the 1390 'BC' and the 1595–1599 'BC' peaks. Both are from the same core, both are plotted against a background of 2.2µ equiv. H+/kg, both show heightened acidity over five years. In addition we are going to assume, as Hammer et al. did with 1390 'BC', that the 1595–1599 'BC' peak relates to Santorini. Doing this, we find that the enhanced acidity from 1595–1599 'BC' represents 30% of the acidity of the 1390 'BC' event. Since all other factors are equal, we can presumably work on the basis that this represents approximately 37 million tons of acid fall-out. Not only that, but, it is noticeable that between 1595 and 1599 'BC' there appears to be structure in the record (if we were to break this down year-by-year the acidity would appear to be running at between 5 and 10 million tons annually).

However, the final twist in this exercise relates to the dating. Because we know, from (4) above, how the estimated ice-core dates, used in 1980, relate to the tree-ring dates, we can estimate the correction necessary at points between the dated ice-core layers. Making the assumption that the ice-core layer at 1120 'BC' is the tree-ring event at

119

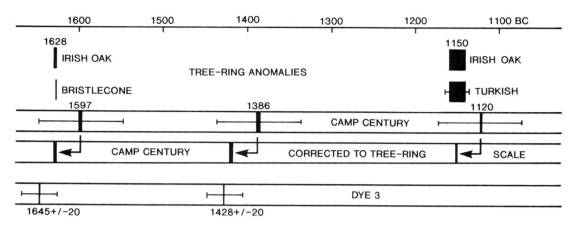

7.4 How the spacing of large acid layers in the Camp Century and Dye 3 ice-cores can be brought into alignment with the volcano-related tree-ring effects, by moving the Camp Century record back 30 years. This implies that this section of the Dye 3 record should move 15 years towards the present

1150 BC and that the ice-core layer at 3150 'BC' is the tree-ring event at 3190 BC, and given that all the acidities are in the same core, it is most likely that the five acid years (1595–1599 'BC') should move back by about 30 to 40 years and fall within a few years of 1628 BC. So a possible solution to the whole 'discrepancy' debate is an ice-core acidity layer, in a reliable core, suggesting acid fall-out – only a factor of two different from the estimated acid output of Santorini – at a date compatible with the volcano-related tree-ring effects of 1628 BC. It only remains to repeat again 'magnitude estimates . . . could easily be wrong by a factor of 2' (Hammer *et al.* 1980: 232) and QED.

Now I can hear the cries of 'special pleading' already – but there is worse to come. Imagine that there are just the two ice-core records and the tree-ring record. Consider the following:

1) In Camp Century, between 1350 and 1700 'BC' there are two notable heightened acidities which Hammer (1980: 369) places at 1386 and 1597 'BC'.

2) If we now return to the Dye 3 record for the same period we find that Hammer *et al.* (1987: 519) specify (using their own free will) two dates in the same period, namely, 1428 'BC' and 1645 'BC'.

3) We know from the links with the Irish trees that the Camp Century dates should probably be about 30–40 years older.

4) The spacing 1386–1597 is 211 'years'.

5) The spacing 1428–1645 is 217 'years'.

Taking points 3, 4 and 5 together, are we not justified in asking whether the 1645 'BC' acidity is actually the same event as the 1597 'BC' acidity, and that both are the same as the tree-ring 1628/7 BC event? **Fig. 7.4** illustrates the logic. Should we even be surprised that two different ice-cores might indicate different acidity levels? After all, if the whole ice-core process is so variable that Dye 3 can consistently fail to record large eruptions, why be surprised if it overestimates one?

So, was there, lurking in the ignored Camp Century record, the solution to the problem all the time? Is it the case that there is an acidity signal just at 1628/7 BC exactly as the tree-rings suggested? What appears to come out of this solution is that the connection to Santorini is the weakest link. However, the five years of enhanced acidity in the Camp Century record do not rule out Santorini as a candidate, though they may suggest something about multiple eruptions.

Out of all this comes one clear fact. The only fixed points in the whole affair are the 1628 BC Irish and the 1627 BC American tree-ring dates for a volcano-related environmental event. Whether these fixed points date the eruption of Santorini only time will tell. The Camp Century acidity scenario at least reconciles some of the issues. Currently, despite all the arguments, no-one can prove that the 1628 BC environmental event is not related to Santorini. The obvious solution is of course a 'high-precision wiggle match' on a tree which was killed by the eruption, if one could be found; alternatively Santorini tephra in the ice layers at 1645±20 BC would answer the question. What is abundantly clear is that without excruciatingly tight chronological control, reconciling volcanoes with their global effects is a virtual impossibility.

Two final twists

After this chapter was originally written, Mt. Pinatubo erupted in the Philippines (1991) and finally destroyed any belief that volcanologists could reliably estimate the amount of sulphur from ancient volcanoes. Pinatubo was the second anomalous volcano in a decade; the first was El Chichon in Mexico in 1982. Both of these eruptions, and the aerosols from them, were observed by the TOMS (Total Ozone Mass Spectrometer) satellite which could directly measure the amount of sulphur in the atmosphere. So no guesswork; volcanologists could visit the sites, collect magma samples, estimate the likely amount of sulphur and compare their estimates with the measured TOMS data. El Chichon rock analysis suggested an output of 23 thousand tons of sulphur dioxide, the satellite data suggested 2.7 *million* tons (Andres *et al.* 1991; M.J. Rutherford pers. comm.). For Pinatubo the figures were 0.3–3.0 million tons of sulphur dioxide estimated compared with 19 million tons measured – a factor of around 20 different (Bernard *et al.* 1991; M. J. Rutherford pers.comm.). The results were devastating and the implications for Santorini were quickly picked up by Sturt Manning (1992). Now all bets are off on the volcanological estimation of the real amount of sulphur put out by Santorini. It transpires that the only mineral which can give an accurate assessment of the amount of excess sulphur from an eruption is anhydrite, a soluble mineral which

is likely to be missing in ancient deposits. Who knows how environmentally effective Santorini may have been?

The second revelation came in a new 1992 ice-core paper. In assessing the new GRIP core from Summit Greenland, Johnsen *et al.* (1992) note that they can identify layers in GRIP which were previously identified and dated in Dye 3. They chose to note only three volcanic acid signals, in a very wide time-window spanning AD 900–6500 BC, the layers being at 49±5 BC, 1646±7 BC and 2050±10 BC. These ice-core dates coincide remarkably with the only three bristlecone frost events at 43, 1627 and 2036 BC originally cited by LaMarche and Hirschboeck (1984) and pretty well have to be the same events. If we take that as a reasonable suggestion, then, it is also clear that the three Dye 3 /GRIP ice-core dates are all slightly too old compared with these tree-ring dates and we can interpolate that a more realistic date for the original 1645±20 BC acid layer would be *c.* 1630 BC. So yet again, and this time on the basis of ice-core evidence, we can feel confident that the late seventeenth-century ice-core and tree-ring evidence is all pointing at the one event.

So the four main lines of counter-argument, against LaMarche and Hirschboeck's original suggested 1627 BC date, involving archaeology, sulphur, ice layers and other candidate eruptions, have all weakened since 1989. In effect, volcanologists have been forced to withdraw from the Santorini debate by the new lines of evidence. The volcanological aspects of the puzzle are no longer of any significance. The situation resolves itself to a volcano-related environmental event at 1628 BC and the question whether that event is related to Santorini. The archaeologists are still divided on the issue. The tree-ring dates haven't moved! It is also now clear that the only definitive solution to the debate will be the location and identification of Santorini tephra shards in one, or both, of the Summit cores and the temporal linking of these ice records with the tree-ring chronologies.

8 Socio-economic information from tree-rings

It is clear that it is the dating aspects of dendrochronology which provide the real strength of the method. The results are tangible: they are here and they are already solidifying the basic archaeological chronology in Europe in the same way that dendrochronology from the 1930s solidified the archaeology of the American south-west. Similar things can be said about some of the environmental aspects of dendrochronology and dendroclimatology. There are several distinct types of environmental information recorded in either the individual rings or in the ring patterns, as well as in such things as the history of tree deposition and regeneration. However, it is also clear that there is a whole spectrum of what might be called 'socio-economic' information which can be produced as a by-product of tree-ring studies, for example direct information on aspects of medieval trade.

Overall, in northern Europe, there seem to be a number of episodes where such things as sample depletion or increased felling activity tell us something about human activity over and above telling us when the episode occurred. This chapter seeks to document a series of episodes, indicated by tree-ring analysis, where we can add to existing historical or archaeological information. In some cases the results might have been expected, in others they appear to offer a completely new insight. It has to be stated that in many cases, just as it is not possible to ascribe a narrow ring to a unique cause, it is similarly difficult to infer particular historic circumstances from the tree-ring evidence. However, there are cases where sufficient circumstantial information exists to allow an educated guess as to the cause of a particular tree-ring phenomenon. The value of this type of tree-ring evidence lies in its ability to define and often refine the chronology of events, and in its ability to demonstrate the reality of historical events. What follows should be representative of the types of socio-economic information which are likely to become available from tree-ring studies.

Seventeenth-century building in the north of Ireland

In the early 1970s, when the Belfast oak chronology was being pieced together, timbers were collected from a range of early houses and other sources. These samples served a dual purpose in that they supplied ring patterns to build the chronology and in many cases provided precise dates or, where sapwood was incomplete, estimated felling dates for timbers from the structures. As tree-ring dates accumulated, there were hints, even on early plots of the results, that the dates seemed to respect the two major periods of political unrest in seventeenth-century AD Ulster – namely the 1640s and the late 1680s. The history of seventeenth-century Ulster is dominated by two major political episodes: the Rebellion of 1641, when the Irish attempted to drive out the English settlers who had been planted in the area earlier in the century, and the Revolution of 1688, when the battles, to decide the English succession, were fought out between James II and William III on Irish soil. It might be expected that at these times, associated with the loss of confidence and outright conflict, people would stop building houses; conversely, when conflict stopped and confidence returned, it might be expected that domestic building would recommence. So, seventeenth-century Ulster buildings would seem to offer a test of that socio-economic hypothesis – if enough examples with complete sapwood (i.e. exact felling dates) could be obtained.

Dated tree-ring records

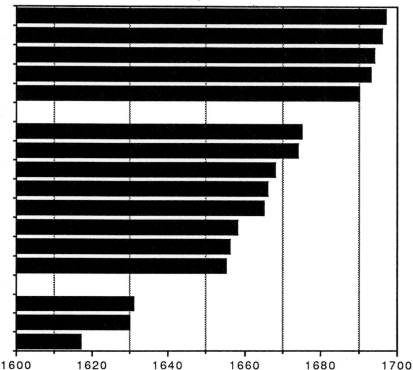

Date AD

8.1 Building phases in seventeenth-century Ulster as shown by accumulated felling dates. Periods of social unrest around 1641 and in the 1680s are reflected by pauses in building

Over the years, as further structures have been dated, we have accumulated those examples where the timbers retained complete sapwood. We now find we have some 16 felling dates from the century. As expected, they do show patterns of building activity following the known periods of unrest. When we look at the tree-ring dates (**Fig. 8.1**) we see, in this quite reasonable sample, no sign of building between 1631 and 1655 or between 1675 and 1690. In the period 1655–75 we have eight 'acts of building' and in the period 1690–1700 we have five. This is useful because it demonstrates that tree-ring dates can give a direct reflection of the results of human activities. We couldn't have told a rebellion from a revolution, but we could have noted, even in the absence of historical documentation, the pauses in building and inferred some sort of disruption at the correct times. The usefulness of this information lies in the confidence which it gives us to make similar inferences when we see

interruptions of building activity in the past, whether at the time of the Black Death, or in the Early Christian period in Ireland when we see, in the tree-ring evidence, considerable building activity in the periods AD 550–648 and AD 720–930 but none at all between AD 648 and 720 (see below).

Before leaving this seventeenth-century example it should be noted that the exercise only worked satisfactorily with timbers which retained total sapwood. Given the short interval between the two historical building episodes (about 30 years between the 1660s and the 1690s) and the fact that average sapwood on Irish oaks is 32±9 years, it is inevitable that sapwood is the limiting factor in deriving felling dates/ranges. Had the building episodes been further apart, say in excess of 50 years, then the building hiatus might have been detected even with incomplete wood samples.

123

The Black Death

A great deal of difficulty was experienced in attempting to build a chronology across the fourteenth century AD in the north of Ireland (see Fig. 1.8) (Baillie 1977a, 1979, 1982). Long ring patterns from timbers of the sixteenth and seventeenth centuries consistently ran back only as far as the later fourteenth century. Similar problems were encountered in the Dublin area where the medieval chronologies covered AD 855–1306 and AD 1357–1556 (Baillie 1977b); workers in Britain found similar problems. So it is possible to show, from tree-ring results, a clear picture of use of oak timbers up to the fourteenth century and regeneration from c. AD 1350. The original, and still current, suggestion is that the one-third culling of population due to the Black Death caused a hiccup in building activity and allowed a lot of marginal land to go back to forest – forest which would be exploited for building purposes in the succeeding centuries.

With the essentially routine use of dendrochronology to date buildings, dates continue to accumulate and it is now apparent that a detailed history of building activity around the fourteenth century can be demonstrated in a number of areas in Europe. **Fig. 8.2a** shows the building dates obtained by Hollstein (1980) in the western portion of Germany. **Fig. 8.2b** shows the distribution of building dates obtained in Greece by Kuniholm and Striker (1983, 1987). In both cases the number of buildings from the second half of the century is noticeably reduced.

To this we can add the observations of detailed dating in Lübeck, in north Germany, by workers from the Hamburg laboratory. In Lübeck they see broad phases of house construction. An early phase ends at AD 1350 after which there is an effective gap from 1350 to 1425 followed by a building episode from 1425 to 1500. Interestingly in the Lübeck local oak chronology they have been unable to find any tree crossing AD 1353 so that this year is effectively missing in Lübeck dendrochronology (S. Wrobel pers. comm.). Apparently there is also a change in the character of the wood in consequence of this hiatus. Up to c. 1350 most of the timbers are

Dated tree-ring records

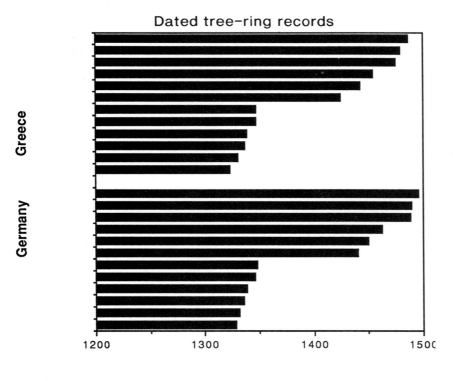

8.2 A simplified diagram showing the building hiatus in (a) Germany (Hollstein 1980) and in (b) Greece (Kuniholm and Striker 1983, 1987) just at the time of the Black Death. This diagram on its own would suggest a possible pandemic in the absence of history (Baillie 1993)

Date AD

long-lived and narrow-ringed. The buildings of the fifteenth century frequently use short-lived and wide-ringed material. This was noticeable in the original Irish work and has already been cited for the latest bridge building phase at Caerlaverock Castle in Scotland (Chapter 4) where timbers of the mid-fifteenth century were extremely wide-ringed and short-lived. It has been suggested that this wide-ringed material could be due either to rapid growth from existing root stocks (e.g. coppiced or pollarded oaks) or to growth in initial open conditions.

So tree-ring dates offer an opportunity to analyse geographically one aspect of the human response to the Black Death, as reflected in a significant hiatus in building, and a significant change in the nature of available timber. It is also interesting to consider whether, in the absence of written history, we might have been able to *infer* plague, in the mid-fourteenth century, purely from the tree-ring information? After all, there are a limited number of possibilities when it comes to interpreting an exactly synchronous building hiatus from Ireland to Germany to Greece; it would either have to have been some major, widespread, socio-economic collapse or a pandemic. When one adds in the second tree-ring suggestion, of regeneration of trees on marginal land, with the implications that that must have for population contraction, my feeling is that pandemic would be the only possible realistic interpretation.

A missing generation of oaks in Ireland

Having seen, in the case of both Ulster buildings and the fourteenth-century Black Death, that gaps in the building record are associated with problems for human populations, one is forced to become conscious of the whole question of 'gaps' in the chronology building process. The concept of a 'missing generation' of Irish oaks came about due to the difficulties experienced in completing the Irish chronology across AD 900 (Baillie 1979, 1982). As with other 'gaps', timbers could be found which grew up to the late ninth century and which grew from the late ninth century onwards. It proved impossible to find a suitable Irish link to

consolidate the chronology, i.e. there seemed to be no timbers available which had grown across AD 900. (It has to be remembered that to form a tree-ring link, long overlaps are necessary; so to bridge across AD 900 requires ring patterns which extend from c. AD 800 to c. 1000.) As it turned out, the problem was eventually circumvented by using English timbers from Exeter and London (see Chapter 1). However, despite the resolution of the problem, the fact remained that in Ireland no archaeological oak timbers have ever dated to the later tenth century. This was a piece of purely dendrochronological information.

The second part of the story came from the analysis of a detail in the tale of Mebd and Ailill in the Ulster Cycle. The detail is tortuous and is published elsewhere (Mallory and Baillie 1988); suffice to say that in an early rendition of the description of Mebd and Ailill's palace, attributed to the eighth century AD, it is called an 'oaken' house. In a later rendition of the same tale, in the ninth or tenth century, the description is materially altered when the palace is changed from oak to pine. In many ways this is a strange thing to do because pine is certainly rare in Ireland at this time (being effectively extinct in the north). The two lines of evidence, dendrochronological and textual, just possibly suggest some hiatus in the availability of oak. Allowing for missing sapwood the latest Early Christian structures had been built around AD 926±9. The next datable archaeological structure of any kind used timbers felled in AD 1033±9. Here then was a missing century in terms of site construction.

It was only when a diagram was being produced to illustrate this point, that all the available first-millennium tree-ring dates were plotted out. This produced two surprises. The known lack of buildings in the tenth century showed up quite clearly (**Fig. 8.3**). When the timber start-dates were also plotted, they showed a period AD 759–833 when no oaks had begun growing. Here, then, was a defined episode where to all intents and purposes we have a missing generation of oaks: no trees starting between AD 759 and 833 and none felled between AD 930 and 1030. From the point of view of a possible link with the textual evidence, we could now cite something happening to the overall oak population just at a period when someone writing a version of an earlier tale changes the text from oak to pine. Is it possible that we are seeing something along the lines of the following? There is intense building activity involving oak timbers between AD 720 and AD 840. Pressure of building activity, population pressure and animal grazing reach a point where few oaks are regenerating. Eventually, by around AD 900, the lack of oaks is so critical that people recognize the oak as a diminishing resource. Perhaps it is at this time that the laws were enforced which made the oak a valuable tree and prescribed the penalty for unlawful felling of an oak as 'the forfeit of two milsch cows' (Mitchell 1986).

Such an explanation would fit well with the wholesale felling of oaks which took place once the Normans arrived in Ireland in the twelfth century; the Normans would have felt under no obligation to respect ancient Irish laws. As with so much of the non-dating evidence, inferred from dendrochronological results, the case here is circumstantial. It is perhaps worth repeating a footnote to the original paper: 'The two lines of evidence, tree-ring and textual, were truly independent and the coincidence of the suggestions, implicit in both, argues that they may relate to a very similar, presumably the same, phenomenon' (Mallory and Baillie 1988). It is the fact of its complete independence that is one of the great strengths of tree-ring information.

However, while plausible, this scenario is only one of a number of possibilities which might be used to interpret the observations around AD 900. An alternative would be to add in further information to broaden the picture. For example, it can be pointed out that various German workers ran into problems when trying to extend their medieval chronologies back across AD 800. At various times the longest German oak chronologies ran back to AD 832 (Huber and Giertz-Siebenlist 1969), to AD 822 (Hollstein 1965) and to AD 820 (Becker and Delorme 1978). Similarly, before their chronologies were eventually linked to the present, Leuschner and Delorme (1984) had a chronology extending forward to AD 785 while Becker had a chronology extending forward to AD 755 (Becker and Delorme 1978). So, in Germany, an effective tree-ring 'gap' occurs just when we see intense building in Early Christian Ireland. In fact, this German 'gap' falls just at the time when we see the majority of horizontal mills being constructed in Ireland; of 27 dated mill sites which fall between AD 630 and 1222 no less than 15 (56%) were constructed with timbers felled between AD 770 and 850. This is an observation which may well suggest increased agricultural activity and pressure on land. So, the essential failure to find regenerating oaks around AD 800 in Ireland and Germany may be part of a larger pattern. The impression of 'something going on' around this period is compounded by the additional observation that in Ireland we have no oaks which were felled in the century between AD 930 and 1030. No mills have been found dating to this

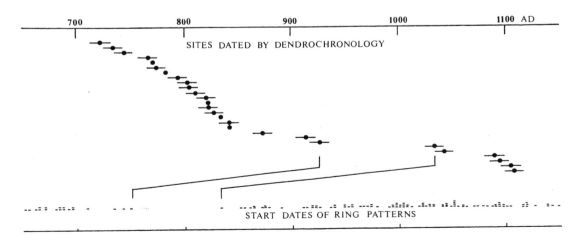

8.3 Plotting start-dates and felling dates for Irish oaks through time highlights a 'missing generation'. We don't find oaks which were felled between 930 and 1030 or which started growing between 750 and 820

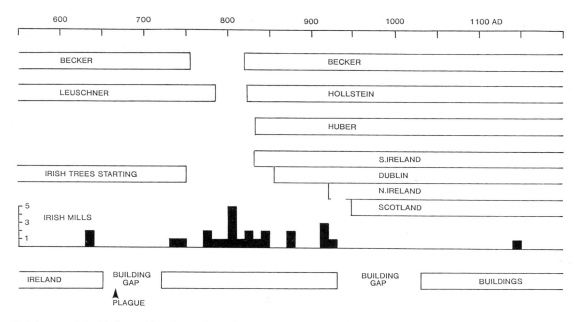

8.4 Accumulated information from chronology construction and the dating of Irish horizontal mills suggests population pressure and cereal production around AD 800. Later, a building gap and forest regeneration suggest reduced human pressure

century. In Germany, Hollstein (1980) also observed a building hiatus between AD 966 and 1030. This accumulated information (**Fig. 8.4**) suggests a picture of human activity around 800 and decreased activity after 930, with the widespread regeneration of oaks from the ninth century hinting at reduced human pressure and quite possibly reduced population.

A building pause in Ireland, AD 648–720

Arising directly out of the documenting of the missing generation of Dark Age oaks was an even more unexpected result. Numerous Early Christian sites had been dated during the construction of the overall Irish chronology. More had accumulated during routine dating for interested archaeologists. By 1988 when the dates were plotted to illustrate the tenth-century building gap some 43 dated sites or phases were available between AD 524 and 1107. When these dates were plotted, a dramatic break was obvious between AD 648 and 722±9 (**Fig. 8.5**). This had never been a tree-ring problem – there are plenty

of trees available which grew across the period, so it didn't show up as a 'gap' – but it does appear to be archaeologically significant. Why should people have stopped building (with oak at least) for about 70 years from AD 648 to 722? Did anything happen which might have led to a significant reduction in building activity? A partial answer may lie in several references in the annals for the period. From AD 664 ('the plague reached Ireland on the first of August') to 668 ('the great plague') there are four references to pestilence in five years. So, is this building hiatus simply an earlier version of the effects observed at the time of the Black Death seven centuries later? It would appear that it might well be. Now a purist might point out that the plague references fall well inside the 648–722 building gap and not at the beginning of the gap, as one would expect if the two phenomena are cause and effect. In fact, there is no reason to see this as a problem. The dendrochronologist is dealing with a small and quasi-random sample of all the buildings of the period; once this is realized, it makes better sense of the observations. We can even generate the hypothesis, for future testing, that as more Early Christian samples are dated in Ireland, the dates

127

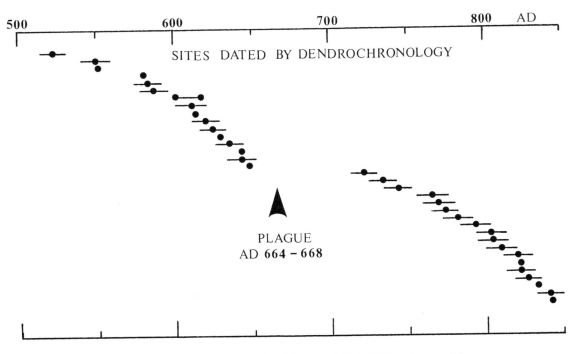

8.5 The notable hiatus in site construction in Ireland from AD 648 to 720 and a possible cause

of those samples should 'squeeze' the gap closer to its true (?) limits, i.e. we might expect with a larger sample to see the gap reduce to perhaps 660–90.

Plague

At this point the discussion can be broadened out to touch on the question of plague and ancient populations. We have already seen that the effects of the fourteenth-century Black Death are well reflected in the tree-ring record, both in terms of sample depletion and a reduction in building activity. We have also seen (Chapters 5 and 6) how the narrowest-ring event at AD 540 focused attention on the issue of plague following famine. From a European perspective the episode would have appeared as dry fog (AD 536/7), famines (late 530s) and plague (early 540s). This raises the question: is the close coincidence between a major environmental event and the spread of a pandemic in fact more than coincidence? Is this a case where volcano-induced famine, in some area of Asia, may have forced population movement

and allowed the disease to break out into the west?

Colin Burgess had already been arguing for the consequences of plague in the past to be taken more seriously. He had posed the question: if you can have a phenomenon like the Black Death once, why not several times? How do we know that there haven't been a series of catastrophic outbreaks of plague in the distant past? This is a concept which might have profound implications for interpretation of the archaeological record. Burgess drew attention to a possible third plague c. 1000–1300 BC at a time when, in his view, all the right conditions existed to allow a plague to spread just as it had done in the sixth and fourteenth centuries AD. In both the latter cases it was clear that trade and movements of people had helped the spread. So between 1300 and 1000 BC, when there was much long-range movement, Burgess believes similar conditions may have prevailed which could have allowed an outbreak of plague to sweep across Europe: 'The abundant contacts between the east Mediterranean world and barbaric Europe in the thirteenth–twelfth centuries BC are well known' (Burgess 1985:

218). Obviously this is a simplification of Burgess' arguments. There would be a complex of factors from population pressure to trade, from climatic change to warfare. What I wish to establish is that someone had already been discussing the possibilities of plague at the end of the second millennium BC. Our interest is in the question of environmentally effective volcanic dust-veils, tree-ring effects and plague.

Having set the scene, let us now review the issue from a dendrochronological perspective. We already know that the Black Death shows up in the tree-ring record – if only as a building hiatus (see above). Following up on LaMarche's 1627 BC suggested date for Santorini (Chapter 5), the dates AD 540 and 1159 BC turn up purely as narrowest-ring events with a strong circumstantial link to volcanoes. In the case of AD 540, it is noted that the tree-ring date impinges on a pre-existing package of information including famines and plague. On a closer inspection we find that the severe tree-ring effect starting at 1159 BC is nicely placed at the start of the Mediterranean Dark Age – broadly 1200–800 BC; a dark age so severe that it has led some scholars to postulate shortening world chronology by some hundreds of years to 'get rid of the problem' (James *et al.* 1987; James 1991). So here we have an earlier Dark Age coupled with a pre-existing suggestion of plague, again close to a volcano-related environmental event which affected the Irish tree-rings!

Given this 'package' of information, it seems fair to ask if there is any independent evidence that what happened in Ireland and Britain, in terms of upland abandonment, and middle to late Bronze Age transition, might just possibly have a plague dimension? Here we have to return to Warner's suggestion about the prehistoric Irish annals having a core of truth. In Chapter 5 we saw that, in Ireland, for whatever reason, a body of literature exists which suggests, with approximate dates, that several catastrophes had befallen the people of Ireland. One of these is 'AM 4020–4169 [1180–1031 'BC'] – plague . . . in which . . . perished . . . a countless number of the men of Ireland' (Warner 1990). Now of course there are many reasons why this may not be significant. We have already noted the difficulty in postulating a mechanism for the handing down of

the information and the criticism of Warner's interpretation of the original references. The mention of plague could just be a brand name for some general catastrophic happening; the whole thing may be no more than a cobbled-together fabrication based loosely on scriptural or ancient historical sources – an attempt by early Irish writers to compose a history for themselves. But there is another way of looking at this. It is just possible that, through a period just a little longer than that for which the New Zealand Maoris carried their oral traditions, some folk-memory of a devastating plague survived in Ireland. In Chapter 5 I listed the packages of information relating to dust-veil events. If we simplify those lists we can make the following comparisons:

c. 1159 BC	*c.* AD 540
Tree-ring event	Tree-ring event
Volcanic dust-veil	Volcanic dust-veil
Population collapse	Population collapse
Dark Age	Dark Age
Plague (?)	Plague

Maybe Burgess was on the right lines and plague should be considered more. As he has said, 'My hope is that prehistorians will now think more about catastrophic population disasters, and will re-examine some of their models with this possibility in mind' (op. cit. 216). The only novel addition to Burgess' original hypothesis is the concept of a volcano-related environmental trigger for the initiation of plague.

It is impossible to leave this discussion without posing the following question: if, and it is a big if, environmentally effective volcanoes triggered plagues in the twelfth century BC and the sixth century AD, why is there no obvious volcanic trigger for the Black Death of the fourteenth century? Intuitively there ought to be some sort of environmental trigger. Ironically, Zeigler (1970: 14), in his book on the Black Death, records events in the East which sound very like the environmental trigger:

in the East, hard by Greater India . . . unheard of tempests overwhelmed the whole province for the space of three days . . . on the third day there fell fire from heaven and stinking smoke which slew all that were left of men and beasts and burned up all the cities and towns in those parts. By these tempests the whole province was infected . . .

Perhaps something volcanic or tectonic was indeed involved in this pandemic after all. A new frost-ring event in foxtail pines from the Sierra Nevada in AD 1331 may just be a hint that this hypothesis needs further investigation (Tony Caprio and Chris Baisan pers. comm.).

Sourcing – ships' timbers and others

It will be obvious to anyone following the development of dendrochronology in Europe that progress has tended to be regional. Local chronologies were developed on the assumption that successful cross-dating was more likely at a local level. As chronology coverage developed, it also became obvious that cross-dating could obtain over considerable distances. Replicated chronologies from Ireland would match reliably with those from Scotland and England. English chronologies would match with the grid of German chronologies which in turn would match those from Poland and the eastern Baltic (an early example of stepwise cross-dating is shown in Fig. 1.11). Thus by the mid-1980s a completely integrated suite of chronologies had been created. At greater distances, for example from Ireland to Germany, or from England to Poland, comparisons between precisely dated chronologies showed that correlation values fell to near random levels. So clearly there was a fall-off in the matching component of the tree-ring signal with distance; though, even at long distances, some matching could be found for short periods or if the master chronologies being compared were very long.

It was also clear, as more and more chronologies were produced, that, although there was underlying consistency, there were undoubted regional differences. This raised the question as to whether timbers could ultimately be sourced. Might it be possible to compare, say, ships' timbers against a whole grid of chronologies and contour the results in order to indicate either where the ship was built or where the timbers

grew? Exactly such an exercise was attempted on some boat timbers from the Dublin medieval excavations in the 1970s. At that time there were still very few available chronologies and the ring patterns were compared with chronologies from Dublin, northern Ireland, Scotland, England and Germany. The results were interesting but disappointing. Most of the timbers dated easily, and gave highest correlation values, against the Dublin chronology (Baillie 1978b). The interest lay in the fairly conclusive evidence for boat/ship building in the Dublin vicinity but the results were nevertheless disappointing because it would have been more stimulating to demonstrate the presence of exotic craft. Later, in a repeat exercise with timbers from a large ship, from the Woodquay site in Dublin, it was again shown that the timbers matched best with the Dublin chronology (Baillie 1982: 239).

By the mid-1980s the picture had begun to broaden. As discussed in Chapter 3, once redated, the English (and Netherlands II) art-historical timbers showed every sign of having been imports from the Baltic (Baillie *et al.* 1985) and this was confirmed by their better correlations at the same date against a new Polish chronology constructed by Wazny (Eckstein *et al.* 1986). So exotic origins could be conclusively demonstrated purely on dendrochronological grounds. Indeed, in tree-ring dating exercises it is possible that difficulty in dating, coupled with signs of mutual exclusion, may be clues to exotic origins. Ironically these were exactly the indications given by the English art-historical chronologies: they were based on oak but there were severe dating problems and a whole debate on their 'different growth response' compared to known English timbers (Fletcher 1978a, 1980). There are other facets of the general problem of exotic timbers which should at least be raised. Let us imagine that an exotic timber turns up on an excavation in a well-dated context but is not recognized as exotic. It fails to date against the 'local' chronology. The archaeologist, who wants the refined dating provided by dendrochronology, asks, 'If I can tell you the likely date can you look for a match within this narrow time-window?' or 'Can you give me any correlation values around such-and-such a date?' Any 'date' coming from this sort of exercise would certainly not be

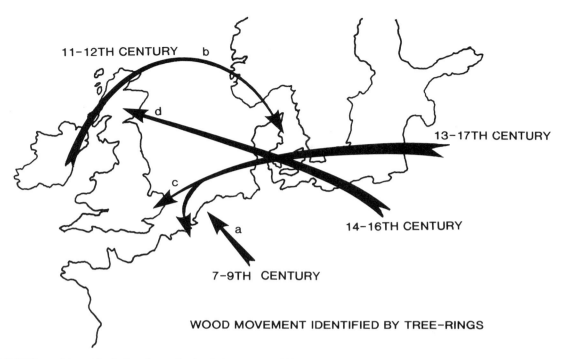

11–12TH CENTURY

13–17TH CENTURY

14–16TH CENTURY

7–9TH CENTURY

WOOD MOVEMENT IDENTIFIED BY TREE-RINGS

8.6 With a wide grid of site chronologies it is now possible to source timbers across northern Europe and to show concrete evidence of medieval trade in oak

an independent tree-ring date and, in this partic-ular example, dealing with an exotic timber, will probably not be a date at all. This is an extreme example used to illustrate a general point. Exotic timbers by their very nature are unlikely to date against chronologies in the locality where they are found. Such exercises inevitably lead to dendrochronologists examining the best of the non-matches; the trick is to avoid accepting these as dates (see Chapter 3).

We can now look at a few of the successes in tracing timbers to source. As early as 1975, Eckstein *et al.* had been able to demonstrate that timbers preserved in the medieval settlement at Dorestad gave every appearance of having been brought some 300km down the river Rhine. This study took the ring patterns of barrel staves from the Dorestad excavations, from levels of the eighth and ninth centuries AD, and compared them with 24 contemporary, local German chronologies. The resulting correlation values contoured beautifully and allowed Eckstein to conclude that 'the oak trees were used for making wine barrels in the Rhineland, which were shipped to Dorestad and after they had been

emptied [they] were sunk into the ground to function as wells' (Eckstein *et al.* 1984). Now the nice thing about this example, as with ships' tim-bers, is that it relates to timbers which are intuitively likely to be exotic. Barrel staves would always be suspected, because of their connection with trade, of not being native to the site on which they are found. The timbers themselves warn the archaeologist and the dendrochronolo-gist to be on guard. However, there is a twist to this statement. A critic could justifiably say that the dendrochronologist should not need to know the origin of the timber. If a timber isn't local it shouldn't date locally; that should be the clue for the dendrochronologist to test for dating against a wide grid of distant chronologies. Interestingly we have some excellent examples of timbers which originally failed to date 'locally' and which subsequently were shown to date against distant chronologies.

Two recent examples of just such cases are pro-vided by samples from the east coast of Scotland. In the late 1970s the chronology for south-cen-tral Scotland was published for the period AD 946 to the present (Baillie 1977c). Of the east-coast

131

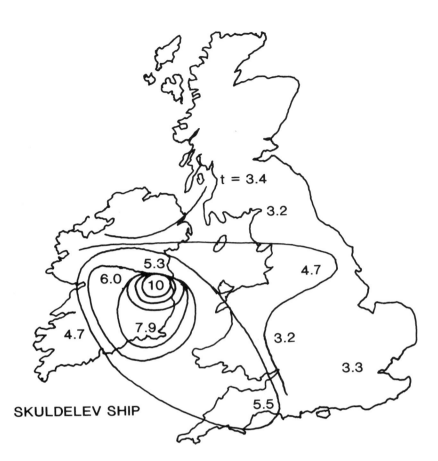

8.7 Correlation values contouring around Dublin, showing the undoubted Irish origin of the Skuldelev 2 ship from Roskilde Fiord, Denmark

buildings sampled in the course of chronology construction, timbers from two failed to date with the Scottish chronology or with each other. These came from Queen Mary's House in St Andrews and from Midhope Castle on the Firth of Forth. In each case the timbers were excellent and provided long, clear ring records. Their failure to date against the Scottish chronology was therefore both interesting and puzzling, and one obvious possibility had to be importation. When the art-historical problem was resolved with the re-attribution of the English art-historical timbers to the Baltic, possibly Lithuania, this again raised the question of the undated Scottish timbers. Unfortunately no definitive match could be found between any of the Scottish ring patterns and the art-historical reference chronologies. However, in 1990 we were kindly supplied with a copy of Wazny's Polish (Gdansk) oak chronology. Immediately the timbers from Queen Mary's House dated to AD 1286 ($t = 7.1$) and Midhope

dated to AD 1505 ($t = 5.3$). Here, apparently, was the solution to the Scottish east-coast problem. Oaks were being imported from the southern Baltic (**Fig. 8.6**). More interesting still is that we can be fairly sure that there are distinct differences between the sources supplying the English art-historical boards and those supplying the Scottish builders (as noted above, the Scottish timbers failed to match the art-historical chronologies). Indeed this division within the Baltic area could already have been suspected because the correlation value ($t = 6.5$) between the art-historical chronologies and the Gdansk chronology was really not high enough (with well-replicated chronologies) to ensure a common source. So sourcing is not only proving successful in terms of archaeological provenancing, it is also allowing a potentially better understanding of the tree-ring patterns from remote areas where local chronologies have not yet been constructed.

So far no specifically exotic timbers have been

identified in Ireland, with the exception of post-medieval beams and furnishings and some pine planks from Viking levels in Dublin – which presumably came from Scandinavia. However, by good fortune an example of long-distance Viking transportation turned up in 1989. Neils Bonde from the Royal Museum in Copenhagen was analysing one of the famous Roskilde boats. These ships were discovered in the 1960s and subsequent excavation showed that they had been deliberately filled with stones and sunk, probably in the early twelfth century to block the fiord and prevent marauding Norwegian Vikings from attacking Roskilde, then Denmark's capital. The five ships included two warships, two trading vessels and a fishing boat. Bonde was studying one of the warships, originally 30m in length and constructed of oak planks. Initial attempts to match ring patterns from the boat with German and Scandinavian chronologies produced no obvious dating. However, at some point it was suggested by nautical experts that there were characteristics of the ship's construction which might indicate an origin in the British Isles. Bonde therefore dug out the various published oak chronologies from Britain and Ireland and ran comparisons (Bonde and Crumlin-Pedersen 1990). Immediate high correlation values, up to $t = 10$, were obtained against the Dublin chronology (Baillie 1977b). The result was a flurry of publicity for dendrochronological sourcing:

> The ship was built of Irish wood in Dublin around 1060 and within the next 60 years it was sailed to Denmark. It may have been built to take part in mercenary raids organised by Irish Vikings along the coast(s) of Britain and France. It was presumably also used as a warship in the Skagerrak, the Kattegat and the Baltic. (Cooney 1990)

The chronology from the ship totalled 246 years spanning AD 778–1023 and felling would have been in the range 1055±9. This in itself raises interesting questions about the importance of Irish Vikings in the period after their defeat by local Irish forces at the Battle of Clontarf in AD 1014. Subsequent comparison of the ring patterns with chronologies from other Irish sources showed that the timbers matched best with the Dublin chronology and indicate that the ship probably derived from a source within 25km of Dublin (**Fig. 8.7**). One continuing puzzle relates to the ship's mast-step. This timber, with complete sapwood (which would have allowed precise dating) and a long ring pattern, failed to date against the Dublin chronology or indeed any other chronology; so the Roskilde story is not yet complete and it is possible that some future attribution may change some aspects of the story.

Ironically, from a tree-ring viewpoint, these timbers represent samples otherwise missing from Ireland. It was noted above how it had proved impossible to find any oaks in Ireland which ran across the 'gap' in the ninth century AD. Here were just such oaks – which in the mid-1970s would have completed the Irish chronology immediately had they been available – lying at the bottom of a Danish fiord (well, actually sitting in a Danish museum). These timbers fit remarkably closely the already observed 'missing generation' of Irish oaks between AD 759–833 and AD 930–1030 (Fig. 8.3).

Conclusion

Some exquisite dating examples now exist which shed completely new light on past human practices. For example, Bonde (1994) has successfully demonstrated that it is possible not only to date the construction of the ship used in the Norwegian Oseburg burial to around AD 820, but to date the actual burial chamber within the ship to the summer of AD 834, thus establishing that a nearly new, high-value ship was used in the burial rite. We can now look forward to the ultimate shipwreck studies where dendrochronology will allow us not only to date and source the ship's timbers but to date and source the timber cargo. I hope this chapter has demonstrated how useful information can emerge from all levels of the dating activity associated with chronology building and routine archaeological dating. Simply by accumulating the dates, patterns begin to emerge relating to periods when things were happening or not happening. Even these early results suggest that the overall story of the past tends to be punctuated rather than uniformitarian.

The importance of the information relating to trade is considerable, not just for tracing ancient trading patterns but equally because it demonstrates that dendrochronology as a discipline is capable of recognizing when tree-ring patterns *don't* match locally. We now know that if the 'English' art-historical chronologies, or the St Andrews or Midhope ring patterns had been forced to 'date' against chronologies from the British Isles, the resulting 'dates' would almost certainly have been wrong. So users of the method need to recognize that not every timber should automatically date; the power of the method is that, when it suggests a lack of correlation against local chronologies, that may be a perfectly valid piece of information about the piece of wood in question.

9 Environmental reconstruction from tree-rings

Humankind inhabits a planet which until recently seemed to be vast, benign and forgiving. This impression was fostered by the climate from the mid-nineteenth century to the mid-twentieth century which tended to suggest that environmental conditions were very stable. Milankovitch cycles and ice ages were on timescales so vast that they could be effectively ignored by beings whose lifespan and reproductive cycle could be measured in decades. So a couple of decades ago, if you asked the average scientist in the field what had happened since the last ice age you would be told that (a) it had been warmer (the climatic optimum) about 6000 years ago when temperatures had been perhaps two degrees higher than at present and (b) within the last millennium we had gone through an episode called the Little Ice Age when, perhaps, it had been 0.5 degrees cooler on average. This was the broad-brush approach. Of course, even for this recent cold episode, things were not well understood and both its length and severity were open to varied interpretation. Anyone wanting to get to grips with the topic of the Little Ice Age, which forms a good model for any study of environmental change, would be well advised to read Jean Groves' book *The Little Ice Age* (Grove 1988).

Overall, ideas about environmental change tended to suffer from poor chronological resolution: there were cool periods, warm periods, wet periods, often thought of in terms of change over centuries. Now of course things have begun to change. Everyone is gripped in the vice of the 'greenhouse' effect and projected world warming – concepts involving potentially rapid change. People now want to know how rapidly systems can alter: can humankind really change the entire climate system of the Earth on a timescale of decades or a few centuries? Anyone wanting the fuller story on greenhouse warming should consult *Climate Change* edited by Houghton *et al.* (1990). However, as noted above, the case is not yet proven. Although greenhouse gases are increasing it is not certain that the warming, which we certainly appear to be seeing, is directly related. Some workers believe that the current warming has more to do with changes in solar activity. This highlights the main problem for the environmental scientist. Attempts to study current change are hampered by the lack of good long-term records of natural variability. What were the maximum rates of change within the pre-industrial natural system, and what were the limiting extremes? Such questions are not all that easy to answer. The obvious approach is to look at the records of past environment locked up in ancient systems. There is a wide range of such records from actual historical documents to cores taken from the ocean floors, from Greenland ice-cores to lake sediments, from sections through peat bogs to tree-ring series. Although these records have already been widely exploited, the next decade will undoubtedly see major effort directed towards padding out the picture of the limits of natural change on all relevant timescales. Obviously our interest here is in the information available from tree-rings. Dendrochronologists increasingly find their data the object of intense interest. An environmentally responsive biological system with precise time-control is a significant resource.

Environmental records from tree-rings

It has always been obvious that there must be climatic or environmental information stored in tree-ring patterns; the very existence of cross-dating between patterns suggests the existence of a common, presumably climatic, signal. So, the year-by-year tree-ring chronologies can be viewed as the response of a biological system to prevailing environmental conditions. With the availability of tree-ring chronologies we can actually look at any period, in the last seven millennia or so, and see what trees thought of the conditions. This ability to look across virtually the whole span of humankind's history as a farming animal, at annual resolution, is destined to provide all research into the past with that essential environmental backdrop which has previously been missing from the story. As we have seen in Chapters 5, 6 and 8, by and large, in northern Europe (and certainly in the British Isles), when oak trees didn't like the conditions in which they were growing people seem to have had a pretty thin time as well. So the environmental story in the tree-rings is important for any better understanding of what happened to people in the past. The problem is how to extract the environmental information locked away in the tree-rings.

It has to be understood that there are clear divisions between attempts to reconstruct climate (which tends towards specific, instrumental style, information) and attempts to reconstruct environment (where information can be much more general and much less quantified, at least in the first instance). Unfortunately, extracting the recorded climatic/environmental signal is not straightforward, and so far, despite a great deal of expectation, only the surface has been scratched. In Chapter 1 there was reference to a failed prediction for the 1980s: 'It seems likely that between . . . widths, densities and isotopic ratios . . . it should be possible to make adequate reconstructions for the last thousand years . . .' (Baillie 1982: 250). Ironically, rather than being fulfilled, one could make the same prediction today looking forward to the next ten years. It is fair to say that there has been only limited success in the reconstruction of past climate information during the last decade. There is still a tendency to talk about the potential for climatic reconstruction from tree-rings rather than actual reconstruction. Why is this? In part it may be that research simply takes time; models and approaches have to be set up and tested, reconstructions made and verified – the 1980s have seen a good deal of this basic work. The slow start is also, to some extent, a function of the variable quantity and quality of the available tree-ring data.

It has to be recognized that tree-ring records are of variable quality. For simplicity we can look at modern records anchored at the present. At one extreme there is the record of a single tree. Next there is the site chronology where the records of a number of trees from a small locality are 'averaged' for a common period. In concept the site chronology has the advantage of ironing out the 'noise' associated with individual trees and concentrating the common 'signal'. Site chronologies can be extended into grids of chronologies – chronologies from different sites which cover some common period. Most recent research on temperate climate reconstruction has moved away from the study of single trees or single chronologies to the analysis of widespread grids of chronologies. Grids can be created for Britain or Europe or America, or even the whole northern hemisphere. Very large grids will, of course, cross species boundaries and may well be highly variable in time depth. So far a lot of progress has been made on the establishment of a widespread 'modern' or 'living tree' grid: hundreds of modern chronologies exist. Virtually all such areal, or grid, studies have as their primary aim the reconstruction of some aspect of the existing instrumental record.

Unfortunately, as soon as we step back in time the situation changes significantly: grids, in the sense of site chronologies, break down. In relative terms there are only dozens of medieval and Dark Age chronologies and only a handful of long prehistoric chronologies. So, overall, there are both quantitative and qualitative differences between the modern chronologies and the long historic and prehistoric chronologies. The principal problem is that most of the long chronologies were not built with climatic reconstruction specifically in mind. They were mostly built as outline chronologies, aimed at creating a firm chronological framework against which to date things. With living trees we know that the 'recorder' has been permanently in the one geographical position and this limits the number of variables. Once we move to the long, composite chronologies, with overlaps from living to ancient timbers, we have to recognize that the response of the trees may have altered with both time and site. This is particularly important when modern tree-ring patterns are calibrated against observed climatic variables. Do those calibrations hold up when we try to interpret the information from ancient chronologies? To give a hypothetical example, if we take oaks from a well-drained modern site and establish a good relationship between tree-growth and temperature/rainfall, can we be sure that the same relationship obtains when we move to look at archaeological timbers whose precise origins are unknown? Worse still, what chance is there of this calibration holding up for oaks which grew rooted on the surface of peat bogs? It is this type of problem which has so far limited the use of the individual long chronologies. However, this is where grids of chronologies may supply better results. If it is possible to produce good calibration relationships between climate variables and grids of chronologies, and if these relationships are sufficiently robust to overcome changes in response, then we may have a way forward.

In this chapter we will look at four themes of environmental reconstruction including some more tangential ways of deriving environmental information from dendrochronology. The approaches are:

1) To read off some specific tree-ring parameter as a direct indicator of some past phenomenon, e.g. fire-scars, moon rings, small early vessels, etc.
2) To measure some physical property of individual growth rings in the same way that measurement of carbon-14 concentrations allowed reconstruction of past variations in radiocarbon concentrations in the atmosphere.
3) To perform regressions between tree-ring data and climate variables in the hope of forming predictive relationships.
4) To use a 'proxy' or indirect approach wherein parameters such as periods of tree abundance, episodes of growth initiation or synchronous tree death are used to *infer* environmental change.

The fourth approach might equally be called 'inferred environmental information'. In this latter area we can deduce that certain things happened in the past because of their effects on factors such as tree-survival rates, dying-off phases, etc. Initially they take the form of little more than hints. However, even preliminary investigation shows that some of them may well

be significant environmental time markers and suggests that more careful analysis may provide some significant insights into the time of occurrence and duration of past environmental change. So this type of proxy information is currently one of the few with direct implications in the prehistoric period. As such, it is perhaps the approach with the greatest relevance to archaeology. In fact it might be justifiable to claim that it is the type of information most useful to archaeologists.

To give an example, an archaeologist might see an episode of abandonment or an apparent act of colonization – evidence for significant going or coming by human populations. Given the nature of most archaeological chronology, the dating of the 'event' is probably no closer than one or two centuries. In such a case the archaeologists, in the first instance, are hardly going to be interested in the May temperatures or even the decadal pressure patterns (were they available). They are much more likely to be interested in whether, around the general period, any significant change occurred which might have some bearing on why people migrated. A major dying-off phase in bog oaks, at about the right time, might, in the first instance, be more useful than the annual weather. If from such juxtaposed information a scenario could be constructed for testing then it might be useful to know something about summer temperatures, growing seasons, etc. We will look at examples of each approach to environmental reconstruction below.

1 Direct indicator approach

One attractive line of research is the identification of some specific phenomenon in a tree-ring record which is directly attributable to a specific set of environmental conditions. With such direct causal relationships it would be possible to search back through even single-tree records and read off the years when the phenomenon occurred. It turns out that this procedure works quite well with some types of environmental phenomena. One of the most straightforward cases relates to the identification of fire-scars as a means of tracing the role of fire in forest history. In North America, where fire history has been studied extensively, records can be carried back for hundreds or even thousands of years. Plots of fire frequency against time then show periods when fires were rare/common (Swetnam 1993). This proxy information can then be compared with environmental and archaeological information in order to separate out natural from man-induced change.

Other phenomena include 'light rings' in subarctic conifers. These light rings are defined as 'light coloured due to incomplete latewood cell wall development' and their occurrence has been related to abnormally cool summers (Yamaguchi *et al.* 1993). We have already looked at the similar case of the frost-damage rings in upper tree-line bristlecone pines (Chapter 5) with their implications for the dating of past episodes of extreme cold within the western United States. In this context, we should note that although the specific cause of the bristlecone frost damage is self-evident, the same cannot be said of the narrowest rings in Irish oaks. These effects can only be classified in general terms such as 'conditions severely detrimental to oak growth' and could be due to a range of effects from severe cold to physical damage to waterlogging, to chemical poisoning, etc. So interpretation of specific phenomena in European tree-ring records is by no means straightforward. This is well exemplified in the case of an anomaly in European oak rings, known as 'small early vessels' (SEVs).

These anomalous rings make themselves obvious in that the hollow vessels, formed at the beginning of an oak ring in April to May, are abnormally small – diameters perhaps 0.06mm, or less, compared to the normal 0.12mm. These vessels fall below the resolving power of the human eye and the ring therefore appears as blurred or indistinct. The phenomenon tends to be rare, certainly in oaks in the British Isles, with only a few trees exhibiting such rings; indeed even those trees which exhibit SEVs may only exhibit one or two in a lifetime of several hundred years. So SEVs can be spotted fairly easily and it would be attractive if they could be related directly to some climatic variable. Existing literature from the Soviet Union (Bolychevtsev 1970) suggests that such rings are associated with severe frost causing damage to the growing tissue. Interestingly, Fletcher (1975) did observe

very clear and consistent SEVs 17 years apart, in the years AD 1437 and 1454, in many of the oak panels which he used in the construction of the, supposedly English, art-historical chronologies.

These observations were out of line with most other work in the British Isles, where no obvious SEV consistency has so far been observed. Indeed, this unusual feature served as a clue that the oaks concerned were probably not of English origin. The situation was resolved and the SEVs better explained when it was demonstrated that the oaks in question had come from the eastern Baltic (see Chapter 3). Despite that false start, even in the temperate British Isles it may be worth checking to see if there are areas, or periods in the past, in which SEVs are genuinely more common, as a clue to extreme conditions. One excellent example of an SEV, which appears to link to a historic reference, is in the growth ring for AD 1861 in an oak from Cadzow in central Scotland. In this case the spring vessels are only 25% of normal size and the effect is so severe that ray tissue is also disrupted. Jones (1959) cites a reference to oak being 'the only indigenous deciduous tree to suffer notably from the severe weather of Christmas 1860', which seems to be evidence for a link between this Scottish SEV and the previous cold winter in Britain. Unfortunately, few trees show the effect in this year and it seems possible that the presence of the SEV may register no more than a single night of extreme cold, or wind chill, in a single exposed individual. The SEV anomaly, even if a little problematic, does require proper analysis as their precise dating does give them an immediacy which increases their significance. Overall, the identification of various forms of damage or anomaly in tree-rings can enhance our understanding of extreme events in the past.

2 Physical measurement approach

The scientific community successfully calibrated the radiocarbon timescale by measuring the radiocarbon activity in consecutive samples of wood from all periods of the last nine millennia. So there is now a continuous record of past variation in the atmospheric concentration of radiocarbon (Pearson and Stuiver 1986; Stuiver and Pearson 1986; Pearson *et al.* 1993). Although initially produced for correction of archaeological radiocarbon dates, this record is now regarded as a useful proxy record of past solar variation. Although not overtly climatic, the radiocarbon to solar activity to earth climate relationship has led to attempts to compare the past radiocarbon variations with proxy climatic records deduced from glacial activity (Wigley 1988). (This attempt ran into the inevitable problem that the radiocarbon variations were based on an absolute tree-ring chronology whereas the glacial information was based on the radiocarbon chronology – exactly the same problem as observed with attempts to date volcanoes in Chapter 7.)

In addition to the radioactive carbon isotope, there are several isotopic ratios which can be used for climatic study, including the stable isotopes of carbon, hydrogen and oxygen. Unfortunately, isotopic studies have a somewhat checkered history. The ratio of oxygen-16 to oxygen-18 in wood cellulose in theory holds the best hope for temperature reconstruction. One early study on German oak produced a reconstructed temperature curve so similar to the Central England Temperature curve as to be almost unbelievable (Libby *et al.* 1976). Unfortunately other workers were less than convinced (Wigley *et al.* 1978), and no attempt appears to have been made to extend the record into the distant past. The controversy remains and oxygen isotopes in tree-rings are one of the great underexploited areas of climatic research.

Libby *et al.* also measured hydrogen/deuterium ratios and discerned a warming trend during the nineteenth century. Those results are borne out by Epstein and Krishnamurthy (1990) who measured the same ratios in trees from 23 different geographical locations and found very consistent agreement over the same period. Epstein and Krishnamurthy also reported carbon-13/12 ratios in growth rings and suggested quite strong and consistent climate signals, basically confirming the earlier observations of Mazany *et al.* 1980. So the potential for detailed, widespread measurements of oxygen, carbon and hydrogen stable isotopes seems considerable especially when coupled with the existence of precisely dated, 7-millennia-long, tree-ring chronologies from a

number of areas. Perhaps the pressure from environmental scientists will make stable isotopes as important in the next decade as radiocarbon was in the last.

Another physical parameter which has been widely favoured in studies on conifers in Europe and America is maximum late-wood density. This is taken to represent a relatively clear temperature record (Schweingruber *et al.* 1979; Hughes *et al.* 1984). The potential of the method is well exemplified in recent reconstructions of summer temperatures in Fennoscandinavia (Briffa *et al.* 1990; 1992). In this work a linear regression equation relates summer temperature to both ring width and maximum late-wood density in current and succeeding years. The resulting reconstruction, back to AD 500, is the longest so far reported at annual resolution. Their main initial conclusion was that, for Fennoscandinavia at least, the prevailing views on a centuries-long Medieval Warm Epoch followed by the centuries-long Little Ice Age did not seem to hold, i.e. initially they failed to see any long-term warm and cool trends; most variability in their record was on a scale from years to decades. However, in the later paper (op. cit. 1992), by employing a different standardization procedure to the same tree-ring data, they were able to reconstruct some centuries-long trends while retaining the short-term variability in their record – an example perhaps of the difficulties associated with attempting these pioneering reconstructions. Nevertheless, the overall results do seem to prove a useful summer temperature record. As it is a proxy temperature record, it is interesting to compare it with the completely independent, temperature-related, record produced on pines from the Sierra Nevada by Scuderi (1990). Sections from both records are shown in **Fig. 9.1.**

As is inevitable in reconstructions from different limiting environments the reconstructions are not identical. It is, however, interesting to see how the American record does broadly duplicate the Fennoscandinavian record from 1100 to 1700. In particular it shows good agreement in 'the cycle of temperature change that occurred in the twelfth century (cooling to *c.* 1140, rapid warming to *c.* 1160 and subsequent cooling)' (Briffa *et al.* 1990). What is perhaps most inter-

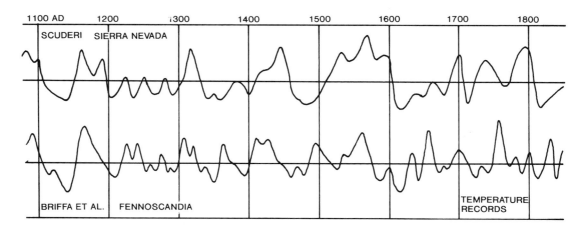

9.1 Smoothed temperature reconstructions from American and Fennoscandinavian temperature-sensitive pine chronologies, showing interesting levels of similarity from 1100–1730

esting is the fairly radical disagreement in the later part of the record, especially around 1760. This demonstrates many of the potential dangers for reconstructions which depend on modern calibrations. However, as more and more long records become available it may be possible to circumvent such problems.

One other approach, with particular relevance to pollution studies, involves the identification of trace elements in tree-rings. The uptake of heavy metals by trees can allow workers to date the onset of various effects subsequent to the Industrial Revolution. Mining and smelting are two industries which have been observed to leave significant traces of Fe, Ti and Zn in the rings of adjacent trees; similarly Pb from petrol allows assessment of the environmental impact of road traffic. Techniques used in the identification process include neutron activation, X-ray fluorescence and atomic absorption spectrometry (Kairiukstis and Kocharov 1990). Of particular interest, in the light of Chapters 5, 6 and 7 in this book, is the potential for the further study of ancient volcanic dust-veils. It may prove possible to identify the date of uptake of elements such as Fe, Ti, Cu, Mn and Zn mobilized in the soil by acid fall-out from volcanic eruptions (Leavitt 1992).

Overall, the potential in both isotope, density and trace element studies has to be considerable. Unfortunately their impact on archaeological understanding has so far been minimal. The 1980s have really seen no more than a few pilot projects. The contrast between this lack of progress and the massive effort put into radiocarbon calibration work is interesting. Why was one isotope so massively favoured over the others? Perhaps it was a reflection of the lobbying power of the archaeological community – in search of better chronology. On that basis it should be the turn of the environmentalists in the 1990s.

3 Grid approach

Ideal situations for climate reconstruction are clearly those areas where growth is limited by one principal climate variable; reconstructions of rainfall in the arid American south-west was where dendroclimatology started. Unfortunately, in temperate areas such as Europe, simple reconstructions are unlikely to be successful. The preferred approach in Europe, following the lead of Fritts in America (1976; Fritts *et al.* 1979), has been the establishment of wide spatial grids of tree-ring chronologies and their regression on to climate variables such as temperature, rainfall and atmospheric pressure. The obvious complexity of regressing large grids of tree-ring data with large grids of climatic variables has led inevitably to some simplification of approach, admirably stated by Briffa *et al.* (1983) in their explanation of Fritts' procedures:

They have used a transfer function approach where a set of dependent variables or predictands (such as atmospheric pressure at each of several locations, or the loadings on principal components of pressure patterns) is related, using canonical regression techniques, to a multivariate set of regressors or predictors (ring width series from a network of sites). (op. cit. 234)

This type of highly mathematical approach, applied to large grids of data, has so far been restricted to the study of modern chronologies. In part this is because of the need for large numbers of chronologies, something not yet available for the distant past. It is also because most of the existing studies have involved attempts to verify reconstructions against existing instrumental records. Most of these exercises have been successful in showing that regression equations can produce reconstructions which account for significant proportions of the variance in the climatic data. Examples include reconstructions of English temperature and rainfall from a grid of 14 mostly British Isles chronologies (Briffa *et al.* 1983) and atmospheric pressure from a similar grid (Briffa *et al.* 1986). With more chronologies it becomes possible to undertake major experimental exercises. Briffa *et al.* (1987) used a grid of 75 modern chronologies to attempt 'a series of exploratory reconstructions of European mean-sea-level pressure variations [over Europe] encompassing a number of . . . seasons . . . back to 1750'. Their results were markedly good at reconstructing the known pressure patterns for

the most extreme years but much less good for the remainder.

One example of this relates to the year AD 1816 when the northern hemisphere suffered the consequences of the Tambora eruption of 1815. Both Fritts (1976: 471) and Briffa *et al.* (1987: 52) reconstructed pressure patterns for this year, and their combined results show something of the effects of the dust-veil event on the hemispheric circulation pattern in that extreme year (**Fig. 9.2**). Note that this indicates, as Kelly and Sear (1985) have pointed out, how low pressure tends to occur over the British Isles in the years following large eruptions and possibly helps to explain why the Irish bog oaks appear to record such events (see Chapters 5, 6 and 7). It seems reasonable to assume that the current mathematical approaches will be refined and new approaches will be developed given the availability of the chronologies and the instrumental records. However, there seems little urgency to attempt long-term reconstructions until dendroclimatologists can maximize their success in explaining climatic variance from the tree-ring grids.

As noted above, one of the major problems with attempting to extend such areal reconstructions back in time, beyond recent chronologies, relates to the different quality of the ancient chronologies. So, built into any long chronology will be potential changes in tree response to climate. Such considerations, in conjunction with the relatively small number of long chronologies, and the limited success in reconstructing climate variables, has so far inhibited attempts at long reconstructions. With this problem in mind, one

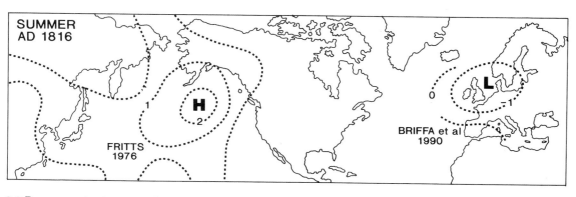

9.2 Two separate elements of the hemispheric pressure pattern for AD 1816 derived from grids of American (Fritts 1976) and European (Briffa et al. 1987) tree-ring chronologies

different approach to reconstruction has been tried. This sought to exploit the observation that in some years virtually all oak chronologies in northern Europe respond similarly – so-called 'signature' years (Baillie 1983b). For example, in 1890 over 80% of 39 oak chronologies, from Ireland to Denmark, registered a wider ring than the previous year. Similarly 1893 and 1898 were consistently narrow. Such signatures occur quite frequently and imply some strong controlling influence on oak growth over wide areas. Kelly *et al.* (1989) studied pressure patterns over northern Europe in the 20 signature years between 1868 and 1970 and were able to conclude that they had 'identified recurrent patterns of climatic conditions associated with [these] large scale signature years' (op. cit. 59). This could be important because signature years can be identified in ancient chronology grids with little regard for site conditions. Kelly *et al.* conclude that this 'suggests that climatic information could be derived from archaeological chronologies, which was previously considered prohibitive as trees . . . could not be accurately provenanced' (op. cit. 59). There appears to be hope on all fronts.

4 Proxy approach

There is no doubt, from the above, that tree-ring chronologies have considerable potential for the reconstruction of past climate. However, we do have to ask, at least in the first instance, just which sort of information is likely to be most useful. Climatologists would like to know about rates of change and extreme limits of variability. Archaeologists, as pointed out above, may have much more basic requirements. Climatologists would like quantitative data while archaeologists might be happy with something more qualitative. Climatologists would like to know 'how hot was the hottest decade in the last 10,000 years', while archaeologists might accept that 'around such and such a time there was a change from cooler to warmer conditions'. In many ways it is the question of 'change' which is of potential archaeological significance; the degree of change is of secondary importance to the change itself and can be the subject of more intensive study after the important periods have been identified.

So one approach, exemplified for better or worse in Chapters 5–8, is that we should be interested in phenomena in the tree-ring record which allow 'archaeological' style inferences to be made about environmental change. Such phenomena may provide markers in the record of the ancient past which at least point to periods where detailed analysis might be worthwhile. After all, so poor is our knowledge of past environments that any information is potentially valuable; so proxy information has a role to play. Furthermore, it is possible to make an early start; ideas about change, or extreme events, can be produced from existing data.

The types of information which we can glean immediately from the precisely dated tree-ring records relate to phenomena such as episodes of tree death, episodes of growth initiation, episodes of widespread depletion in the sub-fossil record and episodes of extreme growth reduction (presumably episodes of extreme growth enhancement would also be of interest). To give an example: if oak trees have been growing continuously on the surface of a bog for 1500 years and, suddenly, that bog no longer supports trees, then something has changed (**Fig. 9.3**). We can hazard a guess that the change was environmental and that it was detrimental for tree-growth; a useful working hypothesis might be that conditions became wetter or simply more variable. A qualification would have to be put in to separate local effects from widespread effects. For example, oaks dying out on a single bog could be explained by some local change in drainage pattern; if oaks die out synchronously on different bogs then we are probably seeing the effects of more general environmental change (Leuschner and Delorme 1988).

Once we have specified any environmental event, we can look for other precisely dated information with which to test our hypothesis. We can also pose the question of the likely effects of any significant increase in wetness, or variability, on early agricultural societies: if things are bad enough to wipe out oaks on bogs, how were things on dry land? We can then look to the archaeological record for signs of associated change. Unfortunately, most of the time, the current archaeological record (or the record of change provided by pollen studies) lacks the time-

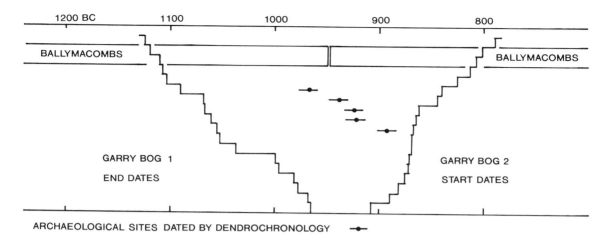

9.3 The decline of oaks across the tenth century BC at Garry Bog, Co. Antrim, plotted with the cluster of Irish archaeological sites dated by dendrochronology. There is a one-year gap in the Ballymacombs chronology at 948 BC

control necessary to make direct comparisons with suggested environmental effects derived from tree-rings, though that situation is bound to change as dendrochronology, high-precision radiocarbon dating and tephrochronology begin to put serious pressure on both archaeological and palynological chronology.

We saw in Chapters 5 and 7 how tree-ring studies drew attention to environmental effects in the 1620s BC. Interestingly, if we hypothesize increased wetness in the seventeenth century BC we already know (Chapter 2) that bog-oak systems which had been continuously regenerating on both East Anglian and Lancashire peatlands since 3200 BC, were interrupted some time after 1680 BC (Baillie and Brown 1988). So it appears that independent information can be drawn together to focus attention on specified episodes.

The remainder of this chapter looks at two case studies where environmental deductions can be linked, for discussion, with archaeological or palaeoecological information.

Case study 1: More on the 208 BC event

In Chapter 2 we saw how, during the construction of the Belfast long chronology, some thousands of sub-fossil oaks were collected from northern Irish bogs. It proved possible to construct continuous year-by-year chronologies from

5289 to 949 BC and from 947 to 229 BC. At 229 BC (197±9 BC estimated death date allowing for missing sapwood) bog oaks cease to be represented in the random collections. What happened? We now know about a major dust-veil event in 208 BC with effects lasting for several years (see Chapter 5). One aspect of this event relates to the observation of the initiation of a major phase of river gravel deposition around that time (Becker and Schirmer 1977).

The Becker and Schirmer case is particularly interesting from a dendrochronological point of view. They made a point of stressing a depositional phase of river-gravel oaks beginning in 226 BC: 'About 220 BC a renewed phase of flooding began to destroy the riverine forest . . . [shown by] 46 cross-dated trunks from eight exposures . . . [this was] obviously the most important horizon of [the] Holocene Main valley . . . simultaneously evident in the Main and Danube area . . .' (1977: 307). When this horizon was being referred to in the early 1980s (Baillie 1982: 236) no specific environmental event was known about, so the 226 BC date for the initiation of a flooding phase was not regarded as significant. However, with a 208 BC dust-veil event, with its implications for the demise of the Irish bog oaks around 200 BC, the date 226 BC from Germany takes on an added importance. Does it, as appears at face value, represent some sort of environmental downturn starting before the 208 BC event? If so the 208 BC

143

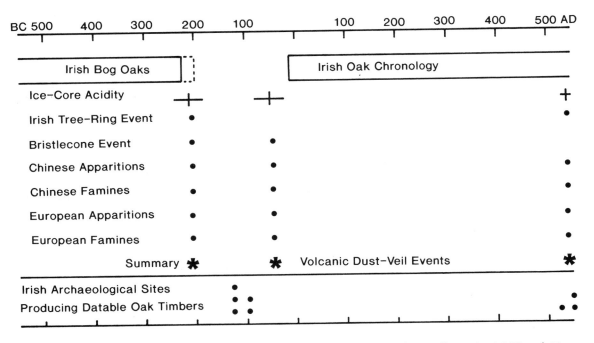

9.4 The 200–13 BC gap in the Irish bog-oak chronology plotted with the dust-veil events at 208 and 44 BC and the cluster of archaeological dates between 150–95 BC

event may simply be superimposed on some pre-existing change and the entire character of the event would change. The reason for raising this issue is because of the very high chronological resolution provided by dendrochronology and historical information; a few years become important in interpretation of events. It becomes important to know if Becker and Schirmer's depositional phase really started pre-208 BC.

One key element in their 1977 paper related specifically to the dating: '. . . the Iron–Roman Age tree-ring patterns have been dated absolutely, following their successful correlation with the ring-sequences of Roman oak bridges . . . (Hollstein 1967)' (op. cit. 307). So their ring patterns were actually dated against Hollstein's chronology. However, we know that until the late 1970s Hollstein had a 26-year error in his Roman-period chronology: he had mistakenly allowed the dating of his chronology, for the period before the fourth century AD, to be based on an historical reference to the bridge at Köln having been built in AD 310. By 1980 this error had been corrected by 26 years and his entire chronology before AD 310 moved forward by 26 years: a tree-ring date of AD 310 after correction

became AD 336 (Hollstein 1980).

So it seems that Becker and Schirmer's 226 BC initiation of a German flooding event, dated against Hollstein's uncorrected chronology, should be moved forward by 26 years and actually refers to an initiation in 200 BC. The deduction is borne out by contemporary comments by Becker and Delorme (1978: 59) and by a 26-year forward move of the River Main chronology (Becker 1985). So we now know that a '350-year depositional phase' was initiated immediately after the 208 BC event. This suggests some significant environmental trigger mechanism. It is interesting in this vein that Leuschner and Delorme (1988) also record a demise of oaks on two German bogs at essentially the same time. So, is the observed demise of bog oaks in the north of Ireland, and the north of Germany, together with the deposition of river-gravel oaks in central Germany, direct evidence for a climatic downturn which registered around (though not necessarily everywhere around) the northern hemisphere? Is the combined evidence sufficient to confirm that, after the 208 BC dust-veil, conditions in northern Europe became a lot wetter?

The possible archaeological significance of

these events becomes more apparent when we add in the other dust-veil event at 44–42 BC. **Fig. 9.4** illustrates the situation. It really looks as if the break in the Irish oak record is environmentally driven. Interestingly, David Weir, who has been undertaking detailed environmental reconstructions using pollen analysis in the north of Ireland, sees a 'period of general woodland regeneration, evident in the majority of Irish pollen diagrams' at this time and suggests that there must have been at least local 'large scale reductions in population' (Weir 1993). In this vein it is probably worth pointing out that there are also suggestions of higher lake levels in Europe and attempts to build long, prehistoric, pine chronologies in Fennoscandinavia have run up against a serious gap in the first few centuries BC (Keith Briffa and Penti Zetterberg pers. comm.). A coincidence?

Case study 2: An early Neolithic 'event'?

If we trace back slightly further in the history of the development of the Belfast oak chronology, there was a time, before its extension to 5289 BC, when the Long Chronology started at 3938 BC (see Chapter 2). Indeed, quite a lot of difficulty was encountered in splicing the extension on to the Long Chronology. It should by now be apparent that such chronology building problems are normally due to depletions in the number of available trees.

The date 3938 BC begins to take on some potential significance when, in the course of outlining the English prehistoric chronology (Chapter 2) it is discovered that in Lancashire it is possible to build a bog-oak chronology back to 3916 BC and another from 4023 to 4989 BC. Extensive random sampling failed to turn up any bog oaks crossing the period 4023–3916 BC. So in two areas, at around the same time, difficulties are associated with chronology construction using oaks which had grown on the surface of peat bogs! More interesting still, around the very period at which there is a depletion in bog oaks is a period when English tree-ring workers were able to find oaks from an archaeological site, from river gravels and from submerged coastal sources (Hillam *et al.* 1990). Overall, there is sufficient evidence to suggest an episode during which there was environmental change. We don't know anything about rainfall or temperature figures but the proxy data suggests real change. Now the interesting thing about this case is that we are able to bring in some archaeological information. It has long been recognized that the start of the Neolithic in the British Isles – the arrival of agriculture – took place somewhere around 3200–3000 bc (raw radiocarbon years). This suggests, taking calibration into consideration, that a major change in the archaeological record may have occurred in the British Isles around 4000 BC (calendar years).

In chronological terms, one way to look at this Neolithic arrival is to examine the radiocarbon dates which archaeologists received when they submitted samples from what they believed to be Neolithic contexts. Of course we could predict, without ever looking at the distribution, that there would be a statistical tail. After all, radiocarbon is, at best, a statistical process and even point events give rise to spreads of radiocarbon dates (Fig. 7.1). So, in order to look at the chronology of the beginning of the Neolithic, all the British and Irish Neolithic and Mesolithic radiocarbon dates, accumulated by the Council for British Archaeology up to 1980, were tabulated. These form a quite reasonable sample and they are plotted in **Fig. 9.5**. The problem for anyone trying to work with Neolithic radiocarbon dates *and* tree-ring dates is that the two are incompatible. It is extremely difficult to convert radiocarbon dates into any sort of useful real-age ranges without extending their ranges to the point of absurdity. However, with the availability of the high-precision radiocarbon calibration curve it is now possible to convert tree-ring dates into relatively tight ranges of radiocarbon years! At first sight this appears to be a surprising thing to do – to move from precise dates to less precise dates – but it is probably preferable to attempting to work with calibrated routine radiocarbon ages. This type of exercise, converting precise dates to tight radiocarbon ranges, could be aptly called 'de-calibrating' and it can be useful in some circumstances. So, de-calibrating the tree-ring dates, we can look at the proxy environmental information in terms of radiocarbon years and compare this with the archaeological radiocarbon dates.

145

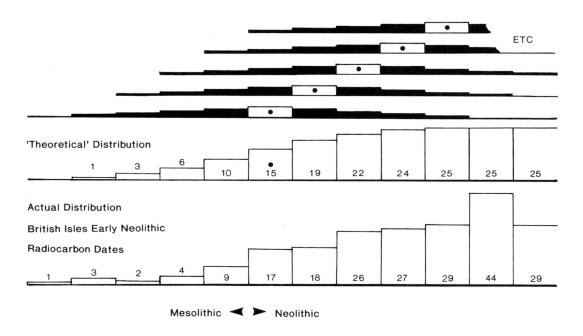

ETC

'Theoretical' Distribution

1 3 6 10 15 19 22 24 25 25 25

Actual Distribution

British Isles Early Neolithic

Radiocarbon Dates

1 3 2 4 9 17 18 26 27 29 44 29

Mesolithic ◄ ► Neolithic

9.5 The actual tail-off in Neolithic radiocarbon dates in the British Isles compared with a theoretical distribution, indicating a realistic start-date for the Neolithic around 5200 BP (raw radiocarbon dates). The distribution of Mesolithic dates tends to support this hypothesis (reproduced with permission of The British Academy)

One obvious question in this context is: when does the Neolithic in the British Isles start? Other workers have been seduced into belief in an 'earliest' Neolithic by the handful of very early radiocarbon dates for the Neolithic site at Ballynagilly in northern Ireland (Williams 1989) and by the occasional occurrence of cereal-sized grass pollen in pre-elm decline deposits (Edwards and Hirons 1984). None of this evidence is very convincing and if Ballynagilly were taken out of the equation there would be essentially no archaeological evidence for an 'earliest' Neolithic in the British Isles, i.e. in the absence of this early 'tail' the radiocarbon dates for the Neolithic would mostly begin around 3200 bc. To a non-believer in the early Ballynagilly dates, a different approach is advocated.

Although the 'tail' of Neolithic radiocarbon dates extends back to almost 5800 BP (thirty-ninth radiocarbon century bc), common sense and a realistic approach to the smearing of radiocarbon dates would suggest that the first serious Neolithic activity is around 5300 BP (thirty-third radiocarbon century bc). This can be justified by

crudely modelling the likely spread of radiocarbon dates from the first century of Neolithic activity and accumulating similar spreads from each successive century (Fig. 9.5). This approach can be justified on the strength of the eight-century spread of 90% of the 62 routine radiocarbon dates associated with the English Neolithic tree-ring complex (Baillie 1990a). The effect of such modelling is also shown in Fig. 9.5 and the fit to the observed distribution suggests that this approach is on the correct lines. It is interesting to note that the main cluster of Mesolithic radiocarbon dates ends around 5400 BP consistent with 'change' at that time.

In **Fig. 9.6** this simplified Mesolithic–Neolithic transition is indicated, along with the spread of radiocarbon dates for the (almost certainly synchronous) elm decline (Edwards 1985), the accurate 'radiocarbon' dates for the English bog oak 'gap', the Sweet Track and the original end of the Belfast long chronology. It may be an illusion but it is possible that in this figure we may be able to see the Neolithic colonization of the British Isles in an environmental context.

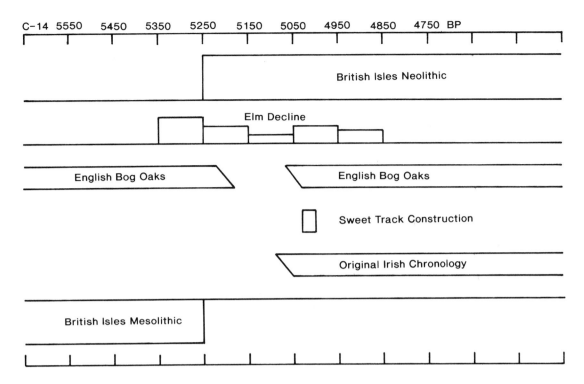

9.6 By plotting the dates of tree-ring gaps in radiocarbon years, and, from Fig. 9.5, plotting the Neolithic start-date at 5200 BP, it is possible to infer an environmental event at the start of the Neolithic (reproduced with permission of The British Academy)

Given the close proximity of something environmental happening at around the time of the colonization, the question then becomes whether the Neolithic colonization was prompted by some environmental pressure. It should be noted in this context that two German tree-ring laboratories also experienced difficulties in their chronology construction around 4000 BC (Leuschner and Delorme 1984, 1988; Becker 1985); so the environmental event, if there was an event, may have been widespread and extended in character.

What does this all mean? We have looked at two episodes where dendrochronology supplies not only time-control but hints of environmental change. Irrespective of the fact that we cannot quantify those changes in degrees centigrade or in millimetres of rainfall, we can assert with some conviction that there is more than a suggestion of both environmental and social change at these times. We can also reasonably ask what else was going on at the same times which might be traced in the archaeological record. Dendrochronology is opening up a new kind of window into the past and suggesting significant events which until now have been virtually invisible. We have looked at two examples here but, as we have already seen, there are others with every bit as much substance at 1159, 1628 and 3195 BC; obviously there must be others. At least some of these are periods of abrupt change and they raise the issue of marker dates, i.e. dates which may break up prehistory and which, by their very nature, might show up in different records (Baillie 1991a). They suggest that the concept of punctuated equilibrium requires further consideration in the archaeological record.

Conclusion

Having looked at the four basic approaches to environmental reconstruction from tree-rings it is clear that the issue could be simplified into two. Approaches 1 and 4 are both low-tech and might be classed as interpretive. In contrast, approaches 2 and 3 require sophisticated analyses, one or more steps removed from the tree-rings themselves. As discussed above, it is the interpretive approaches which can be plugged most easily into the archaeological system. The analysis methods, aimed as they are at the reconstruction of quantified, instrumental-style records are inevitably going to take longer to make an impact. These latter methods require detailed calibration and their results, whenever they become available, will be of most use to climatologists interested in amplitude and frequency of change. With the exception of the marker dates noted above, archaeological time resolution is such that instrumental-style records are currently irrelevant.

10 Problems with dating the Shang and the New Kingdom

The first nine chapters have covered some of the progress which dendrochronology has made since 1980. We have looked at chronology construction and at least preliminary exploitation of the chronologies for environmental and other information. Hopefully it has been demonstrated that dendrochronology has a major role to play in the elucidation of numerous aspects of ancient chronology. In this concluding chapter I shall look in greater detail at the dating of the New Kingdom in Egypt and the Shang dynasty in China as examples of the overall flexibility available in ancient chronology. The point of the exercise will be to explore how flexible all dating is once one goes back before c. 800 BC. One way to explore the level of flexibility is to attempt to move the chronologies a little, in real time, and gauge what happens. We can do this by introducing some of our dendrochronologically derived dates into the overall chronological equation.

The starting point is the second millennium BC and within it those two volcano-related environmental events, at 1628–1623 BC and 1159–1141 BC, which came out of the original narrowest-ring exercise with the Irish oaks (see Chapter 5 and Baillie and Munro 1988). We can define these events by showing what European oaks thought of the first episode and what Irish oaks thought of the second (see Figs. 5.1 and 5.3). These are the only hard facts in the whole of this discussion because, as the reader is by now aware, the dates are based on dendrochronology and hence we know the actual calendar dates of the two events. It is at this point that dendrochronology leaves off and ancient history and archaeology take over.

Until LaMarche and Hirschboeck published 1627 BC as a date, I had no information whatsoever relating to the seventeenth century BC. Similarly until the Irish trees threw up the extreme events in the 1150s and 1140s BC, I had no information on the twelfth century BC other than the reported ice-core acidity layer at 1120±50 BC. So all historical and archaeological information relating to the seventeenth and twelfth centuries BC is, as far as I am concerned, completely independent of the tree-ring dates. However, by 1990 it was possible to draw together several observations by other workers which relate to these two centuries (see Chapter 5). The information, when combined, suggests something rather strange. First we have the evidence from Pang and his co-workers relating to the dating of the Shang dynasty in China. Working on refining the Shang, i.e. attempting to tie down the start and end of the dynasty by astronomical retrocalculations, they arrived at the following suggestions (Pang et al. 1989):

Start of Shang 1600±30 i.e.1630–1570 BC
End of Shang 1100+80/-60 i.e. 1180–1040 BC

(These dates can be compared with the so-called 'traditional' dates for the Shang which is supposed to have had 29 kings and lasted 496 years from 1617 to 1122 BC (Chang 1980).)

This in itself is interesting. Why, if scholars of ancient China know how *many* emperors there were, has the dating become so vague? In addition, given that dating is regarded as precise in China back to about 841 BC, just where does the flexibility come in and why is the younger end of the Shang actually less well dated than the more remote start? However, those are questions for Chinese scholars. What interests me is that Warner (1990b), in extracting the major catastrophic events from the prehistoric section of the Irish annals (which, we will remember, are regarded as purely mythological by most workers), suggests that there are two events, in these early records, relating to the second millennium

BC. These are assigned to broad dating windows as follows:

> A catastrophe 'dated' within 1620-1544 'BC'
> A catastrophe 'dated' within 1180-1031 'BC'

The similarity of these dates to the dates suggested for the start and end of the Shang is astonishing given that the two systems of king lists have to be completely independent. There are three things about this similarity. The dates are not arrived at by picking from a list of possible dates; they are, in each case, the only dates of their type in the second millennium BC: the Shang has only one start and one end, while in Warner's opinion there are only two catastrophic references for Ireland in the millennium. Secondly, neither range was picked by me. Thirdly, we have to remember that the start and end of the Shang are specifically associated with records suggestive of dust-veil effects, i.e. summer frosts and failed crops, etc., leading to dynastic change (see Chapter 5).

In fact, if one wants to play around with these ideas, it is even more curious that, with respect to the seventeenth-century BC events, the Chinese talk about 'the floods were followed by a severe drought that lasted *seven years* [my italics] into the next [Shang] dynasty' (Pang *et al.* 1989), while the Irish annals note that 'This reign was followed by *seven years* [my italics] "without a king"' (Warner 1990b). All in all this appears to be a set of coincidences of the first order. Before going on to consider this further we should look at the other area of the world where an ancient history is based on a king list, namely Egypt. The ancient history of Egypt is divided up into dynasties, 31 in all, which are in turn blocked into 'Kingdoms'. From a recent source (Renfrew and Bahn 1991) these are as follows:

> Old Kingdom   2575–2134 BC
> Middle Kingdom 2040–1640 BC
> New Kingdom   1550–1070 BC
> Late Period   712–332 BC

What interests us here are the gaps between the various Kingdoms; these are rather woolly bits in the chronology and are termed Intermediate periods. So in Egypt in the second millennium BC there are two (again, only two) hiccups in the dynastic chronology:

> The Second Intermediate period
> (2IP) 1640–1550 BC
> The Third Intermediate period
> (3IP) 1070–712 BC

We don't have to go very far to discover that the Intermediate periods in Egypt reflect chronological problem areas: 'Unfortunately, the lengths of a good number of reigns are not completely known, *or are not known at all* [my italics], and in the Intermediate periods national unity breaks down with . . . lines of kings reigning contemporaneously,' (Kitchen 1991). Indeed it transpires that nothing is regarded as precisely dated before the Late Period.

So we can now look at three areas of the ancient world where scholars note both hiatus and dating difficulties. It should by now be obvious what is coming. This information is entirely from ancient history (plus astronomy in the case of China). But, we have already noted that dendrochronology, in conjunction with ice-core acidity evidence, has suggested two significant environmental events, related to volcanic activity, in 1628–1623 BC and 1159–1141 BC. We can now bring these four items together:

China	1630–1570 BC	1180–1040 BC
Ireland	1620–1544 BC	1180–1031 BC
Egypt	1640–1550 BC	1070–712 BC
Tree-rings	1628–1623 BC	1159–1141 BC

In the second millennium BC, in three areas of the ancient world, there is apparently hiatus at or around the times when it is known that there were environmental problems; moreover, environmental problems which, by their apparent volcanic nature, are likely to have been hemispheric in character.

Personally I wouldn't care to venture an opinion on this list (I might be biased). However, given the remarkable coincidence between these sets of dates, it can't be impossible that the events are cause and effect, i.e. the catastrophic natural events recorded in the tree-rings *caused* (or were somehow involved with) the hiatus in the various records. We can play this game by imagining that the environmental events did cause the problems in the various historical records, i.e. the events of 1628–1623 BC caused the collapse of the Hsia Dynasty and the start of the Shang; it caused the problems in Ireland and it caused the 2IP in Egypt. Similarly, the 1159–1141 BC event caused the collapse of the Shang, more problems in Ireland and the 3IP. Now, imagine that this scenario of cause and effect were true, what would it do to the various chronologies? At face value it would be perfectly acceptable in China and Ireland given their avowedly flexible chronologies.

This leaves Egypt. What would the ramifications be for Egyptian chronology if the 2IP *started* in 1628–1623 BC and the 3IP started in 1159–1141 BC? There would be no obvious problem at the older of the two events. Several recent authors indicate that the start of the 2IP is around 1640 BC (e.g. Renfrew and Bahn 1991) which at face value would suggest they could live with 1628–1623 BC as a possibility. However, as with all chronological issues, nothing is simple. Kitchen (1991) does not define the 2IP in the same way as Renfrew and Bahn; to the latter the 2IP is the fifteenth–seventeenth dynasties, whereas to Kitchen it is the thirteenth–seventeenth dynasties defined as 1786–1550 BC. This difference of opinion is explained as follows: when the Middle Kingdom ended c. 1786 BC the Egyptian-dominated civilization broke down and Egypt was gradually infiltrated by Asian intruders whose leaders were known as the Hyksos. 'The Hyksos formed two dynasties that ruled over much of Egypt between 1675 and 1567 BC' (Fagan 1992). So, the 2IP is not a neat package with an abrupt start, as far as ancient historians are concerned. However, from the point of view of whether an extreme environmental event at 1628–1623 BC would actually cause any major upset to current thinking on the chronology of the 2IP, it would seem that it wouldn't. At the other end of the New Kingdom there would be a much greater clash. Traditionally the 3IP begins c. 1070 BC, so there appears to be too big a gap between 1159–1141 and 1070 BC to allow that event to be involved in the initiation of the 3IP, or so it would seem.

However, if we stand back from what ancient historians *think* they know, there is a rather strange element of spacing involved with the Intermediate periods. The tone of Egyptologists is that the New Kingdom is really very well understood, i.e. it is a robust unit of chronology made somewhat flexible by the woolly bits at either end – the Intermediate periods. The suggested length of the New Kingdom is c. 1550–1070 (Renfrew and Bahn 1991). Or again 'The Hyksos were expelled c. 1567 BC. The Theban liberator and re-unifier was Amosis (Ahmose) (ruled c. 1575–1550 BC) . . . The total timespan of the New Kingdom . . . was nearly five centuries (c. 1575–1087 BC)' (Toynbee 1976). Fagan (1992) uses 1567–1085 BC. So people seem agreed that the New Kingdom was around 480–90 years in length. If we take the two independently dated tree-ring events at 1628–1623 and 1159–1141 BC the mean separation is of the order of 475 years (maximum span 488 years).

So, we have a robust ancient-historical chronology of approximately 480–90 years, bracketed historically by two Intermediate periods, and we have two independently observed environmental events, which we might expect to cause upsets, almost exactly the same distance apart. We know that the New Kingdom chronology unit is not precisely dated, i.e. it is to some extent floating (see Kitchen above). The question has to be asked: could the New Kingdom fit from 1628 to 1141 BC? While there will be howls from some ancient historians and Egyptologists, it is interesting that (apparently) completely independent work on the Shang dynasty sees it starting between 1630 and 1570 BC and ending between 1180 and 1040 BC, so their mean spacing is approximately 490 years and Pang and his colleagues have already pointed out those references to dust-veil phenomena at the start and end of the dynasty.

Moreover, in the case of the Egyptian king list we already know that the existing date system is not truly calendrical. To quote Kitchen, again referring to the likely errors in the Egyptian chronology, 'from about 30 years in 2000 BC, through 20/10 years by 1500 BC, to 11 years in the 13th century BC . . . dates come exact from 664 BC' (op. cit. 205). Here is an interesting concept for the student of chronology; a chronology which is *almost precisely dated*. How does one get to the stage where a chronology is almost precisely dated?

This is an interesting philosophical point. Are Egyptian scholars trying to say that they really know the error limits on the dates associated with their chronology? An outsider might reasonably be forgiven for thinking that if there is any error at all then it might not be limited to 'just a few years'. Why might it not be just a few decades? Why not 40 years or 70 years? We have to remember that the evidence for Egyptian dating is a complex package involving synchronisms with adjacent civilizations, astronomical retro-calculations, king lists, archaeological inscriptions etc. The real question has to be whether or not there is any circularity built into the arguments. Do the neighbouring chronologies merely feed upon each other? For example, Kitchen says, 'Given the very precise Mesopotamian dates available during 911–630 BC, and such dates accurate to within *a decade or so* [my italics] during the fifteenth to tenth centuries BC these correlations help to set closer limits for Egyptian dates' (op. cit. 204). This gives the impression that the Egyptian chronology depends on the Mesopotamian chronology – but does it? It is widely held that it is Egypt which is the yardstick for all the chronologies of the eastern Mediterranean; now it seems that it may be the other way round! This argument smacks of circularity and that could easily be the case if each chronology was constructed or fine-tuned looking sideways at the other, i.e. can we be sure that they are truly independent? The critical point is this: if there is any circularity in the dating of the Egyptian chronology, then the existing dating may be wrong and there may be no reason why the New Kingdom shouldn't move to conform to a 1628–1141 BC range.

The reason for raising this, as a non-historian, is that in chronological terms there are some interesting analogies between this ancient historical problem and a previous scientific-dating problem, about which we know a great deal. So we will now take a small chronological excursion into the 'absolutes' of chronology.

The concept of 'fixed points' in chronology

When a chronology of any kind is being constructed it would be ideal if there was some reference standard against which to either anchor or check it. Dendrochronologists recognized that there were not going to be any fixed points in pre-history against which to check their chronologies, which is why they underpin the chronologies with replication at three levels; independent chronologies serve to check each other. However, we can demonstrate the example of two scientific chronologies which lacked any absolute standard, namely the art-historical chronologies discussed in Chapter 3. These examples form an excellent parallel to the dating of the Egyptian New Kingdom. In the art-historical case, workers, having mis-identified the source of some oak timbers, were working with chronologies which were incorrectly dated. As was noted in that discussion, the English art-historical chronology cross-dated with the Netherlands II chronology, i.e. their correct relative dates were known, but different absolute dates were used for each chronology. The analogy with the Egyptian and Mesopotamian chronologies is that both the art-historical tree-ring chronologies were wrongly dated but their similarity, and the apparently good dates they produced, encouraged the erroneous belief that they must both be nearly correct. We have to remember that the art-historical problem was only resolved by reference to an independent standard, i.e. by cross-dating with correctly dated chronologies. The correctly dated chronologies served as the 'fixed point' to resolve the issue. Without some fixed point with which to date definitively the art-historical chronologies the system would have continued being wrong due to the circularity in the dating procedure used. That procedure could have allowed the chronologies to be wrongly dated by a considerable margin while appearing to be nearly correct.

It is to try to get around just such problems that Pang and his colleagues have been isolating those rare Chinese references to ancient astronomical observations, noted in Chapter 5. If they can really pin a reference in a particular year of a particular Chinese king to an astronomical date, then they have achieved a fixed point for that chronology. What Egypt lacks (at least so far) is any equivalent fixed point.

Attempts to provide fixed points for the Egyptian chronology

Sothic dating is the Egyptian equivalent of the Chinese astronomical retrocalculations, and in theory could provide fixed points in the Egyptian chronologies. It works, very briefly, as follows: the Dog Star Sothis was important to the Egyptians because, in July, just as the Nile flood rose, the Dog Star – after being invisible because it was too far south – 'first became visible again at dawn just before the rising sun swamps its fainter glow. This phenomenon is known as the heliacal rising of Sothis' (Kitchen 1991: 205). Because the Egyptians apparently used a year length of 365 days – as if the Egyptians, who were capable of running a major civilization didn't know that the year was very close to 365.25 days long – there are long tortuous discussions concerning the supposed 'fact' that the Egyptian calendar moved out of synchronization by one day every four years. If this were the case and if, for instance, the heliacal rising of Sothis occurred one year on 20 July, then it wouldn't occur again on 20 July for another 1460 years. Ancient historians, on fairly flimsy evidence, have decided that they can believe a report that Sothis rose heliacally on the Egyptian New Year in AD 139–42. They thus 'know' that this happened previously around 1313 BC. Now, if (and it's a very big if) Egyptologists could find an ancient Egyptian reference, in some year in the reign of some particular pharaoh, to a heliacal rising of Sothis in relation to a New Year, then they could compute the calendar year of the reference. At least, they could provided their base point is correct; however, that is not the only difficulty. Kitchen summarizes some additional problems, namely that such references are rare, are at best good to a four-year period, and depend on the geographical location of the original observation within Egypt (because the further south you are the earlier the star appears).

So, a good astronomical fix at any one year in the reign of any one pharaoh of the New Kingdom would do the trick and the robust chronology unit of the New Kingdom could be specified absolutely (well, within four years). However, were that the case, there would be no need for this discussion because the New Kingdom chronology would be fixed to a four-year period. It is fairly clear that the ancient historians have no fixed point which they can stand over, remember that Kitchen (1991: 205) says, '. . . through 20/10 years by 1500 BC, to 11 years in the 13th century BC . . . dates come exact from 664 BC'. This sounds very like the confident statements from the art-historical dendrochronologists 'of the dating to within ±1 years or at the most ±2 years there is no doubt' (Bauch 1978) and we know that they, largely by luck, were wrong by 4 or 5 years (Fletcher) and 6 years (Bauch).

Ironically, there would be a way round this whole problem if the date of the eruption of Thera was known, and if the Egyptians had recorded the consequences of the eruption in a particular year of the reign of a particular pharaoh. At a single stroke this information, if it existed, could potentially tie down a long section of Egyptian chronology. Of course we saw in Chapter 7 just how little agreement there is, at the minute, on the date of Thera; it may have erupted in 1628 BC *or* sometime between *c.* 1670 and 1530 BC depending on which of the arguments you happen to believe. However, there is no reason why, with sufficient application, the date of Thera cannot be confirmed; Renfrew obviously sees this as a possibility given his concluding prediction at the Thera III conference (Renfrew 1990). So, if we consider some future time when Thera is finally dated, it would only then be necessary to locate a definite mention of the eruption in Egyptian records and the Egyptian chronology would be tied down. Obviously, as was laboured in Chapter 7, there has to be a finite possibility that the date of Thera will be 1628 BC but that is not the main issue here.

Thera and Egypt

We can start with the question of whether we could reasonably expect that Egypt should be adversely affected at the time of significant volcanic events. Surprisingly there is some relevant information. Forsyth, in discussing one of two famines in the reign of Cleopatra notes:

> one of them occurring about 43–42 BC . . . at BC 4.61 (43 BC) we are told that Cassius had requested aid from Cleopatra; the queen, however, refused, claiming that Egypt was inthe grip of famine and pestilence. (Forsyth 1988: 54)

This is interesting because, in Chapter 5, we saw how there was a major dust-veil event at 44–42 BC. So here is a documented case of serious happenings in Egypt at the time of a known dust-veil. In fact, Forsyth goes on to make a useful synthesis of the likely cause of the Egyptian famines, by linking failure of the Nile floods to the consequences of hemispheric cooling. These are: failure of the spring monsoons in Ethiopia affecting the Blue Nile; failure of rainfall in central Africa affecting the White Nile, and reduced snow melt at the Mountains of the Moon in Uganda affecting the Albert system of the Nile. In summary: 'Clearly the Nile system would be deprived of water from all its sources should the monsoons and rains of Africa be eliminated or reduced' (op. cit. 56). But we already know that Handler (1989) has postulated that volcanic dust-veils trigger El Niño events which in turn can affect the whole monsoon system. We can also note that in the AD 536 package, the Justinian plague is said to have started (or first appeared) in Egypt in AD 542, following severe famines in the Near East (Rampino et al. 1988). So here we have a package of information which borderlines on suggesting that we should almost expect Egypt to be adversely affected by the knock-on environmental effects of a large dust-veil.

So, if Egypt is known to have suffered at the time of the 44 BC and AD 536 events, Egypt might well have been in the front line in the case of earlier, large dust-veil events, particularly if the eruption, in the case of Thera, was relatively close to Egypt. In fact, irrespective of whether the 1628 BC event is Thera or not, we do know that there seem to have been large dust-veil events in the 1620s BC and c. 1150 BC and we

can hypothesize that they may have had consequences for Egypt.

The next question is whether there is any record in Egypt of the consequences of a large dust-veil, Thera or otherwise. The answer, rather strangely, is that, not only is there one record of a possible dust-veil event, there appear to be two. The first 'possible' reference relates, of course, to the catastrophic events described in the biblical Exodus (Rampino et al. 1988); the second 'possible' reference is to 'a storm in Egypt during the reign of Ahmose' – the first pharaoh of the New Kingdom (Davis 1990). The latter possibility is relatively benign. Davis tells us that a fragmentary stele from Thebes 'documents a destructive storm accompanied by flooding' during the reign of Ahmose (op. cit. 232). If this were a direct reference to the Thera eruption, then since it appears to relate to a date before year 22 of Ahmose's reign, 'this would place the event either between 1550 and 1528 BC or between 1539 and 1517 BC . . . [which] . . . would support the traditional chronology' (op. cit. 234). This is a nice straightforward statement and the only remaining question is whether the record relates to a 'volcanic' storm or just an exceptionally severe 'ordinary' storm? It's a hard one to call; the fragmentary descriptions certainly suggest things were bad and the buzz words 'tempest' and 'darkness' do appear along with 'all that had existed had been annihilated' (op. cit. 233) – but is it a dust-veil? There are two ways to view this 'possible' record, either (a) it is not a dust-veil and it can be dropped from consideration, or (b) it is a dust-veil. If the record is of the Theran dust-veil then again there are two possibilities: (a) Thera erupted between 1550 and 1517 BC if we accept the traditional chronologies, or (b) Thera erupted in 1628 BC and the traditional Egyptian chronology is too low.

Here is a classic chronological dilemma. We started this section exploring the possibility of using the eruption of Thera to date the Egyptian chronology. Here we find the traditional Egyptian chronology being used to date a storm which might possibly represent the Theran eruption. If the reader reflects carefully on this issue, it will become apparent that this traditional approach betrays the underlying circularity of much ancient historical reasoning: of course dating the event against the traditional Egyptian chronology will support the traditional Egyptian chronology! That Davis supports the traditional chronology is evident from the following statement: 'major issues have been raised . . . regarding the validity of the scientific methods of evaluating the absolute date of the volcanic destruction of Thera. Until these questions are resolved . . . the evidence of the "Tempest Stele" deserves consideration' (op. cit. 234). This can only be read as an exhortation to date Thera against Egypt and preserve the traditional chronology unless and until Thera is proven to be earlier. So basically Davis, like Warren (1984), rather than consider the implications of a seventeenth-century BC date for the eruption would rather ignore the possibility and argue for the status quo until such time as the date of Thera is proven.

Yet, it is to try to break out of the danger of circularity that scientists want to use Thera to date Egypt. Given that there is even a possibility of the eruption being in the seventeenth century BC, the scientists are asking that the possibility be considered rather than ignored.

In a nutshell, traditional arguments effectively get us nowhere in the quest to try to date the New Kingdom. So let us move on to the other, less straightforward, 'possible' record of Thera in Egypt – the biblical Exodus. This possibility opens a veritable Pandora's box, because the question of the dating of the biblical Exodus was the driving force behind the great twentieth-century revisionist, Immanuel Velikovsky. Curiously, Velikovsky is usually ignored on this issue, although the rules of 'prior work' would suggest that he should at least be mentioned. Part of the problem is that people are actively uneasy about mentioning Velikovsky because of the danger of being somehow associated with his views. I have no such qualms because the European oak chronologies (and my own work) have been actively attacked by 'followers' of Velikovsky (see, for example, Newgrosh 1988, 1990). In fact, it is unlikely that a dendrochronologist will be a supporter of Velikovsky because the tree-ring chronologies, and the radiocarbon calibration curves based on them, prove that Velikovsky's basic thesis, on radically redating the Egyptian chronology, is impossible

(Baillie 1990c).

How therefore does Velikovsky fit into the arguments in this section? Velikovsky, in studying the Exodus, had asked the perfectly reasonable question, if the Exodus from Egypt was so important to the Israelites why is it not mentioned in Egyptian sources? He then proceeded to show that there are considerable similarities between the biblical Exodus story and several Egyptian texts, particularly the Papyrus of Ipuwer, the inscriptions on the el-Arish shrine and the Ermitage papyrus. Now the details of Velikovsky's arguments are not relevant here (because it is advisable to stay out of ancient historical arguments, particularly those conducted by Velikovsky), but there is no doubt that Velikovsky had read a lot of ancient history. What is rather strange is that his *Ages in Chaos* (Velikovsky 1973; originally published in 1952) contains the following statements in relation to the Exodus:

> The biblical story does not present the departure from Egypt as an everyday occurrence, but rather as an event accompanied by violent upheavals of nature. . . clouds of dust and smoke darkened the sky and coloured the water they fell upon with a bloody hue . . . wild beasts, plagued by sand and ashes, came from the ravines of the wasteland to the abodes of men. A terrible torrent of hailstones fell, and a wild fire ran upon the ground . . . blasts of cinders blew in wave after wave, day and night, night and day, and the gloom grew to a prolonged night, and blackness extinguished every ray of light. (op. cit. 10)

Obviously this draws heavily on the biblical Exodus story. However, it is Velikovsky's conclusion which is of interest (remembering that he was originally writing in 1952):

> If we . . . turn our attention to the many other passages in the various books of the Scriptures referring to the Exodus, we soon feel bound to make the unusual admission that, if the words mean what they say, the scope of the catastrophe must have exceeded by far the extent of the disturbance that

could be caused by one active volcano. Volcanic activity spread far and wide. (op. cit. 15)

So, from his reading of the texts, and (admittedly) because of his belief in extraterrestrial catastrophe, he sees the Exodus as happening at a particularly catastrophic time. But it is the time which is the most interesting. Velikovsky convinced himself that 'the Exodus of the Israelites preceded by a few days or weeks the invasion of the Hyksos' (op. cit. 45). Now there is a package to contemplate. It really doesn't matter about his reputation, or how he arrived at his decision, the fact is that Velikovsky, back in 1952, was arguing for major volcanic activity, involving Egypt, at the beginning of the Hyksos period! We are now considering, for completely different reasons – tree-rings and ice-cores and radiocarbon among others – whether Thera might have erupted in 1628 BC, how it might have affected Egypt, and we have already seen that some modern writers place the start of the Hyksos period – for whatever reasons – around 1640 BC. Not a bad effort on Velikovsky's part, to call a volcanic episode, affecting Egypt, within twelve years of a postulated volcanic event in the Aegean!

Now, yet again, the real problem is that it is impossible to use this sort of information to prove anything. Velikovsky was using the biblical Exodus, and volcanoes, and the Hyksos, as part of an argument to shorten the Egyptian chronology by some six centuries. So even if he called one aspect of the story fairly close his thesis overall was untenable. Important chronological issues cannot be resolved by such semantic arguments. It is scientific methods and chronologies based upon them which must eventually arbitrate on the issue of the dating of the Egyptian chronology.

So we have to conclude that the 'possible' references to the effects of Thera in Egypt are of no help in anything other than maintaining the traditional dating of the New Kingdom. Most sobering, from a chronological point of view, is Davis' (1990) statement that:

the 'Tempest Stele' cannot be precisely dated within Ahmose's reign, but it must have been erected before year 22 . . . . This would place the event either between 1550 and 1528 BC or between 1539 and 1517 BC . . . . Since the stele was erected to commemorate the repairs at Thebes, some time must have elapsed between the storm itself and the erection of the stele upon completion of the repairs. (op. cit. 234)

Here is an ancient-historical/archaeological record of a severe storm which may or may not be related to the Theran eruption. The storm lasted a few days. Davis dates this point event to some time in or before the range 1550–1517 BC. This extended range, of about 40 years or more, is unlikely ever to be improved upon, with the result that, even if Thera were precisely dated tomorrow, the storm record could never be definitively linked to the eruption. Imagine, for the sake of argument, that Thera had actually erupted in 1527 BC; would this confirm the stele? Or how about 1555, or 1580, or 1628, could any of these dates for Thera *ever* establish a link to Ahmose's poorly dated storm? The answer of course is no. Yet Davis is quite willing to state that 'the evidence of the "Tempest Stele" deserves consideration' (op. cit. 234). The fact of the matter is that the stele inscription can never be anything other than 'of interest'; it can never prove anything.

In contrast, the biblical Exodus at least has all the attributes of a dust-veil event (dust, darkness, hail, fish kill, undrinkable water, sycamores destroyed by frost, vines destroyed by hail, cattle killed by hail, flocks killed by thunderbolts, plagues of flies, water breaking out of rocks, the earth opening, etc. (Wilson 1985)) and its dating is only marginally worse than the range suggested by radiocarbon. Joseph – of seven years' famine fame – died 'before 1635 BC', whence appears Moses and the whole Exodus saga, dated 'before 1491 BC'. If that isn't saying that the Exodus was between 1635 and 1491 BC, what is? (This biblical span of 145 years is almost exactly the same as the calibrated radiocarbon range of 140 years: how's that for improvement in chronology since biblical times!).

I hope it is by now clear just how difficult it is to date anything pre-c. 800 BC with any reliability – other than by dendrochronology. The suggestion (made above on the basis of the similarity of the length of the New Kingdom to the spacing of the two volcano-related tree-ring events) that the New Kingdom would fit well between 1628 and 1141 BC, certainly cannot be ruled out by ancient history, because ancient history has serious problems of its own, both in terms of dating and in terms of the positive identification of events. Thera has to be a key issue in the whole business of ancient chronology, and really has to be dated precisely at some stage.

Conclusion

This discussion has strayed over a lot of ground, some of it very shaky indeed. However, it is possible to draw the discussion in this chapter together as a lesson in chronology and environment. It is clear that when we attempt to look at environmental change or abrupt environmental events in the past, we are continually let down by inadequate chronology. Everything, with the exception of the replicated tree-ring chronologies, is flexibly dated. Extensive labour on the dating of that most fundamental of ancient historical chronologies – Egypt – has singularly failed to provide absolute dates. The lesson of the volcanoes is that environmental events cannot be sensibly studied without firm chronology. So chronology needs to be improved on all sides. That is why this book is heavily weighted towards chronology, because chronology underpins our understanding of everything else.

Some of the tone of this book is necessarily pessimistic. There are problems: we can't date Thera (yet); we can't adequately date the Egyptian New Kingdom. However, there is some light on the horizon. Even though no definitive link can be substantiated between volcanoes and El Niño and Egyptian droughts and famines and plagues, the mere accumulation of this information does allow the formulation of some very interesting hypotheses for testing. If, as seems entirely plausible, a major volcanic eruption or several synchronous volcanic eruptions caused a major environmental upset in the 1620s BC, then we can set out to test whether, in reality, that event had serious socio-economic effects in both China and Egypt. If that could be

proven, it would weld together world chronology.

An interim note on the dating of the Shang Dynasty

It will, I hope, be obvious to the reader that the seventeenth-century and twelfth-century 'events' and their possible relationship to the chronological limits of the Shang dynasty are entirely outside the writer's control: 1628–1623 BC and 1159–1141 BC turned up purely from narrowest Irish tree-rings, while the suggested dates for China, Egypt and Ireland are derived from the published statements of other workers. However, it will also be obvious that one cannot force 496 years (one suggested length for the Shang) between 1628 and 1141. So, one has to be open to the possibility that the Irish dates may not be the answer. This became even more likely when Pang (1991) published further information on the end of the Shang. In a nutshell (according to Pang) there is clear evidence for environmental effects due to volcanic activity in the fifth year of King Chou (the last Shang ruler) who ruled somewhere around 1100 BC. As Pang states:

> Additional evidence . . . comes from a reference to a lunar eclipse that took place in the thirty-fifth year of King Wen, who lived one generation before Chou. This event has been precisely dated by astronomers, at January 29, 1137 BC.

If Pang, and indeed the astronomical fix, is correct, then the end of the Shang must be *after* 1137 BC. This would break the link between the Irish tree-ring event at 1159–1141 BC and the Shang termination event. Now such a situation is untidy: obviously it would have been nice if the circumstantially volcano-related events in Ireland could be linked to those recorded in China. However, in chronology one has to be realistic. As the evidence has accumulated it has become more and more clear that the 1628 BC event really was related to volcanic activity (because of the 1627 BC bristlecone frost rings and their increasingly definite relationship with the environmental effects of large eruptions and the new ice-core evidence suggesting that the 1645±20 BC acid

157

layer should in fact date close to 1630 BC, see Chapter 7). However, any such specific volcanic link was missing for the 1159–1141 BC event; the circumstantial case still existed but no smoking gun evidence (such as bristlecone of foxtail pine frost rings) had turned up.

It was with considerable interest, therefore, that on a visit to the Laboratory for Tree-Ring Research at the University of Arizona, in late 1993, I learned from Tony Caprio and Chris Baisan that they had evidence for frost rings in a new foxtail pine chronology, from the Sierra Nevada, at 1132 BC. Here was a marvellous revelation. We know frost rings are very good indicators of explosive volcanic eruptions; now we have frost rings at 1627 BC (LaMarche and Hirschboeck 1984) and at 1132 BC. From 1627 to 1132 BC is a total span of 496 years. So now we have tree-ring evidence suggestive of two volcanic events at exactly the right interval to fit *precisely* with one of Chang's (1980) prior suggestions for the length of the Shang, with its own volcanic evidence. Even more impressively, Chang has stated that the traditional start and end dates for the Shang were thought to be 1617–1122 BC; within a decade of the frost-ring dates in the American trees. It would seem to me that the Shang dynasty can now be dated 1627–1132 BC, *until proven otherwise*. So, we can see that the concept of the dating of the Shang by dating volcanoes has evolved from the original suggestion by Pang and Chou (1985), through the attempts with the Irish trees (Baillie 1989b), to a more plausible scenario with the new data of Caprio and Baisan.

Conclusion

In many ways people have been unprepared for the injection, into a predominantly radiocarbon-based chronological framework, of precise calendar dates; one immediate consequence has been the exposure of the inadequacy of routine radiocarbon dating. For example, in Chapter 7 we saw how attempts to date the Bronze Age eruption of Santorini, using radiocarbon, led to discussion of a range spanning approximately 140 years – for an eruption which undoubtedly happened within a few days. So we should be aware that other instantaneous events in the past may have gone unrecognized because the dating – mostly radiocarbon based – has smeared events into periods. Smearing has been an obvious danger for some time yet it is only now, with the yardstick of dendrochronology, that the extent of the problem is being made visible. Santorini was one example, the routine radiocarbon dates associated with the Neolithic Sweet Track form another; in this latter case 90% of the dates associated with the structure fall in a bracket of 800 radiocarbon years, making sensible appraisal of the true date of the track impossible (Baillie 1990a).

There is now the danger of a new chronological problem. This is the effect whereby the specification of a dendrochronological horizon tends to suck in loosely dated archaeological, environmental and even ancient-historical information. The danger, in such cases, is that the precisely dated 'event' may be used to explain a wide spread of previous, loosely dated, observations. A good example of the suck-in problem is offered by those events in the sixth century AD (see Chapter 6). We know there was a significant environmental event at AD 536–45. We also know that it is possible to compile a long list of things which happened within about 50 years of AD 536. It is also possible to invoke cause and effect, i.e. to suck in all the various strands of loosely dated evidence and suggest an economical solution, with the environmental event

causing all the archaeological and ancient-historical phenomena. This is a dangerous game because we could, if we are not careful, create an artificial horizon due to this sucking in of evidence. So smeared dating evidence can hide significant short-period events while precisely dated events, badly used, can conceivably create artificial short-duration horizons, by sucking in evidence (Baillie 1991b). These are chronological problems which have to be watched out for as dendrochronology increasingly rivals radiocarbon as a routine dating tool.

However, despite such warnings, there is no doubt that the last decade has seen some real progress in chronological refinement. As I hope I have shown in the last ten chapters, there is the possibility that we will eventually be able to link chronologies of various kinds from tree-rings to ancient histories, from pollen records to ice-cores. If we succeed we will start to make some real sense of the short-term changes in the later Holocene. The fact is that studies at annual resolution are effectively within our grasp. Having said that, one equally strong message from this book is that, currently, we know quite remarkably little about some aspects of our planet's recent history. Take Santorini: we still don't know exactly when it erupted or what its effects were. Take AD 536: was the dust-veil really volcanic? What was happening to the population of Europe in AD 538 or 539 or 540 or 541? What happened in Ireland in 1159 to 1142 BC to make some oaks, growing up to 300km apart, show reduced growth for *exactly* the same number of years? I could go on but these examples will suffice. The point is that, by and large, such specific questions are not easily answered; we simply don't know. This contrasts with the impression given by historians, archaeologists, geologists and even physicists, that we know a great deal about everything from the first second after the Big Bang right up to the present. In fact we don't know very much at all about short-term events, and yet this is a time when we are tinkering with the planet's atmosphere and planning a radical increase in the world population of people and cars within a few decades.

It will also have become apparent to the reader that, as soon as dendrochronologists start to date aspects of either human activity or environmental change, the concept of environmental determinism raises its head; there are strong hints of it in Figs. 5.4, 5.5 and 9.6 among others. So, although we've only started down the dendroclimatological road, there are indications that human populations are passengers on a system which is ultimately environmentally driven. Archaeologists and historians have allowed environmental determinism to go out of favour and have given people a quite possibly false impression of somehow being in control; when it is realized how little we know about the recent past, that comfortable feeling of control evaporates rather quickly. In this vein, anyone who still thinks we have a good handle on how the world has been, how it works and where it is going is referred to Clube and Napier's *Cosmic Winter* (1990). Even though written by people with a 'bee in their bonnet' about comets, its message is inescapable. In 1908 an extraterrestrial object exploded over Siberia with a force estimated at up to 30 megatons. If Clube's thesis is correct we should expect

a collision of several megatons energy to occur somewhere on Earth every 200 years or so . . . . a few dozen sporadic impacts in the tens of megatons, and a few in the 100 to 1000 megaton range, must have occurred in the past 5000 years. (op. cit. 246)

When we look at tree-ring patterns over the last 5000 years we see major unexplained changes. If even one of these was due to a 1000 megaton extraterrestrial visitor, humankind's view of the universe would never be the same again. Moreover, cometary debris is only one of a list of imponderables; we could add in other potentially catastrophic factors such as extreme solar variations, ocean outgassing, simultaneous large volcanic eruptions and interstellar dust clouds. The modern world sails on as if none of these phenomena exists, yet each could be a potential threat to civilization. The problem centres on the fact that scientists are forced to assume that nothing unpleasant has happened 'recently' because there is no evidence for any of these phenomena having affected human populations during the Holocene (apart from Tunguska). What I hope this book has shown is that there are huge gaps in our knowledge about the past; many events are invisible until properly dated. *Chronology is the key to better understanding and until recently there was no good chronology.* Now, dendrochronology, dendroecology and dendroclimatology have the potential to provide a much better understanding of world events in the Holocene. Who knows what future tree-ring research may reveal.

Finally, remember, the trees don't lie – and they were there!

Bibliography

Abram, A. 1909, *Social England in the Fifteenth Century*, Routledge, London

Alley, R.E., Meese, D.A., Shuman, C.A., Gow, A.J., Taylor, K.C., Grootes, P.M., White, J.W.C., Ram, M., Waddington, E.D., Mayewski, P.A. and Zielinski, G.A. 1993, 'Abrupt increase in Greenland snow accumulation at the end of the Younger Dryas Event', *Nature* 362, 527–9

Andres, R.J., Rose, W.I., Kyle, P.R., Desilva, S., Francis, P., Gardeweg, M. and Moreno Roa, H. 1991, 'Excessive sulphur dioxide emissions from Chilean volcanoes', *Journal of Volcanology and Geothermal Research* 46, 323–9

Apsimon, A.M. 1976, 'Ballynagilly and the beginning and end of the Irish Neolithic' in S.J. De Laet (ed.) *Acculturation and Continuity in Atlantic Europe*, Ghent, 15–30

Baatz, D. 1977, 'Bemerkungen zur Jahrringchronologie der Romischen Zeit', *Germania* 55, 173–9

Baillie, M.G.L. 1973, 'A recently developed tree-ring chronology', *Tree-Ring Bulletin* 33, 15–28

Baillie, M.G.L. 1977a, 'The Belfast oak chronology to AD 1001', *Tree-Ring Bulletin* 37, 1–12

Baillie, M.G.L. 1977b, 'Dublin medieval dendrochronology', *Tree-Ring Bulletin* 37, 13–20

Baillie, M.G.L. 1977c, 'An oak chronology for south central Scotland', *Tree-Ring Bulletin* 37, 33–44

Baillie, M.G.L. 1978a, 'Dendrochronology for the Irish Sea Province', *British Archaeological Reports* (British Series) 54, 25–37

Baillie, M.G.L. 1978b, 'Dating of some ships' timbers from Woodquay, Dublin', *British Archaeological Reports* (International Series) 51, 259–62

Baillie, M.G.L. 1979, 'Some observations on gaps in tree-ring chronologies', in Aspinall, A. (ed.) *Proceedings of the Symposium on Archaeological Sciences* (January 1978), University of Bradford, 19–32

Baillie, M.G.L. 1982, *Tree-Ring Dating and Archaeology*, Croom-Helm, London

Baillie, M.G.L. 1983a, 'Belfast dendrochronology – the current situation', in Ottaway, B.S. (ed.) *Archaeology, Dendrochronology and the Radiocarbon Calibration Curve* Occasional Paper No. 9, University of Edinburgh, 15–24

Baillie, M.G.L. 1983b, 'Is there a single British Isles oak tree-ring signal?', *Proceedings of the 22nd Symposium on Archaeometry* (1982), University of Bradford, 73–82

Baillie M.G.L. 1984, 'Some thoughts on art-historical dendrochronology', *Journal of Archaeological Science* 11, 371–93

Baillie, M.G.L. 1985, 'Dendrochronology and radiocarbon calibration', *Ulster Journal of Archaeology* 48, 11–23

Baillie, M.G.L. 1988a, 'The dating of the timbers from Navan Fort and the Dorsey, Co. Armagh', *Emania* 4, 37–40

Baillie, M.G.L. 1988b, 'Irish oaks record prehistoric dust-veils drama', *Archaeology Ireland* 2, 71–4

Baillie, M.G.L. 1989a, 'Hekla 3 – just how big was it?', *Endeavour* 13, No. 2, 78–81

Baillie, M.G.L. 1989b, 'Do Irish bog oaks date the Shang dynasty?', *Current Archaeology* 117, 310–13

Baillie, M.G.L. 1990a, 'Checking back on an assemblage of published radiocarbon dates', *Radiocarbon* 32, 361–6

Baillie, M.G.L. 1990b, 'Irish tree-rings and an

event in 1628 BC', in D.A. Hardy (ed.) *Thera and the Aegean World III* vol. 3, The Thera Foundation, London, 160–6

Baillie, M.G.L. 1990c, 'Difficulties associated with and radical revision of Egyptian chronology', *Journal of the Ancient Chronology Forum* 3, 29–36

Baillie, M.G.L. 1991a, 'Marking in marker dates; towards an archaeology with historical precision', *World Archaeology* 23, 233–43

Baillie, M.G.L. 1991b, 'Suck-in and smear: two related chronological problems for the 1990s', *Journal of Theoretical Archaeology* 2, 12–16

Baillie, M.G.L. 1993, 'Archaeological wood in Northern Ireland', *Archaeomaterials* 7, 139–50

Baillie, M.G.L. 1994, 'Dendrochronology raises questions about the nature of the AD 536 dust-veil event', *The Holocene* 4, 212–17

Baillie, M.G.L. and Brown, D.M. 1988, 'An overview of oak chronologies', *British Archaeological Reports* (British Series) 196, 543–8

Baillie, M.G.L. and Munro, M.A.R. 1988, 'Irish tree-rings, Santorini and volcanic dust-veils', *Nature* 332, 344–6

Baillie, M.G.L. and Pilcher, J.R. 1973, 'A simple cross-dating program for tree-ring research', *Tree-Ring Bulletin* 33, 7–14

Baillie, M.G.L. and Pilcher, J.R. 1988, 'Make a date with a tree', *New Scientist* 117, 48–51

Baillie, M.G.L., Pilcher, J.R. and Pearson, G.W. 1983, 'Dendrochronology at Belfast as a background to high-precision calibration', *Radiocarbon* 25, 171–8

Baillie, M.G.L., Hillam, J., Briffa, K. and Brown, D.M. 1985, 'Re-dating the English art-historical tree-ring chronologies', *Nature* 315, 317–19

Bauch, J. 1978, 'Tree-ring chronologies for the Netherlands', *British Archaeological Reports* (International Series) 51, 133–7

Bauch, J. and Eckstein, D. 1970, 'Dendrochronological dating of oak panels of Dutch 17th century paintings', *Studies in Conservation* 15, 45–50

Bauch, J. and Eckstein, D. 1981, 'Woodbiological investigations on panels of Rembrandt paintings', *Wood Science and Technology* 15, 251–63

Becker, B. 1974, 'Eine Eichenchronologie der Alamannischen Totenbaume und Grabkammerbretter von Hufingen, Oberflacht und Zobingen', *Fundberichte aus Baden-Wurttemberg* 1, 545–64

Becker, B. 1981, 'A 2350-year South German oak tree-ring chronology', *Fundberichte aus Baden-Wurttemberg* 6, 369–86

Becker, B. 1983, 'The long-term radiocarbon trend of the absolute German oak tree-ring chronology 2800 to 800 BC', *Radiocarbon* 25, 197–203

Becker, B. 1985, 'Die Absolute Chronologie der Pfahlbauten Nördlich der Alpen im Jahrringkalender Mitteleuropas', in Becker, B. *et al.* (eds) *Dendrochronologie in der Ur-und-Frühgeschichte*, Schweizerische Gesellschaft für Ur-und-Frühgeschichte, Basel, 8–13

Becker, B. and Delorme, A. 1978, 'Oak chronologies for Central Europe: their extension from medieval to prehistoric times', *British Archaeological Reports* (International Series) 51, 59–64

Becker, B. and Schirmer, W. 1977, 'Palaeoecological study on the Holocene Valley development of the River Main, southern Germany', *Boreas* 6, 303–21

Becker, B. and Schmidt, B. 1982, 'Verlangerung der Mitteleuropaischen Eichenjahrringchronologie in das Zweite Vorchristliche Jahrtausand (bis 1462.Chr.)', *Archäologisches Korrespondenblatt* 12, 101–6

Becker, B. and Schmidt, B. 1990, 'Extension of the European oak chronology to 9224 years', *PACT* 29, (ESF) Strasbourg, 37–50

Bernard, A., Demaiffe, D., Matielli, N. and Punongbayan, R.S. 1991, 'Anhydrite-bearing pumices from Mount Pinatubo: further evidence for the existence of sulphur-rich silicic magmas', *Nature* 354, 139–40

Betancourt, P.P. 1987, 'Dating the Aegean late

Bronze Age with radiocarbon', *Archaeometry* 29, 1, 45–9

Bolychevtsev, V.G. 1970, 'Annual rings in oak as an index of secular cycles of climatic fluctuation', Lesoved, Moskva, 15–23 (English translation in J.M. Fletcher and W. Linnard, *Russian Papers on Dendrochronology and Dendroclimatology 1962–1972*, Research Laboratory for Archaeology, Oxford University, 1977)

Bonde, N. 1994, 'The dating of the Norwegian Viking Age ship burials: a successful Norwegian–Danish research project', *Nationalmuseets Arbejdsmark*, 128–48

Bonde, N. and Crumlin-Pedersen, O. 1990, 'The dating of Wreck 2, the longship, from Skuldelev, Denmark', *NewsWARP* 7, 3–6

Bradley, J. 1985, 'Excavations at Moynagh Lough 1984', *Riocht na Midhe* 7, 79–92 (1985–6)

Briffa, K.R., Jones, P.D., Wigley, T.M.L., Pilcher, J.R. and Baillie, M.G.L. 1983, 'Climate reconstruction from tree-rings: Part 1, basic methodology and preliminary results for England', *Journal of Climatology* 3, 233–42

Briffa, K.R., Jones, P.D., Wigley, T.M.L., Pilcher, J.R. and Baillie, M.G.L. 1986, 'Climate reconstruction from tree-rings: Part 2, spatial reconstruction of summer mean sea level pressure patterns over Great Britain', *Journal of Climatology* 6, 1–15

Briffa, K.R., Wigley, T.M.L., Jones, P.D., Pilcher, J.R. and Hughes, M.K. 1987, 'Patterns of tree-growth and related pressure variability in Europe', *Dendrochronologia* 5, 35–57

Briffa, K.R., Bartholin, T.S., Eckstein, D., Jones, P.D., Karlen, W., Schweingruber, F.H. and Zetterberg, P. 1990, 'A 1400-year tree-ring record of summer temperatures in Fennoscandia', *Nature* 346, 434–9

Briffa, K.R., Jones, P.D., Bartholin, T.S., Eckstein, D., Schweingruber, F.H., Karlen, W., Zetterberg, P. and Eronen, M. 1992, 'Fennoscandian summers from AD 500: Temperature changes on short and long timescales', *Climate Dynamics* 7, 111-19

Brown, D.M. and Baillie, M.G.L. 1992, 'Construction and dating of a 5000-year English bog oak tree-ring chronology', *Lundqua* Report 34, 72–5

Brown, D.M., Munro, M.A.R., Baillie, M.G.L. and Pilcher, J.R. 1986, 'Dendrochronology – The absolute Irish standard', *Radiocarbon* 28, 279–83

Bryson, R.A., Lamb, H.H. and Donley, D.L. 1974, 'Drought and the decline of Mycenae', *Antiquity* 48, 46–50

Bunney, S. 1985, 'Tree-ring dating for paintings is thrown into doubt', *New Scientist* 105, no. 1440, 37

Burgess, C. 1985, 'Population, climate and upland settlement', *British Archaeological Reports* (British Series) 143, 195–229

Burgess, C. 1989, 'Volcanoes, catastrophe and global crisis of the late 2nd millennium BC', *Current Archaeology* 117, vol. X, no. 10, 325–9

Carpenter, R. 1966, *Discontinuity in Greek Civilization*, Cambridge

Chang, K-C. 1980, *Shang Civilization*, Yale University Press, London

Chester, D.K. 1988, 'Volcanoes and climate: recent volcanological perspectives', *Progress in Physical Geography* 12, 4, 1–35

Clark, R.M. and Morgan, R.A. 1983, 'An alternative statistical approach to the calibration of floating tree-ring chronologies: two sequences from the Somerset Levels', *Archaeometry* 25, 1, 3–16

Clube, S.V.M. and Napier, B. 1990, *The Cosmic Winter*, Blackwell, Oxford

Clymo, R.S., Oldfield, F., Appleby, P.G., Pearson, G.W., Ratnesar, P. and Richardson, N. 1990, 'The record of atmospheric deposition on a rainwater-dependent peatland', *Phil. Trans. R. Soc. Lond.* B 327, 331–8

Coe, M.D. 1992, *Breaking the Maya Code*, Thames and Hudson, London

Cook, E.R. and Kairiukstis, L.A. 1990 (eds) *Methods of Tree-Ring Analysis – applications in the environmental sciences*, Kluwer Academic

Bibliography

Publishers, Dordrecht

Cooney, J. 1989, '1060 Viking ship was built in Dublin', *Irish Times* (9 November 1989), 1

Davies, O. 1950, *Excavations at Island MacHugh*, supplement to the Belfast Natural History and Philosophical Society, Belfast

Davis, E.N. 1990, 'A storm in Egypt during the reign of Ahmose', in Hardy, D.A. (ed.) *Thera and the Aegean World III* vol. 3, The Thera Foundation, London, 232–5

Dobbs, M.E. 1956, 'Lough Neagh', *Ulster Journal of Archaeology* 19, 113–14

Douglass, A.E. 1919, *Climatic Cycles and Tree Growth I*, Carnegie Institute, Washington

Douglass, A.E. 1938, 'Estimated tree-ring chronology: 450–600 AD', *Tree-Ring Bulletin* 4, no. 3, 8

Dugmore, A.J. and Newton, A.J. 1992, 'Thin tephra layers in peat revealed by X-radiography', *Journal of Archaeological Science* 19, 163–70

Eckstein, D. and Bauch, J. 1969, 'Beitrag zu Rationalisierung eines Dendrochronologischen Verfahrens und zu Analyse seiner Aussagesicherheit', *Forstwis Centralblatt* 88, 230–50

Eckstein, D., Baillie, M.G.L. and Egger, H. 1984, *Dendrochronological Dating, Handbook for Archaeologists* no. 2, European Science Foundation

Eckstein, D., Brongers, D.A. and Bauch, J. 1975, 'Tree-ring research in The Netherlands', *Tree-Ring Bulletin* 35, 1–13

Eckstein, D., Wazny, T., Bauch, J. and Klein, P. 1986, 'New evidence for the dendrochronological dating of Netherlandish paintings', *Nature* 320, 465–6

Edwards, K.J. 1985, 'The elm decline', in Edwards, K.J. and Warren, W.P. (eds) *The Quaternary History of Ireland*, Academic Press, 288–9

Edwards, K.J. and Hirons, K.R. 1984, 'Cereal pollen grains in pre-elm decline deposits: implications for the earliest agriculture in Britain and Ireland', *Journal of Archaeological Science* 11, 71–80

Epstein, S. and Krishnamurthy, R.V. 1990, 'Environmental information in the isotopic record in trees', *Phil. Trans. R. Soc. Lond.*, A330, 427–39

Fagan, B.M. 1992, *People of the Earth* (7th ed.) HarperCollins, New York

Ferguson, C.W. 1969, 'A 7104-year annual tree-ring chronology for bristlecone pine, pinus aristata, from the White Mountains, California', *Tree-Ring Bulletin* 29, 2–29

Ferguson, C.W. and Graybill, D.A. 1983, 'Dendrochronology of bristlecone pine: a progress report', *Radiocarbon* 25, 287–8

Fletcher, J.M. 1975, 'Relation of abnormal earlywood in oaks to dendrochronology and climatology', *Nature* 254, 506–7

Fletcher, J.M. 1977, 'Tree-ring chronologies for the 6th to 16th centuries for oaks of southern and eastern England', *Journal of Archaeological Science* 4, 335–52

Fletcher, J.M. 1978a, 'Oak chronologies: England', *British Archaeological Reports* (International Series) 51, 145–56

Fletcher, J.M. 1978b, 'Tree-ring analysis of panel paintings', *British Archaeological Reports* (International Series) 51, 303–6

Fletcher, J.M. 1980, 'A list of tree-ring dates for building timber in southern England and Wales', *Vernacular Architecture* 11, 32–8

Fletcher, J.M. 1982, 'Panel examination and dendrochronology', *The J. Getty Museum Journal* 10, 39–44

Fletcher, J.M. 1986, 'Dating of art-historical artefacts', *Nature* 320, 466

Fletcher, J.M., Tapper, M.C. and Walker, F.S. 1974, 'Dendrochronology: a reference curve for slow-grown oaks AD 1230 to 1546', *Archaeometry* 16, 31–40

Forsyth, P.Y. 1988, 'In the wake of Etna, 44 BC', *Classical Antiquity* 7, 1, 49–57

Forsyth, P.Y. 1990, 'Call for Cybele', *The*

Ancient History Bulletin 4, 4, 75–8

Fritts, H.C. 1976, *Tree-Rings and Climate*, Academic Press, London

Fritts, H.C., Lofgren, G.R. and Gordon, G.A. 1979, 'Variations in climate since 1602 as reconstructed from tree-rings', *Quaternary Research* 12, 18–46

Fulford, M.G. 1989, 'Byzantium and Britain: a Mediterranean perspective on post-Roman Mediterranean imports in western Britain and Ireland', *Medieval Archaeology* 33, 1–6

Garmonsway, G.N. 1962, *The Anglo-Saxon Chronicle*, Dent and Sons, London

Grove, J. 1988, *The Little Ice Age*, Methuen, London

Hall, V.A., Pilcher, J.R. and McCormac, F.G. 1994, 'Icelandic volcanic ash and the mid-Holocene Scots pine (*Pinus sylvestris*) decline in the north of Ireland; no correlation', *The Holocene* 4, 79–83

Hammer, C.U. 1977, 'Past volcanism revealed by Greenland ice sheet impurities', *Nature* 270, 482–6

Hammer, C.U. 1980, 'Acidity of polar ice-cores in relation to absolute dating, past volcanism, and radio-echoes', *Journal of Glaciology* 25, 359–72

Hammer, C.U. 1984, 'Traces of Icelandic eruptions in the Greenland ice sheet', *Jökull*, 34, 51–65

Hammer, C.U. and Clausen, H.B. 1990, 'The precision of ice-core dating', in Hardy, D.A. (ed.) *Thera and the Aegean World III* vol. 3, The Thera Foundation, London, 174–8

Hammer, C.U., Clausen, H.B. and Dansgaard, W. 1980, 'Greenland ice sheet evidence of post-glacial volcanism and its climatic impact', *Nature* 288, 230–5

Hammer, C.U., Clausen, H.B., Friedrich, W.L. and Tauber, H. 1987, 'The Minoan eruption of Santorini in Greece dated to 1645 BC?', *Nature* 328, 517–19

Handler, P. 1989, 'The effect of volcanic aerosols on global climate', *Journal of Volcanology and Geothermal Research* 37, 233–49

Hankey, V. and Warren, P. 1974, 'The absolute chronology of the Aegean Late Bronze Age', *Bulletin of the Institute of Classical Studies*, 21, 142–52

Harington, C.R. 1992 (ed.) *The Year Without a Summer? World Climate in 1816*, Canadian Museum of Nature, Ottawa

Härke, H. 1987, *Anglo-Saxon Weapon Burials*, D. Phil. thesis, Göttingen

Härke, H. 1991, 'Bede's borrowed eclipses', *Rastar* (newsletter of the Reading Astronomical Society), October 1991, 12

Herron, M.M. 1982, 'Impurity sources of F, Cl, NO and SO in Greenland and Antarctic precipitation', *Journal of Geophysical Research* 87, 3052–60

Heyworth, A. 1978, 'Submerged forests around the British Isles', *British Archaeological Reports* (International Series) 51, 279–88

Hillam, J. 1976, 'The dating of Cullyhanna Hunting Lodge', *Irish Archaeological Research Forum* 3, 1, 17–20

Hillam, J. 1981, 'An English tree-ring chronology, AD 404–1216', *Medieval Archaeology* 25, 31–44

Hillam, J. 1987, 'Dendrochronology – 20 years on', *Current Archaeology* 9, 12, 358–63

Hillam, J. 1992, 'The dating of archaeological sites in the United Kingdom', *Lundqua* 34, 146–9

Hillam J., Morgan, R. and Tyers, I. 1984, 'Dendrochronology and Roman London', *Trans. London and Middx. Archaeological Society*, 35, 1–4

Hillam J., Morgan, R. and Tyers, I. 1987, 'Sapwood estimates and the dating of short ring sequences', *British Archaeological Reports* (International Series) 333, 165–85

Hillam, J., Groves, C.M., Brown, D.M., Baillie, M.G.L., Coles, J.M. and Coles, B.J. 1990, 'Dendrochronology of the English Neolithic', *Antiquity* 64, 210–20

Hollstein, E. 1965, 'Jahrringchronologische von Eichenholzern ohne Waldkande', *Bonner Jahrbuch* 165, 12–27

Hollstein, E. 1973, 'Jahrringkurven der Hallstattzeit', *Trierer Zeitschrift* 36, 37–55

Hollstein, E. 1980, *MittelEuropaische Eichenchronologie,* Phillip Von Zabern, Mainz am Rhein

Horgan, J. 1987, 'Volcanic winter', *Scientific American* 1987, 2, 83–4

Houghton, J.T., Jenkins, G.J. and Ephraums, J.J. 1990 (eds) *Climate Change,* Cambridge University Press

Housley, R.A., Hedges, R.E.M., Law, I.A. and Bronk, C.R. 1990, 'Radiocarbon dating by AMS of the destruction of Akrotiri' in Hardy, D.A. (ed.) *Thera and the Aegean World III* vol. 3, The Thera Foundation, London, 207–15

Huber, B. and Giertz, V. 1969, 'Our 1000 year oak chronology', *Conference Report of the Austrian Academy of Science* 178, 32–42

Huber, P.J. 1977, 'Early cuneiform evidence for the existence of the planet Venus', in D. Goldsmith (ed.) *Scientists Confront Velikovsky,* Cornell University Press, Ithaca, 117-44

Hughes, M.K. 1988, 'Ice layer dating of the eruption of Santorini', *Nature* 335, 211–2

Hughes, M.K., Schweingruber, F.H., Cartwright, D. and Kelly, P.M. 1984, 'July–August temperature at Edinburgh between 1721 and 1975 from tree-ring density and width data', *Nature* 308, 341–4

Ivens, R.J., Simpson, D.D.A. and Brown, D. 1986, 'Excavations at Island McHugh 1985 – Interim Report', *Ulster Journal of Archaeology* 49, 99–103

Jacoby, G.C. and Hornbeck, J.W. (eds) 1987, *Proceedings of the International Symposium on Ecological Aspects of Tree-Ring Analysis, Tarrytown, New York, August 1986,* Carbon Dioxide Effects Research and Assessment program CONF-8608144 U.S. Department of Energy, Washington, DC

James, P.J. 1991, *Centuries of Darkness,* Jonathan Cape, London

James, P.J., Thorpe, I.J., Kokkinos, N. and Frankish, J.A. (eds) 1987, *Studies in Ancient Chronology* 1

Johnsen, S.J., Clausen, H.B., Dansgaard, W., Fuhrer, K., Gundestrup, N., Hammer, C.U., Iversen, P., Jouzel, J., Stauffer, B. and Steffensen, J.P. 1992, 'Irregular glacial inter-stadials recorded in a new Greenland ice core', *Nature* 359, 311–13

Jones, E.W. 1959, Quercus L. in 'Biological flora of the British Isles', *Journal of Ecology,* 47, 169–222

Kairiukstis, L. and Kocharov, G.E. 1990, 'Measuring the chemical ingredients in tree-rings', in Cook, E.R. and Kairiukstis, L.A. (eds) *Methods of Tree-Ring Analysis – applications in the environmental sciences,* Kluwer Academic Publishers, Dordrecht, 229–32

Kelly, P.M. and Sear, C.B. 1985, 'The climate impact of explosive volcanic eruptions', in *Third Conference on Climate Variations and Symposium on Contemporary Climate: 1850–2100,* American Meteorological Society, Boston, 178–9

Kelly, P.M., Munro, M.A.R., Hughes, M.K. and Goodess, C.M. 1989, 'Climate and signature years in west European Oaks', *Nature* 340, 57–60

Keys, D. 1989, 'Fire stones support catastrophe theory', *The Independent* (14 January 1989), 8

Kitchen, K.A. 1991, 'The chronology of Ancient Egypt', *World Archaeology* 23, 201–8

Klein, P. 1989, 'Dendrochronological studies on oak panels of Rogier Van Der Weyden and his circle', *Colloque VII,* Univ. Louvain-la-Neuve, 25–36

Kruse, H.H., Linick, T.W., Suess, H.E. and Becker, B. 1980, 'Computer-matched radio-carbon dates of floating tree-ring series', *Radiocarbon,* 22, 2, 260–6

Kuniholm, P.I. 1990, 'Archaeological evidence and non-evidence for climatic change', *Phil. Trans. R. Soc. Lond.* A330, 645–55

Kuniholm, P.I. and Striker, C.L. 1983, 'Dendrochronological investigations in the Aegean and neighbouring regions,

1977–1982', *Journal of Field Archaeology* 10, 411–20

Kuniholm, P.I. and Striker, C.L. 1987, 'Dendrochronological investigations in the Aegean and neighbouring regions, 1983–1986', *Journal of Field Archaeology* 14, 385–98

LaMarche, V.C. Jr 1970, 'Frost-damage rings in subalpine conifers and their application to tree-ring dating problems', *The University of British Columbia, Faculty of Forestry, Bulletin* 7, 99–100

LaMarche, V.C. Jr 1974, 'Palaeoclimatic inferences from long tree-ring records', *Science* 183, 1043–8

LaMarche, V.C. Jr and Harlan, T.P. 1973, 'Accuracy of tree-ring dating of bristlecone pine for calibration of the radiocarbon time scale', *Journal of Geophysical Research* 78, 8849–58

LaMarche, V.C. Jr and Hirschboeck, K.K. 1984, 'Frost rings in trees as records of major volcanic eruptions', *Nature* 307, 121–6

Leavitt, S.W. 1992, 'Isotopes and trace elements in tree-rings', *Lundqua* 34, 182–90

Leuschner, von H.H. 1992, 'Subfossil trees', *Lundqua* 34, 193–7

Leuschner, von H.H. and Delorme, A. 1984, 'Verlangerung der Gottingen Eichenjahrringchronologien fur Nord- und Suddeutschland bis zum Jahr 4008 v. Chr.', *Forstarchiv* 55, 1–4

Leuschner, von H.H. and Delorme, A. 1988, 'Tree-ring work in Gottingen – absolute oak chronologies back to 6255 BC', *Pact II.5 Wood and Archaeology*, 123–32

Libby, L.M., Pandolfi, L.J., Payton, P.H., Marshall, J. III., Becker, B. and Giertz-Sienbenlist, V. 1976, 'Isotopic tree thermometers', *Nature* 261, 284–8

Long, M.E. and Benn, W. 1990, 'Modern day echoes of Peru's past', *National Geographic* 117, 6, 34–49

Lucas, A.T. 1985, 'Toghers or causeways: some evidence from archaeological, literary, historical and place-name sources', *Proceedings of the Royal Irish Academy* 85, C, no. 2, 37–60

Lynn, C.J. 1981, 'The excavation at Rathmullan, a raised rath and motte in Co. Down', *Ulster Journal of Archaeology* 44, 65–171

Lynn, C.J. 1987, 'Deer Park Farms, Glenarm, Co. Antrim', *Archaeology Ireland* 1, 1, 11–15

Lynn, C.J. 1988, 'Ulster's oldest wooden houses', in Hamlin, A. and Lynn, C.J. (eds) *Pieces of the Past* HMSO, Belfast

McGhee, R. 1983, 'Archaeological evidence for climatic change during the last 5000 years', in Wigley, T.M.L., Ingram, M.J. and Farmer, G. (eds) *Climate and History,* Cambridge University Press, 162–79

Mallory, J.P. and Baillie, M.G.L. 1988, 'Tech ndaruch: the fall of the House of Oak', *Emania* 5, 27–33

Manning, S. 1988, 'The Bronze Age eruption of Thera: absolute dating, Aegean chronology and Mediterranean cultural interrelations', *Jnl. Mediterranean Archaeology* 1.1, 17–82

Manning, S. 1990, 'The Thera eruption: the third congress and the problem of the date', *Archaeometry* 32, 1, 91–100

Manning, S.W. 1992, 'Thera, sulphur, and climatic anomalies', *Oxford Journal of Archaeology* 11, 3, 245–53

Mazany, T. *et al.* 1980, 'Carbon-13 in tree-ring cellulose as an indicator of Past Climates', *Nature* 287, 432–5

Michael, H.N. 1976, 'Radiocarbon dates from Akrotiri on Thera', in *Temple University Aegean Symposium* 1:7–9. Philadelphia, Temple University

Mitchell, F. 1986, *The Shell Guide to Reading the Irish Landscape,* County House, Dublin

Morgan, R.A. 1977a, 'Tree-ring dating of the London waterfronts', *The London Archaeologist* 3, 2, 40–5,

Morgan, R.A. 1977b 'Dendrochronological dating of a Yorkshire timber building', *Vernacular Architecture* 8, 809–14

Morgan, R.A. 1988, 'Tree-ring studies of wood used in Neolithic and Bronze Age trackways from the Somerset Levels', *British Archaeological Reports* (British Series) 184, Oxford

Morgan, R.A., Litton, C.D. and Salisbury, C.R. 1987, 'Trackways and tree trunks – dating Neolithic oaks in the British Isles', *Tree-Ring Bulletin* 47, 61–9

Munro, M.A.R. 1984, 'An improved algorithm for crossdating tree-ring series', *Tree-Ring Bulletin* 44, 17–27

Nelson, D.E., Vogel, J.S. and Southon, J.R. 1990, 'Another suite of confusing radiocarbon dates for the destruction of Akrotiri', in Hardy, D.A. (ed.) *Thera and the Aegean World III* vol. 3, The Thera Foundation, London, 197–206

Newgrosh, B. 1988, 'Scientific dating methods and absolute chronology', *Journal of the Ancient Chronology Forum* 2, 60–8

Newgrosh, B. 1990, 'Still at the crossroads – a response to Mike Baillie', *Journal of the Ancient Chronology Forum* 3, 37–41

Nichols, R.F. and Harlan, T.P. 1967, 'Archaeological tree-ring dates from Wetherill Mesa', *Tree-Ring Bulletin* 28, 13–40

Orton, C.R. 1983, 'The use of student's t-test for matching tree-ring patterns', *Bulletin of the Institute of Archaeology* 20, University of London, 101–5

Oskarsson, N. 1980, 'The interaction between volcanic gases and tephra: fluorine adhering to tephra of the 1970 Hekla eruption', *Journal of Volcanology and Geothermal Research* 8, 251–66

Pang, K.D. 1987, 'Extraordinary floods in early Chinese history and their absolute dates', *Journal of Hydrology* 96, 139–55

Pang, K.D. 1991, 'The legacies of eruption', *The Sciences* 31, 1, 30–3

Pang, K.D. and Chou, H.-h. 1985, 'Three very large volcanic eruptions in antiquity and their effects on the climate of the ancient world', EOS, *Transactions, American Geophysical Union* 66, 816

Pang, K.D., Slavin, J.A. and Chou, H.-h. 1987, 'Climatic anomalies of late third century BC: correlation with volcanism, solar activity and planetary alignment', EOS, *Transactions, American Geophysical Union* 68, 1234

Pang, K.D., Srivastava, S.K. and Chou, H.-h. 1988, 'Climatic impacts of past volcanic eruptions: inferences from ice-core, tree-ring and historical data', EOS, *Transactions, American Geophysical Union* 69, 1062

Pang, K.D., Keston, R., Srivastava, S.K. and Chou, H.-h. 1989, 'Climatic and hydrologic extremes in early Chinese history: possible causes and dates', EOS, *Transactions, American Geophysical Union* 70, 1095

Pearson, G.W. 1980, 'High-precision radiocarbon dating by liquid scintillation counting applied to radiocarbon timescale measurements', *Radiocarbon* 22, 337–45

Pearson, G.W. 1983, *High-Precision Radiocarbon Dating*, PhD thesis, Queen's University, Belfast

Pearson, G.W. 1986, 'Precise calendrical dating of known growth-period samples using a 'curve fitting' technique', *Radiocarbon* 28, 292–9

Pearson, G.W. and Stuiver, M. 1986, 'High-precision calibration of the radiocarbon timescale, 500–2500 BC', *Radiocarbon* 28, 839–62

Pearson, G.W. and Stuiver, M. 1993, 'High-precision bidecadal calibration of the radiocarbon timescale, 500 BC – 2500 BC, *Radiocarbon* 35, 25–33

Pearson, G.W., Becker, B. and Qua, F. 1993, 'High-precision 14-C measurement of German and Irish oaks to show the natural 14-C variations from 7890–5000 BC', *Radiocarbon* 35, 93–104

Pearson, G.W., Pilcher, J.R., Baillie, M.G.L., Corbett, D.M. and Qua, F. 1986, 'High-precision 14-C measurement of Irish oaks to show the natural 14-C variations from AD 1840 to 5210 BC', *Radiocarbon* 28, 911–34

Pilcher, J.R. and Baillie, M.G.L. 1987, 'The Belfast CROS program – Some observations', *British Archaeological Reports* (International Series) 333, 157–63

Pilcher, J.R. and Hall, V.A. 1992, 'Towards a tephrochronology for the holocene of the north of Ireland', *The Holocene* 2, 3, 255–9

Pilcher, J.R., Baillie, M.G.L., Schmidt, B. and Becker, B. 1984, 'A 7272-year tree-ring chronology for western Europe', *Nature* 312, 150–2

Pilcher, J.R., Hillam, J., Baillie, M.G.L. and Pearson, G.W. 1977, 'A long sub-fossil tree-ring chronology from the north of Ireland', *New Phytologist* 79, 713–29

Pyle, D.M. 1989, 'Ice core acidity peaks, retarded tree growth and putative eruptions', *Archaeometry* 31, 88–91

Pyle, D.M. 1990a, 'The application of tree-ring and ice-core studies to the dating of the Minoan eruption', in Hardy, D.A. (ed.) *Thera and the Aegean World III* vol. 3, The Thera Foundation, London, 167–73

Pyle, D.M. 1990b, 'New estimates for the volume of the Minoan eruption', in Hardy, D.A. (ed.) *Thera and the Aegean World III* vol. 2, The Thera Foundation, London, 113–21

Raftery, B. 1990, *Trackways Through Time: Archaeological investigations on Irish bog roads 1985–89*, Headline, Dublin

Rampino, M.R., Self, S. and Stothers, R.B. 1988, 'Volcanic winters', *Annual Review of Earth Planet Science* 16, 73–99

Renfrew, C. 1990, 'Summary of the progress in chronology', in Hardy, D.A. (ed.) *Thera and the Aegean World III* vol. 3, The Thera Foundation, London, 242

Renfrew, C. and Bahn, P. 1991, *Archaeology – Theory, Methods and Practice*, Thames and Hudson, London

Rigold, S.E. 1975, 'Structural aspects of medieval timber bridges', *Medieval Archaeology* 19, 48–91

Robinson, W.R. 1976, 'Tree-ring dating and archaeology in the American southwest', *Tree-Ring Bulletin* 36, 9–20

Robinson, W.R. and Cameron, C.M. 1991, *A directory of tree-ring dated prehistoric sites in the American southwest*, The University of Arizona, Tucson, Arizona

Salisbury, C.R., Whitley, P.J., Litton, C.D. and Fox, J.L. 1984, 'Flandrian courses of the River Trent at Colwick, Nottingham', *Mercian Geologist* 9, 189–207

Salzman, L.F. 1931, *English Trade in the Middle Ages*, Clarendon Press, Oxford

Schmidt, B. 1981, 'Beitrag zum Aufbau der Holozanen Eichenchronologie in Mitteleuropa', *Archäologisches Korrespondenzblatt* 11, 361–3

Schmidt, B. 1987, 'Ein Dendrochronologischer Befund zum Bau der Stadtmauer der Colonia Ulpia Traiana', *Bonner Jahrbucher* 187, 495–503

Schmidt, B. and Freundlich, J. 1984, 'Zur Absoluten Datierung Bronzezeitlicher Eichenholzfunde', *Archäologisches Korrespondenzblatt* 14, 233–7

Schmidt, B. and Schwabedissen, H. 1978, 'Jahrringanalytische Untersuchungen an Eichen der Romischen Zeit', *Archäologisches Korrespondenzblatt* 8, 331–7

Schmidt, B. and Schwabedissen, H. 1982, 'Ausbau des Mitteleuropaischen Eichenjahrringkalenders bis in Neolithische Zeit (2061 v Chr.)', *Archäologisches Korrespondenzblatt* 12, 107–8

Schweingruber, F.H. 1983, *Der Jahrring: Standort, Methodik, Zeit und Klima in der Dendrochronologie*, Paul Haupt, Bern

Schweingruber, F.H., Braker, O.U. and Schar, E. 1979, 'Dendroclimatic studies on conifers from central Europe and Great Britain', *Boreas* 8, 427–52

Scuderi, L.A. 1990, 'Tree-ring evidence for climatically effective volcanic eruptions', *Quaternary Research* 34, 67–85

Scuderi, L.A. 1993, 'A 2000-year tree-ring record of annual temperatures in the Sierra Nevada mountains', *Science* 259, 1433–6

Sear, C.B., Kelly, P.M., Jones, P.D. and Goodess, C.M 1987, 'Global surface-temperature responses to major volcanic eruptions', *Nature* 330, 365–7

Bibliography

Sheldon, H. and Tyers, I. 1983, 'Recent dendrochronological work in Southwark and its implications', *The London Archaeologist* 4, 13, 355–61

Siebenlist-Kerner, V. 1978, 'The chronology, 1341–1636, for certain hillside oaks from western England and Wales', *British Archaeological Reports* (International Series) 51, 157–61

Sigurdsson, B and Pálsson, P.A. 1957, 'Fluorosis of farm animals during the Hekla eruption of 1947–1948', in *The eruption of Hekla 1947–1948*, III, 3, Soc. Sci. Islandica, Reykjavik, 1–12

Sigurdsson, H., Carey, S. and Devine, J.D. 1990, 'Assessment of mass, dynamics and environmental effects of the Minoan eruption of Santorini volcano', in Hardy, D.A. (ed.) *Thera and the Aegean World III* vol. 2, The Thera Foundation, London, 100–12

Sigurdsson, H., Devine, J.D. and Davis, A.N. 1985, 'The petrological estimation of volcanic degassing', *Jökull* 35, 1–8

Simkin, T., Siebert, L., McClelland, L., Bridge, D., Newhall, C. and Latter, J.H. 1981, *Volcanoes of the World*, Hutchinson Ross, Stroudsburg

Sparks, R.S.J. and Wilson, C.J.N. 1990, 'The Minoan deposits: a review of their characteristics and interpretation', in Hardy, D.A. (ed.) *Thera and the Aegean World III* vol. 2, The Thera Foundation, London, 89–93

Starkey, S. 1985, 'Seeing the wood for the trees', *History Today* 35, 4–5

Stothers, R.B. 1984, 'Mystery cloud of AD 536', *Nature* 307, 344–5

Stothers, R.B. 1989, 'Volcanic eruptions and solar activity', *Jnl. of Geophysical Research* 94, B12, 17, 371–81

Stothers, R.B. and Rampino, M.R. 1983, 'Volcanic eruptions in the Mediterranean before AD 630 from written and archaeological sources', *Jnl. of Geophysical Research* 88, 6357–71

Stuiver, M. and Pearson, G.W. 1986, 'High-precision calibration of the radiocarbon timescale AD 1950–500 BC', *Radiocarbon* 28, 805–38

Stuiver, M. and Pearson, G.W. 1993, 'High-precision bidecadal calibration of the radiocarbon timescale, AD 1950–500 BC and 2500 BC–6000 BC', *Radiocarbon* 35, 1–23

Suess, H.E. 1970, 'Bristlecone pine calibration of the radiocarbon timescale from 5200 BC to the present', in Olsson, I.U (ed.) *Radiocarbon Variations and Absolute Chronology*, John Wiley and Sons, New York, 303–9

Sullivan, D.G. 1988, 'The discovery of Santorini Minoan tephra in western Turkey', *Nature* 333, 552–4

Swetnam, T.W. 1993, 'History and climate change in giant sequoia groves', *Science* 262, 885–9

Symonds, R.W. 1946, 'The craft of the joiner in medieval England I and II', *The Connoisseur* 109, 17–23, 98–104

Toynbee, A. 1976, *Mankind and Mother Earth*, Oxford University Press, London

Velikovsky, I. 1973, *Ages in Chaos*, Abacus, London

Vogel, J.S., Cornell, W., Nelson, D.E. and Southon, J.R. 1990, 'Vesuvius/Avellino, one possible source of 17th century BC climatic disturbances', *Nature* 344, 534–7

Warner, R.B. 1985, 'The date of the start of Lagore', *The Journal of Irish Archaeology* 3, 75–7

Warner, R.B. 1990a, 'A proposed adjustment for the "old-wood effect" ', *PACT* 29, (ESF) Strasbourg, 159–72

Warner, R.B. 1990b, 'The "prehistoric" Irish annals: fable or history', *Archaeology Ireland* 4, 1, 30–3

Warren, P.M. 1984, 'Absolute dating of the Bronze Age eruption of Thera (Santorini)', *Nature* 308, 492–3

Warren, P.M. 1991, 'The Minoan Civilization of Crete and the Volcano of Thera', *Journal of Ancient Chronology Forum* 4, 29–39

Watson, G.P.H. 1922, 'The development of

Caerlaverock Castle', *Proceedings of the Society of Antiquaries of Scotland* 57, 29–40

Weir, D.A. 1993, 'Dark Ages and the pollen record', *Emania* 11, 21-30

Weisburd, S. 1985, 'Excavating Words: a geological tool', *Science News* 127, 91–6

Wigley, T.M.L. 1988, 'The climate of the past 10,000 years and the role of the sun', in Stephenson, F.R. and Wolfendale, A.W. (eds) *Secular Solar and Geomagnetic Variations in the Last 10,000 Years*, Kluwer Academic Press, 209–24

Wigley, T.M.L., Gray, B.M. and Kelly, P.M. 1978, 'Climatic interpretation of delta-O and delta-D in tree-rings', *Nature* 271, 92–4

Wigley, T.M.L., Jones, P.D. and Briffa, K.R. 1987, 'Cross-dating methods in dendrochronology', *Journal of Archaeological Science* 14, 51–64

Wilde, W. 1851, *The Census of Ireland for the Year 1851, Part 5: Tables of Deaths*, vol. 1, HMSO, Dublin

Williams, E. 1989, 'Dating the introduction of food production into Britain and Ireland', *Antiquity* 63, 510–21

Wilson, I. 1985, *The Exodus Enigma*, Weidenfeld and Nicolson, London

Yamaguchi, D.K. and Allen, G.L. 1992, 'A new computer program for estimating the statistical significance of cross-dating positions for "floating" tree-ring series', *Canadian Journal of Forestry Research* 22, 1215–21

Yamaguchi, D.K., Filion, L. and Savage, M. 1993, 'Relationship of temperature and light ring formation at subarctic treeline and implications for climate reconstruction', *Quaternary Research* 39, 256–62

Zeigler, P. 1970, *The Black Death*, Pelican, England

Index

Index